EXPLORE

2

English for field-specific success

Vanessa Beal | Sherry Kent

OXFORD
UNIVERSITY PRESS

OXFORD
UNIVERSITY PRESS

Oxford University Press is a department of the University of Oxford.
It furthers the University's objective of excellence in research, scholarship,
and education by publishing worldwide. Oxford is a registered trade mark of
Oxford University Press in the UK and in certain other countries.

Published in Canada by
Oxford University Press
8 Sampson Mews, Suite 204,
Don Mills, Ontario M3C 0H5 Canada

www.oupcanada.com

Library and Archives Canada Cataloguing in Publication
Beal, Vanessa, 1969-, auteur
Explore 2 : English for field-specific success / Vanessa Beal, Sherry Kent.

ISBN 978-0-19-902463-6 (couverture souple)

1. Anglais (Langue)–Manuels pour francophones.   2. Anglais (Langue)–
Problèmes et exercices.   I. Kent, Sherry, 1966-, auteur   II. Titre.   III. Titre:
Explore two.

PE1129.F7B4153 2017   428.2'441   C2017-900997-4

Cover images, top (left to right): © iStock/Tassii; © iStock/DK-photography;
© iStock/cyther5; © iStock/ima_sidelnikov.
Cover images, bottom (left to right): © iStock/hironosov; © iStock/23ducu;
© iStock/asiseeit; © iStock/shironosov
Cover design: Laurie McGregor
Interior design: Laurie McGregor

Oxford University Press is committed to our environment.
Wherever possible, our books are printed on paper which comes from
responsible sources.

Printed and bound in the United States of America

1 2 3 4 — 21 20 19 18

Contents

SKILLS UNITS

UNIT 1 | Personal Development   1

UNIT 2 | The Evolving Workplace   23

UNIT 3 | Creativity: The Number 1 Skill   45

UNIT 4 | Innovation at Work   63

UNIT 5 | The Art of Persuasion 85

UNIT 6 | Modern Solutions to Modern Problems 107

Projects 129

Learning Strategies 135

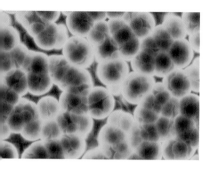

Grammar Guide 185

Abbreviations Used in the Text			
abbr	abbreviation	**n phr**	noun phrase
adj	adjective	**phr v**	phrasal verb
adv	adverb	**tr**	transitive (verb)
exp	expression	**v**	verb
n	noun		

Acknowledgements

I would like to express my sincere gratitude to David Coombes for his expertise and enthusiasm for this project and to both Nicola Balfour and Kathryn Willms for their focused editorial skills. Thanks to my co-author Sherry Kent for the discussions, knowledgeable input, and thorough hard work. To my students, colleagues, family, and friends in ESL and in yoga in Australia, Canada, and England, for inspiration, ideas, and conversations that have fuelled me along this endeavour. To Felix and Zoe, for being the very best. Most of all, to Jean-Fred, for sharing life's adventures and love with me.

Vanessa Beal

I would like to thank the entire team at Oxford for their exceptional work on *Explore*. I would like to thank David Coombes for his support throughout this rigorous process. His passion for the field is contagious. I would like to thank Nicola Balfour for her encouragement, insightful comments, and attention to detail. I would also like to thank Kathryn Willms for her extensive feedback and enthusiasm. Both editors have contributed greatly to the success of this project. I would like to thank my co-author Vanessa Beal for her creativity, dedication, and hard work. It has been a pleasure to work with her. I would like to thank the reviewers for their honest suggestions and comments. Finally, I would like to thank my family, friends, and colleagues for being there for me during this project.

Sherry Kent

Oxford University Press Canada would like to express appreciation to the English teachers who generously offered feedback about *Explore* at various stages of the development process. Their feedback was instrumental in helping to shape and refine the book.

Rebecca Baker Collège Montmorency
Marie-Hélène Belley Cégep de Jonquière
Félix Maranda Castonguay Cégep Lévis-Lauzon
Jennifer Caylor Cégep de Rimouski
Lisa Deguire Cégep de Jonquiere
Cecilia Delgado Collège Lionel-Groulx
Marie-Claude Doucet Cégep de Chicoutimi
Suzie Dufresne Cégep Régional de Lanaudière in Joliette
Barry G. Glebe Collège de Maisonneuve
Rebecca Higgins Cégep Édouard-Montpetit
Liana Jalalyn Cégep Régional de Lanaudière
Nancie Kahan Cégep de Saint-Jérôme
Jerry Kowtalo Cégep de Saint-Jérôme
Christine Lalonde Cégep de Sainte-Foy
Chiara Laricchuta Collège Ahuntsic
Sara Langevin Cégep de Granby
Marie-J. Martineau Cégep Édouard-Montpetit
Darcy Robb Cégep de Rimouski
Maria Pia Smargiasso Collège Montmorency

Scope and Sequence

	Reading	Writing	Speaking	Listening and Watching
UNIT 1 **Personal Development**	• Read about self-awareness and your relationships with others • Read about neuroplasticity and how organizations use it with employees • Strategy Previewing	• Write a paragraph on your personality's contribution to your future career. (**Field of Study**) • Build a mind map (**Field of Study**) • Write a topic sentence, develop supporting ideas, and write a paragraph • **Strategy** Well-structured paragraphs and topic sentences	• Describe your personality, values, skills, and interests • Discuss factors affecting your personality • Discuss use of the Johari Window by organizations • Present results of your personality test • Brainstorm careers that require multitasking • **Strategy** Prepare and deliver an oral presentation • Pronounce ed; / th / sound	• Watch a video about how personality affects our personal and work lives • Listen to an interview about mindfulness meditation and time management • Note-taking
UNIT 2 **The Evolving Workplace**	• Read about generational characteristics and the forces that shape them • Read about companies embracing unlimited vacation time • **Strategy** Identify main ideas and supporting details	• Identify job requirements and write a cover letter (**Field of Study**) • Write a paragraph about the impact of automation on your future career (**Field of Study**)	• Rank job satisfaction factors; describe their role in your career choice (**Field of Study**) • Discuss generation gap in the workplace • Interview a partner about useful skills you have to offer (**Field of Study**) • Practise presenting your soft skills • Discuss automation advantages/disadvantages • **Strategy** Speaking in a job interview • Pronounce three-syllable words	• Watch a video about automation in white-collar jobs • Listen to tips on developing your personal brand and selling your unique skills
UNIT 3 **Creativity: The Number 1 Skill**	• Read about creativity and how to be more creative every day • Read about a fashion designer who has built a successful ethical-fashion business • **Strategy** Note-taking using the Cornell Notes method	• Write a one-sentence definition of creativity • Write a paragraph summarizing a text • Write about a process • **Strategy** Writing a summary • **Strategy** Skimming and scanning	• Discuss what inspires you to be creative • Brainstorm creative inventions/processes in your field of study (**Field of Study**) • Pitch an innovative solution to a problem (**Field of Study**) • Discuss companies committed to sustainable development • Present a process (**Field of Study**) • Pronounce / h / sounds	• Listen to an interview that debunks the myth of creative genius • Watch a documentary excerpt about the fashion industry and how clothing is made
UNIT 4 **Innovation at Work**	• Read about the impact of 3D technology in diverse fields • Read about the impact the Internet may be having on you • **Strategy** Objective and subjective writing; fact and opinion	• Write an opinion paragraph • Write a paragraph comparing objective and subjective articles • Write a short description of important technology (**Field of Study**) • Write an essay outline about an obstacle to innovation (**Field of Study**) • **Strategy** Thesis statement and topic sentences • **Strategy** Simple, compound, and complex sentences	• Describe innovations (**Field of Study**) • Express your opinion about innovation • Discuss how 3D printing might affect your future career (**Field of Study**) • Present on the impact of the Internet on your field of study (**Field of Study**) • Discuss issues related to the use of drones • Propose ideas to reduce obstacles to innovation • Pronounce two-syllable words	• Listen to an interview about the long-term impact of the Internet on how we think • Watch a video about the diverse uses of drones
UNIT 5 **The Art of Persuasion**	• Read about the persuasive power of "nudges" to influence decisions • Read about influencing strategies that reduce shoplifting	• Write sentences using cognates and identify false cognates (**Field of Study**) • Write a formal email proposal • Research and write a paragraph profiling a company (**Field of Study**) • **Strategy** Write a proposal	• Discuss how marketing influences behaviour • Describe an important decision and factors that influenced it • Brainstorm ways nudging could be useful in your future career (**Field of Study**) • Describe the message/impact of activities • Discuss your ideal workplace • Conduct an urban architecture survey, analyze and report findings • Pronounce words with silent consonants	• Watch a video about how Google uses nudges to create a culture, influence behaviour, and boost productivity • Listen to an interview about the influence of urban design and architecture
UNIT 6 **Modern Solutions to Modern Problems**	• Read about the implications of driverless technology • Read about an initiative to use rooftop farming to address food production challenges • **Strategy** Identify author's purpose	• Write a paragraph describing a problems and solutions specific to your field (**Field of Study**) • Write a summary of an article describing a problem and its solution • **Strategy** Recognize organizational patterns	• Discuss modern problems and innovative solutions • Give opinions on whether driverless technology will benefit society • Discuss a technology's impact on your field and other industries (**Field of Study**) • Share your knowledge of obesity statistics and methods of addressing obesity • Debate the value of taking a weight-loss pill • Present an innovative start-up company • Pronounce schwa	• Watch a video about the driverless technology and its potential for widespread impact • Listen to a report about a pill that may prevent obesity and help people lose weight

Grammar	Interpreting Data	Vocabulary	Revising and Editing	Wrap Up
• Simple present, simple past, and past progressive	• Review types of graphs • Learn important graph- and data-related terms • Make comparisons and identify trends • Use the comparative and superlative to discuss charts and graphs	• Cognates • Adjectives to describe personality • Synonyms	• Revise to correct verb tense errors • Revise to organize a well-structured paragraph	• Research and write about a leader or innovator (**Field of Study**) • Write a short text on mindfulness and neuroplasticity • Oral presentation: research and present findings on accuracy and usefulness of personality tests • Review new words
• Future tense and modals	• Analyze information in an infographic	• Verbs and adjectives used in resumé writing • Vocabulary related to soft skills	• Revise a cover letter to correct grammar and formality errors	• Write a cover letter (**Field of Study**) • Write a paragraph about a generational leader • Oral presentation: Role-play a job interview and evaluate interviewees • Review new words
• Passive voice	• Use previewing, predicting, and skimming to identify graph's subject • identify graph types and identify trends shown in graphs • Summarize information in a graph	• Transition words	• Revise sentences from a summary • Rewrite a paragraph to explain a process	• Identify passive voice and transition words • Take notes and write a process outline • Write a summary about a process (**Field of Study**) • Oral presentation: Research and present on the importance of creativity (**Field of Study**) • Write a summary of a video • Write definitions for new words
• Present perfect and simple past • Sentence types	• Analyze bar graph data about the obstacles to innovation	• Determining the meaning of new words from context • Vocabulary related to innovation	• Revise to create compound or complex sentences • Complete a paragraph with past and present perfect tenses	• Research articles and evaluate their credibility • Research and write an essay about an innovation in your field of study (**Field of Study**) • Oral presentation: research and present an innovation (**Field of Study**) • Review new words
• Comparatives and superlatives	• Interpret a graph and understand the main message of data • Use the comparative and superlative to describe data	• Cognates and false cognates • Collocations • Vocabulary related to marketing and persuasion	• Revise to correct errors In spelling, verb tense, and comparative and superlative use	• Research and present a nudge campaign (**Field of Study**) • Write an essay on the ethics of nudging • Oral presentation: make a persuasive speech about your field of study (**Field of Study**) • Review new words learned in this unit
• Nouns: countable and uncountable	• Analyze the information in an infographic	• Compound adjectives • Compound nouns	• Revise to correct errors using articles, singular/plural words, and compound words • Rewrite sentences using compound adjectives	• Research and present on a problem and solutions (**Field of Study**) • Write an essay about a problem (**Field of Study**) • Oral presentation: Debate the ethics of computer-driven cars • Review compound words and phrases learned in this unit

Explore: How to Use the Book

Book Structure

Six theme-based **Skills** units provide contemporary, high-interest, Canadian and international readings, listenings, and watchings chosen to connect with a wide range of students' fields of study and future careers.

Fourteen **Grammar Guide** chapters cover all the key grammar points and give students thousands of practice activities.

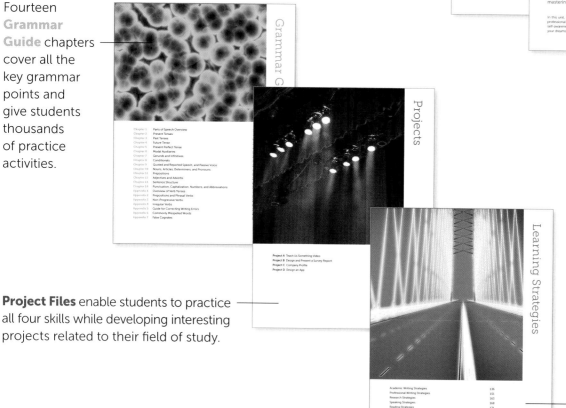

Project Files enable students to practice all four skills while developing interesting projects related to their field of study.

A concise **Learning Strategies** section at the back of the book allows students to become more independent and successful at acquiring new language and transferring it to career and academic situations.

Skills Unit Features

Warm Up

Work with a partner and match each innovation with the correct description. The first one has already been completed.

1. In 1953, James Watson and Francis Crick discovered the molecular structure that encodes the genetic instructions used in the development and functioning of all known living organisms.	a) mobile phone
2. In 1973, Motorola created the first device of this kind. It weighed more than 1 kg and people could use it to talk to each other for only 30 minutes. The battery took 10 hours to charge.	b) airplane
3. Orville and Wilbur Wright invented this flying machine in 1903.	c) penicillium
4. In 1896 Ernest Duchesne, a French medical student, discovered the antibiotic properties of this fungus which was developed into a common antibiotic that is still used worldwide.	d) DNA
5. In 1592, Dutch eyeglasses makers Zacharias and Hans Jansen discovered that objects were magnified when looking through a specially shaped lens. This invention led to innovations in many fields, including science and medicine.	e) bar code

Warm Up activities that practice all four skills connect students to the themes and activate their prior knowledge.

Vocabulary Development

Vocabulary Strategy

Collocations

A collocation is two or more words that are often used together. For example, *dinner party* (not *dinner event*), *health benefits* (not *health advantages*), *heavy workload* (not *big workload*).

The following collocations are taken from the text:

low cost rather than small cost or less cost

tackling crime rather than attacking crime or dealing with crime

contribute to society rather than help to society or contribute for society

1. Working with a partner, find the following words in the text on page 98 and write the missing part of the collocation.

a) *appeal* (para. 3) _____

b) *crime* (paras. 2 & 13) _____

c) *element* (paras. 3 & 12) _____

Dynamic vocabulary development activities ensure that students build a rich vocabulary bank related to their individual **fields of study** and **future careers**

Vocabulary

Fill in the following chart with different forms of the same word. The first one has been done for you. Provide the meaning of the verb or noun.

Noun	Verb	Adjective	Adverb	Meaning
manipulation	manipulate	manipulative	manipulatively	to change someone or something for one's purposes
		persistent		

Vocabulary Activities before texts, audios, and videos ensure students are more successful with reading, listening and watching activities.

Build Your English Vocabulary

How many words do you think you need to know in English? What is the best way to add new words to your vocabulary? Are there specialized words that are essential in your field of study? A combination of these techniques can be used to build your vocabulary.

Word lists

The New Academic Word List (NAWL) and New General Service List (2013)

The New Academic Word List (NAWL) is a list of words that are frequently used in academic texts; they are not field-specific and are also found in newspapers, on television, and in conversation. If you are familiar with the 2800 most frequently used words that make up the New General Service List in English as well as the 963 words that make up the NAWL, you should be able to understand around 90 percent of any text you read.

To find out whether you know the most frequently used words in English, enter the key words vocabulary size online quizzes or lextutor in your web browser.

You can browse the word lists by typing New Academic Word List or Academic Word List website or type Academic Word List in your web browser to find other AWL websites. You will find word lists as well as exercises to practise using this vocabulary.

All vocabulary learning requires active involvement and lots of repetition. Visiting these sites, doing related exercises, and writing down unfamiliar words and their definitions will help you build the foundations of your English vocabulary.

Word forms

When you encounter a new word, use a dictionary to confirm its meaning(s), word forms, or parts of speech. Create a chart like this one to record your new vocabulary words. An X indicates there is no applicable word.

Target NAWL word	Meaning(s)	Verb	Noun	Adjective	Adverb
utilize	use	utilize	utilization	utilized	X
correlate	connect	correlate	correlation	correlated	X
reliability	dependability	rely	reliance	reliable	reliably
impact	effect	impact	impact	impactful	X
spontaneous	unplanned	X	spontaneity	spontaneous	spontaneously

To help students succeed with their academic studies, *Explore* highlights and practises the **New Academic Word List** (NAWL), 963 words derived from an academic corpus containing about 288 million words.

Reading, Listening, and Watching

Making the World a Better Place Tops Generation Z's List for Best Employer

By Tom Turpin, *Financial Post*

1. Twenty years ago when I was starting in the workforce, I was driven, competitive, and engaged—more than anything I'm certain I was a **challenge** to manage.

2. Every generation has its own set of values, aspirations, and characteristics. Boomers were driven to build institutions and **thrive** while growing up in the largest **cohort** of human births in the history of the world. Generation X **withstood** economic **turmoil** to innovate with the developing technologies that are driving the world's economy today. Generation Y's innovations and influence are already being felt, as well as their demands for good work, good pay, and great work–life balance.

3. Now, Generation Z is joining the workforce, with their **quest** for making the world a better place and their drive to be their own boss. With all these generations working together come bias, stereotypes, and perceptions that can hinder a productive working relationship. But we can make the most of our differences simply by initiating an open dialogue, and the good news is that this is exactly what the younger generation is thirsty for.

4. **Getting to know Gen Z.** Like the generation before them, this fresh young cohort places significant value on companies that are socially responsible and are making a positive contribution to their communities.

5. In a survey conducted by Randstad Canada, 87 percent of respondents **revealed** it was important for them to work for a company that helps the community, with specific focus on creating new jobs locally, rewarding

aspiration (n) ambition to achieve an objective

cohort (n) a group of people with a common characteristic

withstood (v) remained unaffected by

bias (n) a personal, often unreasonable judgment

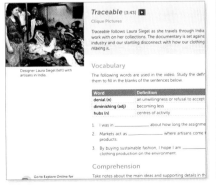

Traceable [3:43]

Clique Pictures

Traceable follows Laura Siegel as she travels through India, work with on her collections. The documentary is set against industry and our startling disconnect with how our clothing making it.

Designer Laura Siegel (left) with artisans in India.

Vocabulary

The following words are used in the video. Study the defin them to fill in the blanks of the sentences below.

Word	Definition
denial (n)	an unwillingness or refusal to accept
diminishing (adj)	becoming less
hubs (n)	centres of activity

1. I was in _____ about how long the assignme

2. Markets act as _____ where artisans come t products.

3. By buying sustainable fashion, I hope I am _____ clothing production on the environment.

Comprehension

Take notes about the main ideas and supporting details in th

Go to Explore Online for

Exercise Pill [6:26]

ABC TV Catalyst

Comprehension

As you watch the report, answer the following questions. For *True/False* if the answer is *False* write the correct answer in the space provided.

1. Why are pharmaceutical companies spending money to develop address obesity?

2. How did Adro Sarnelli lose weight?

3. According to Dr. Boyd Swinburn, what is the problem with usin affect a person's appetite?

4. What have researchers done to deal with the problem of using hu hormone to cause weight loss?

5. Human trials using human growth hormone have shown promise

6. How soon will this new drug using human growth hormone becom

Go to Explore Online for additional practice and comprehension questions.

High-interest readings, audios, and videos connected to pre-university and career programs increase students' involvement and motivation.

Speaking, Pronunciation, and Writing

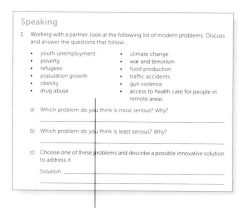

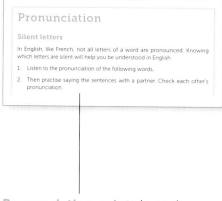

Four to six communicative activities in every skills unit guide students to express themselves on field specific and career related topics.

Pronunciation points in each chapter improve students' speaking skills developing more confident speakers.

Writing activities enable students to master key academic and professional genres and formats.

Field-Specific Practice

 Field-specific activity

Four to six field-specific practice activities in each unit provide students with numerous opportunities to explore and connect to their **fields of study and future careers** making their English language acquisition meaningful and relevant.

Learning Strategies

Two or three carefully chosen **Learning Strategies** in each skills unit make learning easier, quicker, and more enjoyable.

Interpreting Data

An **Interpreting Data** activity in every unit with **authentic graphs and diagrams** helps students develop the skills to evaluate and communicate about data and information that is common in all careers and fields of study.

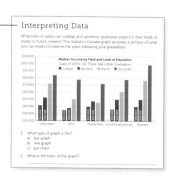

Grammar

Grammar in every skills unit provides a contextualized, student-centred approach that allows students to evaluate their understanding and discover how grammar works in real life.

Explore Online

Explore Online is an easy-to-use website that provides students with hundreds of practice activities related to the content in the student book. Students will improve their English through additional practice in vocabulary, listening, watching, reading, pronunciation, revising and editing, and all aspects of English grammar.

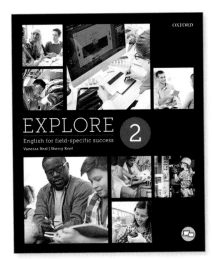

Students have access to a full **eBook** version of the text book to study anytime, anywhere.

All **reading texts**, all **audios** and all **videos** are available on the website so students can complete the interactive activities in one place even without their textbook.

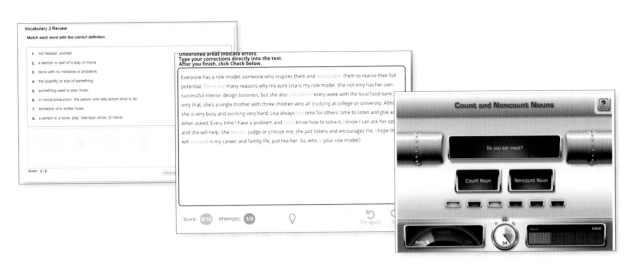

Interactive, self-graded activities, games and tests make learning stimulating and fun!

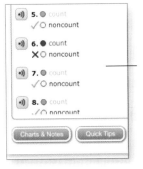

Instant feedback and access to **charts**, and **tips** develops autonomous learning.

Gradebook allows students and teachers to track progress quickly and easily.

Knowing others is intelligence;
knowing yourself is true wisdom.
Mastering others is strength;
mastering yourself is true power.

—Lao Tzu

In this unit, we explore a subject that is key to success in your academic and professional life: personal development. You will discover ways of improving your self-awareness, developing your talents, and boosting your potential to achieve your dreams and aspirations.

Field-specific activity

Warm Up

1. Answer the questions below to create a list of at least 10 words pertaining to your field of study. Share these words with other students.

   a) What program are you in?
   _____

   b) What field-specific courses are you taking?
   _____

   c) Name five key skills you are learning in your courses.
   _____

   d) Name five common jobs in your field of study or future career.
   _____

   e) What type of personality is best suited for your field of study or future career?
   _____

2. a) Teamwork is essential at school and in the workplace and requires a good awareness of others, as well as a good level of self-awareness.
   • What does the word *awareness* mean to you?
   • How self-aware are you?
   • How do you interpret the quotation at the beginning of this unit?

   b) Look at the diagram below and answer the following questions.
   • In the lines beside each section of the diagram write two or three words that describe your personality, values, skills, and interests.
   • Now write a short paragraph that answers the question "Who am I?" Describe your personality, values, skills, and interests.

values (n) beliefs about what is the right or wrong way for people to behave

skills (n) abilities and competencies

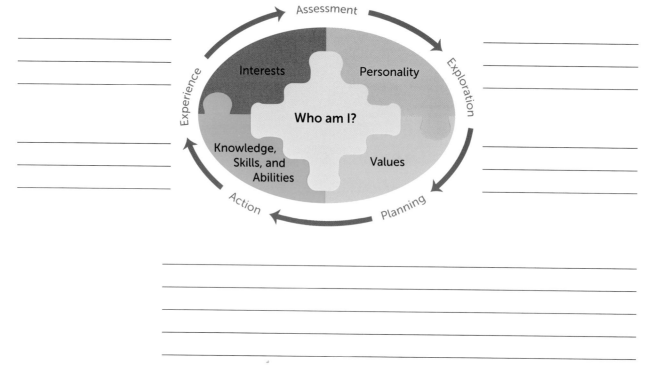

_____
_____
_____

_____
_____
_____

_____
_____
_____

_____
_____
_____

_____
_____
_____
_____
_____

Speaking

In teams of two, use the information that you noted when answering "Who am I?" and introduce yourself to your partner using six to seven sentences.

1. Listen to your partner and ask at least two pertinent questions about what he or she tells you.

2. Working with another team of two, introduce your partner to the group using four to five sentences and listen as he or she introduces you. Be attentive to subject–verb agreement (*he/she likes . . .*) and be ready to answer any questions your partners ask.

Watching

Why do some people work really well together while others don't? Whether the goal is to find the right person to hire or develop stronger teams, evaluating personality gives us valuable insights into how people behave, work, and lead, and how successful they will be.

This video explores the psychology of personality and offers some clues to how personality affects our personal and working lives.

Pre-Watching Activity

The expression "A leopard cannot change its spots" means that a person cannot change who they are (their character) even if they try very hard. Before watching the video, discuss the following questions with a partner.

- What is personality?
- Can personality change? Give examples from your own life to support your point of view.

Vocabulary

Before watching the video, familiarize yourself with the following words. Can you identify which ones are cognates? Listening for cognates can help you understand what people are saying as well as expand your vocabulary. Pay attention to how these words are used in the video to ensure that they are true cognates and their meaning is the same in French and English.

> **S** Several words in the following videos are cognates. Cognates are words from the same origin that have similar, or the same, spelling and the same meaning in both French and English; for example, *disposition*, *interaction*, and *motivation* are cognates. For more information about cognates and false cognates, see Vocabulary Strategies, page 178, and Unit 5 pages 86-87, and Appendix 7, page 284.

Word or phrase	Definition
distinctiveness (n)	the quality of being different from others; individuality
disposition (n)	the qualities of a person's character
behaviour (n)	the way a person acts or behaves
interact (v)	to act on, engage, or communicate with someone or something
motivation (n)	a reason or incentive for doing something
constant (adj)	happening or existing all the time, again and again
hierarchy (n)	system of ranking according to power relationships and status
cooperation (n)	the process of working together; collaboration

What Is Personality? [5:40] ▶

Hogan Assessment Systems

Watch the video on the psychology of personality twice. Follow these steps.

First viewing

1. Watch the video to get a general understanding of its content. Make notes about what the different speakers say about personality.

2. Compare your notes with your answers to the Pre-Watching activity on page 3. With a partner, discuss how they are the same or different.

Second viewing

1. Read the Comprehension questions below. Highlight key words; this will help you better focus on the information you need to find in the video.

2. Watch the video again and answer the Comprehension questions.

Comprehension

Answer the following questions. With *True/False* questions, if the answer is *False* write the correct answer in the space provided.

1. List four words that people on the street use to describe what constitutes personality.

   a) _____

   b) _____

   c) _____

   d) _____

2. List five ways in which the academics interviewed define personality.

   a) _____

   b) _____

   c) _____

   d) _____

   e) _____

3. According to the academics, personality type relates to the probability of a person reacting in a certain way. ☐ True ☐ False

   _____

4. According to the academics, understanding why we are all different makes the difference between getting along and getting ahead. ☐ True ☐ False

   _____

Go to Explore Online for additional practice and comprehension questions.

to get along (with) (exp) have friendly relationships with people and colleagues

to get ahead (exp) become successful in your life or career

5. According to the academics interviewed, all societies are social with three constant characteristics. These are:

    a) _____

    b) _____

    c) _____

6. These generalizations have led psychologists to identify three main motives or core drivers in society:

    a) _____

    b) _____

    c) _____

7. What is the core driver in business, according to the business leaders identified?

    _____

8. According to the business leaders, is it possible to both get along with others and to get ahead at the same time? Do you agree? Why or why not?

    _____

9. What do you think are the advantages of knowledge of personality psychology?

    _____

    _____

Speaking

Working in a group of four students, discuss different events in your life or people you have met that have influenced your personality. Explain how these events or people have affected or helped form the personality you have today. Give one or two concrete examples.

Reading

If someone asked you to describe yourself, what would you say? Self-awareness is our ability to see ourselves and understand how we feel and why we behave the way we do. This text discusses the importance of self-awareness and a technique that can be used to help you better understand your relationships with yourself and others.

Reading Strategy

Previewing

Previewing is a simple strategy that involves seeing what you can learn from the titles, subtitles, introductory and concluding paragraphs, and any bolded words to obtain an overview of the content. Previewing is very quick and helps improve your concentration, comprehension, and memory of what you read.

S For more information about previewing, see Reading Strategies, page 173.

Pre-Reading Activity

Look quickly at the text below and fill in the answers below to preview the text.

1. What is the title of the text? _____

2. What are the three subtitles?

   a) subtitle 1 _____

   b) subtitle 2 _____

   c) subtitle 3 _____

3. Now read the first and last paragraph, and then answer the following question.
   What is the Johari Window?

   a) It is a process for changing your personality.
   b) It is a tool for improving self-awareness.
   c) It is a type of opening in a building or roof.

Vocabulary

Most words have more than one meaning. Find the following words in the text, read the whole sentence surrounding the bolded word and choose the best meaning from the two choices below.

Word	Paragraph	Meaning 1	Meaning 2
contemplate (v)	1	plan	think about
clarity (n)	2	being clear about	being precise about
empowering (n)	2	enable you to do or achieve something	give you power
counterintuitive (adj)	4	not reasonable	contradictory
weaknesses (n)	4	your lack of physical strength	your personal limitations

Self-Awareness—Who Am I?

By the University of Warwick

Introduction

1   We usually identify our existence with our position in society, our friends and family, the needs and desires of our body, and the emotional and intellectual expressions of our mind. For example: We might say "I am a student studying economics, I have three sisters, and live in London." We rarely take the time to **contemplate** the real nature of our existence, to ask the question "Who am I?"

2   Self-awareness is about learning to better understand why you feel what you feel and why you behave in a particular way. Once you begin to understand this concept you then have the opportunity and freedom to change things about yourself enabling you to create a life that you want. It's almost

impossible to change and become self-accepting if you are unsure as to who you are. Having **clarity** about who you are and what you want can be **empowering**, giving you the confidence to make changes.

Is self-awareness important?

3   Self-awareness is often a first step to goal setting. Self-awareness is being conscious of what you're good at while acknowledging what you still have yet to learn. This includes admitting when you don't have the answer and owning up to mistakes.

4   In our highly competitive culture, this can seem **counterintuitive**. In fact, many of us operate on the belief that we must appear as though we know everything all the time or else people will question our abilities, and then perhaps judge us. If you're honest with yourself, you'll admit that really the opposite is true. Because whether you acknowledge your **weaknesses** or not, everyone still sees them. So rather than conceal them, the person who tries to hide weaknesses actually highlights them, creating the perception of a lack of integrity and self-awareness.

The Johari Window

5   The Johari Window is a technique that was created to help people better understand their relationship with themselves as well as with others. It is a model that can be looked at from many angles and provides four basic forms of the Self (the Known, Hidden, Blind, and Unknown Self).

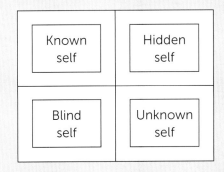

6   The Known Self is what you and others see in you. This is the part that you are able to discuss freely with others. Most of the time you agree with this view you have and others have of you.

7   The Hidden Self is what you see in yourself but others don't. In this part you hide things that are very private about yourself. You do not want this information to be **disclosed** for the reason of protection. It could also be that you feel ashamed of these areas and feel a vulnerability to having your faults and weaknesses exposed. This area equally applies to your good qualities that you don't want to advertise to the world due to modesty.

disclosed (v) to make known; reveal

8   The Blind Self is what you don't see in yourself but others see in you. You might see yourself as an open-minded person when, in reality, people around you don't agree. This area also works the other way. You might see yourself as a "dumb" person while others might consider you incredibly bright. Sometimes those around you might not tell you what they see because they fear offending you. It is in this area that people sometimes detect that what you say and what you do don't match and sometimes body-language shows this **mismatch**.

mismatch (n) not a good fit, contradiction

9   The Unknown Self is the self that you cannot see; others can't see it either. In this category there might be good and bad things that are out of the awareness of others and you. This might refer to **untapped potential**, talents and skills that have yet to be explored by you, your friends, colleagues, or managers.

untapped potential (n) potential that you have not used yet

10 You may find the Johari Window model quite useful as you answer the question "Who am I?" and discover who you are.   **[637 words]**

Comprehension

Go to Explore Online for additional practice and comprehension questions.

Answer the following questions. With *True/False* questions, if the answer is *False* write the correct answer in the space provided.

1. What are the four aspects of identity listed in the introduction?

    _____

    _____

2. How is *self-awareness* defined in this text?

    _____

    _____

    _____

3. What are the benefits of being self-aware, according to the text?

    _____

4. Match the following phrases in paragraph 4 with the most appropriate synonyms below.

    in fact   a)   in place of

    whether . . . or not   b)   regardless of

    rather than   c)   indeed

5. Identify a word in paragraph 4 meaning "not enough." _____

6. Indicate whether the following statements are true or false.

    a)   Self-awareness means knowing the right answers. ☐ True ☐ False

    _____

    b)   Increased self-awareness involves being more competitive. ☐ True ☐ False

    _____

    c)   A person who attempts to conceal a weakness can often unintentionally bring attention to it and appear dishonest. ☐ True ☐ False

    _____

7. Complete the Johari Window with the descriptions on page 9.

Known self	Hidden self
_____	_____
_____	_____
_____	_____
Blind self	**Unknown self**
_____	_____
_____	_____
_____	_____

a) Things neither we, nor others, know about us.
b) Things we know about ourselves and that others also know about us.
c) Things others know about us that we do not know.
d) Things we know about ourselves that others do not know.

8. Using the Johari Window, can you observe and describe the different sides of yourself? How easy is it to observe without judging or evaluating?

Speaking

The Johari Window model is especially relevant today because modern companies and organizations put a high emphasis on the value of employees' soft skills.

Working with a partner, find at least two situations related to your field of study or future career in which using the Johari Window might be beneficial or useful. Explain the situation and how this technique would be useful. You may want to do some research to discover how the Johari Window is used by different organizations and businesses.

 Field-specific activity

soft skills or **people skills (n)**
personal attributes, such as good communication skills, empathy, etc., that enable someone to interact well with others

Writing

 Field-specific activity

Self-awareness means that you have a clear perception of your own personality, including strengths, weaknesses, beliefs, motivations, and emotions.

Write a paragraph (125–150 words) describing yourself.

Before you begin writing, look at the words below and circle four or five adjectives that describe you. Next, brainstorm ideas about how you have become the person that you are today. Think about events and people in the past that have influenced you and ask yourself how you think your personality will contribute to your future in your field of study or career.

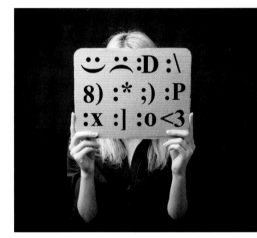

able	experienced	knowledgeable	relaxed
adaptable	extroverted	logical	self-conscious
assertive	friendly	mature	sensible
brave	funny	modest	shy
calm	generous	nervous	silly
caring	happy	observant	spontaneous
cheerful	helpful	organized	stressed
clever	idealistic	patient	sympathetic
complex	independent	proud	trustworthy
confident	intelligent	quiet	warm
dependable	introverted	reflective	wise
energetic	kind		

Speaking

For more information about giving effective oral presentations, see Speaking Strategies, page 168.

Speaking Strategy

Oral presentations

There are two steps to oral presentations: preparation and delivery.

Before preparing your oral presentation, check your teacher's instructions to ensure you prepare properly.

Oral presentations should have an introduction, a body section (with three main points), and a conclusion. Use transition words to move between sections.

When delivering your oral presentation, speak slowly, maintain eye contact with your audience, and use cue cards to remind you of key points. Do not memorize your presentation or read it directly from your cards.

One tool you can use to find out more about your personality is a personality test. Personality tests ask you a series of questions to reveal your personality. They are often used by employers during the hiring process or to learn more about employees. One common personality test is the Myers–Briggs Type Indicator.

Go online and take a personality test. Then present your findings to the class in an oral presentation titled "This is what I learned about my personality."

In the introduction, introduce the test (its name, how many questions it asks, what aspects of personality it focuses on, how it delivers results).

In the body of the presentation, focus on three things you learned about your personality from the test. Give an explanation of each and then a brief example of a time when you demonstrated that aspect of your personality.

Conclude by giving an assessment of why you do or do not think the test gave an accurate reflection of your personality.

Field-Specific Practice

Field-specific activity

For more information about mind maps, see Vocabulary Strategies, page 183.

One way to increase vocabulary is by making mind maps—linking new words to words that you already know.

The mind map on the next page shows how links can be made between words. These links are called associations. Like neural pathways in the brain, the more you think about and use new words, the stronger these pathways become and the more you will remember words and expand your vocabulary.

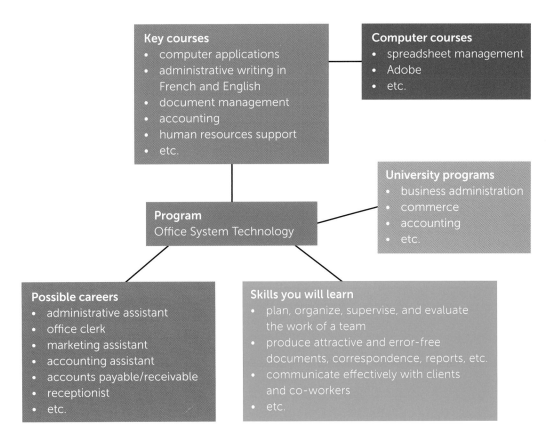

Key courses
- computer applications
- administrative writing in French and English
- document management
- accounting
- human resources support
- etc.

Computer courses
- spreadsheet management
- Adobe
- etc.

Program
Office System Technology

University programs
- business administration
- commerce
- accounting
- etc.

Possible careers
- administrative assistant
- office clerk
- marketing assistant
- accounting assistant
- accounts payable/receivable
- receptionist
- etc.

Skills you will learn
- plan, organize, supervise, and evaluate the work of a team
- produce attractive and error-free documents, correspondence, reports, etc.
- communicate effectively with clients and co-workers
- etc.

1. Work with a partner to brainstorm words to continue building the office system technology mind map.

2. Now build a similar mind map related to your field of study or future career. Researching English college websites may help you to find the information you need to complete this task.

 Field-specific activity

Listening

In this CBC *Spark* interview, David M. Levy, a professor at the Information School at the University of Washington, talks with Nora Young about how contemplative practices such as mindfulness meditation can help us manage our busy, multitasking lives more successfully.

Pre-Listening Activity

Think about the following questions and write a short answer. Then compare and discuss your answers with a partner.

- What does *multitasking* mean to you? How often do you do several things at the same time?
- Do you feel you are more efficient or less efficient when you multitask?
- What does *mindfulness* mean to you?
- What is an example of something you could do to become more mindful?

Vocabulary

Familiarize yourself with the following words before listening to the audio clip.

Word or phrase	Definition
enrolled (v)	signed up to participate
focus (n)	single-minded attention
mindful (adj)	attentive; aware
sustain (v)	continue (something) over a period of time
switching (v)	shifting or moving from one thing to another

Mindful Multitasking [7:20] 🔊

CBC, *Spark*

Go to Explore Online for additional practice and comprehension questions.

Comprehension

Answer the following questions.

1. What is the main idea of the listening?
   a) Doing several things successfully at the same time is impossible.
   b) Mindfulness meditation is a way to help us manage our busy multitasking lives.
   c) Multitasking is part of everyone's professional life.

2. Name three things that mindfulness mediation involves.

   _____

   _____

3. Professor David Levy describes his study of mindful multitasking.

   a) Who was enrolled in the study? _____

   b) Where did the study take place? _____

   c) How many weeks of training did they receive? _____

      10 weeks   8 weeks   2 weeks   4 weeks

4. What were three results of the experiment?

   Participants were _____

   _____

5. Where does David Levy teach and what professional qualifications does he have?

   _____

   _____

6. Why does David Levy think that mindfulness meditation worked?

   _____

   _____

7. What do Levy's students learn in the course he has created?

Students learn _____

_____

_____

8. Is multitasking an individual or cultural phenomenon? Explain.

_____

_____

Speaking

 Field-specific activity

1. Working in a group, come up with an agreed definition of multitasking, then name five jobs that you believe require a high level of multitasking. Discuss which of the five is the job that requires the most multitasking and make a list of ten daily tasks that someone in that job does.

2. Does your field of study or future career require a high level of multitasking? Provide examples of those tasks. Which person in your group has the highest level of multitasking in his or her field of study?

3. Are you good at multitasking? What techniques do you use to prioritize tasks? Explain your answers to the others in your group.

Grammar

Review of the simple present, the simple past, and the past progressive

 Go to Explore Online for additional practice using the simple present, the simple past, and the past progressive.

Working with a partner, read the following passages about the life of Wilder Penfield and put the underlined verbs into the appropriate column in the table below. The two highlighted verbs have already been done for you.

Simple present	Simple past	Past progressive
are	revolutionized	

Wilder Penfield, Professor of Neurology and Neurosurgery at McGill, revolutionized our understanding of the human brain. Penfield was born in 1891 in Spokane, Washington. He studied at Princeton University and obtained a Rhodes scholarship to study at Oxford. He obtained his medical degree from Johns Hopkins University while he was also studying neuropathology.

Penfield's team developed the "Montreal Procedure." While patients are in surgery they remain awake and describe their feelings and reactions while the surgeon stimulates different areas of the brain. Penfield applied this procedure to the surgical treatment of epilepsy

 GG For more information about the simple present tense, see Grammar Guide, page 190.

For more information about the simple past tense, see Grammar Guide, page 200.

For more information about the past progressive tense, see Grammar Guide, page 204.

NEUROCHIRURGIEN · NEUROSURGEON

WILDER PENFIELD 1891-1976

CANADA 40

and <u>used</u> the information <u>collected</u> during hundreds of brain operations to create functional maps of the cortex (surface) of the brain. He <u>mapped</u> areas relating to speech and also <u>discovered</u> that stimulation of the temporal lobes <u>provoked</u> vivid memories. These maps <u>suggest</u> that there <u>is</u> a physical source of memory.

1. Indicate the correct verb tense for each question below.

	Simple present	Simple past	Past progressive
a) Which verb tense is used to express facts, habits, or permanent situations?			
b) Which verb tense is used for events that occurred at a definite time in the past?			
c) Which verb tense is used to express actions that were happening when something else occurred in the past?			

2. Create two *Wh-* information questions about the information in the text.

_____

_____

Reading

More and more employers, especially big companies, are looking at ways to improve employee satisfaction, creativity, and productivity. The secret to changing behaviour involves one of the hottest topics in contemporary science—*neuroplasticity*, a term that describes the brain's ability to change and reorganize its structure, function, and connections with learning.

Pre-Reading Activity

What do you know about the human brain and the process of learning?

1. Work with a partner and decide whether the following statements are true or false. If the answer is *False* write the correct answer in the space provided.

a) The human brain is protected by the skull (cranium), a protective casing that is made up of 30 bones joined together.　　　☐ True　☐ False

_____

b) The brain of an adult human weighs around 1.5 kg. Although it makes up just 2 percent of the body's weight, it uses around 20 percent of its energy.　　　☐ True　☐ False

_____

c) The brain has around 100 million nerve cells.   ❏ True   ❏ False

_____

d) The left side of the brain is largely responsible for
    the left side of the body.   ❏ True   ❏ False

_____

2. Find two more facts about the brain or learning and challenge another team
    to discover whether the information is true or false.

Vocabulary

Find the following words in the text and familiarize yourself with the definitions
before reading.

Word or phrase	Definition
embedded (adj)	fixed into the surface of something
exhausted (adj)	very tired
hone in (v)	focus attention on
mitigate (v)	lessen or minimize
motor cortex (n)	the part of the brain responsible for voluntary muscle activity
unaccustomed (adj)	not used to
willpower (n)	the ability to control your thoughts and how you behave

What It Takes to Change Your Brain's Patterns after Age 25

By **Vivian Giang,** *Fast Company*

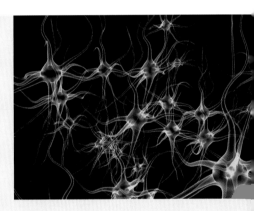

1   "In most of us, by the age of thirty, the character has set like plaster, and will
    never soften again."

2   That quote was made famous by Harvard psychologist William James in his
    1890 book *The Principles of Psychology*, and is believed to be the first time
    modern psychology introduced the idea that one's personality becomes fixed
    after a certain age.

3   More than a century since James's influential text, we know that, unfortunately,
    our brains start to solidify by the age of 25, but that, fortunately, change
    is still possible after. The key is continuously creating new pathways and
    connections to break apart stuck neural patterns in the brain.

4   Simply put, when the brain is young and not yet fully formed, there's a lot of
    flexibility and plasticity, which explains why kids learn so quickly, says Deborah
    Ancona, a professor of management and organizational studies at MIT.

5   "It turns out that we, as human beings, develop neural pathways, and the more
    we use those neural pathways over years and years and years, they become
    very stuck and deeply **embedded**, moving into deeper portions of the brain,"
    she tells *Fast Company*. By the time we get to the age of 25, we just have so
    many existing pathways that our brain relies on, it's hard to break free of them.

The prefix *neuro* relates to a nerve
or the nervous system. Nerves pass
messages through the body. They
are part of the nervous system,
which controls internal functions and
includes the brain and spinal cord.

neuroplasticity the ability of the
nervous system to change

neural pathways the way the brain
communicates to the rest of the
nervous system

neuroscience the study of the nervous
system

neurogenesis the creation of new
neurons

6 One reason why is because our brain is "inherently lazy" and will always "choose the most energy efficient path" if we let it, writes Tara Swart, a senior lecturer at MIT, in her book *Neuroscience for Leadership*.

7 While you'll never learn and change as quickly and easily as you once could, you're also not stuck with your thought patterns from your childhood. In a recent class taught to senior management and executives, Ancona and Swart discussed ways in which people can keep their brain agile—and become better leaders. Below are the steps required to create new connections between neurons.

Focused attention

8 If you want to keep your brain agile, you're going to have to **hone in** on parts of the brain that you use less frequently, says Swart. And this new task has to be so challenging that you'll feel mentally and physically **exhausted** after practising the task because you're forcing your brain to work in ways it's **unaccustomed** to. This is the only way you'll actually grow new neurons strong enough to connect with existing neurons, forming new pathways.

9 For those who want to stimulate their brain, Swart recommends learning a new language or musical instrument. Or do any "energy intensive" challenge that requires "conscious processing of inputs, conscious decision making, complex problem solving, memorizing complex concepts, planning, strategizing, self-reflection, regulating our emotions and channelling energy from them, exercising self-control and **willpower**," Swart says.

Deliberate repetition and practice

10 You can't just learn a new language or musical instrument and never think about it again; you'll forget what you learned. New connections and pathways are fragile, says Swart, and only through repetition and practice can those connections be established enough to become habitual or default behaviours.

11 She writes in *Neuroscience*: "Depending on the complexity of the activity, [experiments have required] four and a half months, 144 days, or even three months for a new brain map, equal in complexity to an old one, to be created in the **motor cortex**."

12 During this time, motivation, willpower, and self-control are necessary to achieve your goal.

The right environment

13 Without the right environment to enable change, your brain won't be able to focus on what's needed to create new neurons. Instead, your brain will be stuck in survival mode, meaning it will choose to travel along pathways it's already familiar with to **mitigate** risk.

14 "[The brain's] need [to survive] focuses attention on the sources of danger and on trying to predict where the next threat will appear, on escape or full frontal battle rather than on an innovative or creative solution, on avoiding risk rather than managing it toward a new suite of products, market, or way of doing business," Swart writes. "And of course, the most important part of our environment is other people and our relationship with them."

15 To have the energy to keep your brain flexible and "plastic," Ancona and Swart say your physical health needs to be in good shape, especially since

your brain sucks up such a massive amount of your body's nutrients. The hydration, nutrients, and rest you need are even more important as your brain learns, unlearns, and relearns behavioural patterns.

16 "Your brain will send its resources through the blood supply to areas that it can tell that you're focusing attention and concentration on," Swart tells *Fast Company*, "or areas that you have a desire to put more energy into."
[782 words]

Comprehension

Answer the following questions. With *True/False* questions, if the answer is *False* write the correct answer in the space provided.

Go to Explore Online for additional practice and comprehension questions.

1. What is the main idea of this reading?
   a) The article describes the history of neuroscience.
   b) The article explains how pathways in the brain can be altered.
   c) The article shows why children learn so quickly compared to adults.
   d) The article explains why patterns in the brain solidify after a certain age.

2. In what ways have current beliefs about the brain changed?
   _____

3. Decide whether the following statements regarding brain plasticity are true or false, according to the text.

   a) The brain changes the most in early childhood. ❏ True ❏ False
   _____

   b) The concept of neuroplasticity was developed by Harvard psychologist William James. ❏ True ❏ False
   _____
   _____

   c) It is possible to create a new neural pathway that is as strong as one you've had your whole life. ❏ True ❏ False
   _____

   d) Adults can teach themselves to learn as quickly as children. ❏ True ❏ False
   _____

4. Does the brain continue to create new neurons after birth? ❏ Yes ❏ No

5. What three abilities will you need to change the patterns in your brain?
   _____

6. The article says that the right environment is very important to changing the brain's pathways. Based on what you learned in the article, what do you think the right environment would look like?
   _____
   _____
   _____

7. In your own words, describe how physical health is connected to neuroplasticity.

_____

_____

_____

8. In what way do you think neuroplasticity might allow someone to become a better leader? Provide an example.

_____

_____

_____

_____

Writing

S For more information about writing paragraphs and topic sentences, see Writing Strategies, page 136.

Writing Strategy

Paragraph and topic sentence

The paragraph is at the heart of all writing—whether it is an essay, report, or presentation. A well-structured paragraph should express one main idea. The main idea is expressed in the topic sentence. The topic sentence is then developed with supporting details (an explanation or description). The concluding sentence of the paragraph should link back to the topic sentence to show how this point is important and relevant.

1. Label the sentences in the following paragraph.

   TS: topic sentence

   SD: supporting details

   CS: concluding sentence

   Self-awareness is important to develop a better understanding of ourselves. It empowers us to build on our strengths, which is why it is often a first step to goal setting. It helps us become conscious of strengths and weaknesses, which allows us to identify areas where we can make improvements. Self-awareness involves admitting errors and learning from our mistakes.

2. Write topic sentences about the following ideas: learning; brain exercises; identity.

3. Work with a partner to develop supporting ideas for *one* of the topic sentences.

4. Write your paragraph. Be attentive to grammar and make sure that you use transitions to logically make links between ideas.

Field-specific activity

5. Select a one-word topic from your field of study. Give this word to another student in your field. Prepare another brief but well-structured paragraph about this topic.

Interpreting Data

What kind of salary can college and university graduates expect in their fields of study or future careers? This Statistics Canada graph provides a glimpse of what you can expect to earn in the years following your graduation.

 We often use the comparative and superlative forms when presenting the results of a graph. For more information about comparative and superlative forms, see Grammar Guide, page 259.

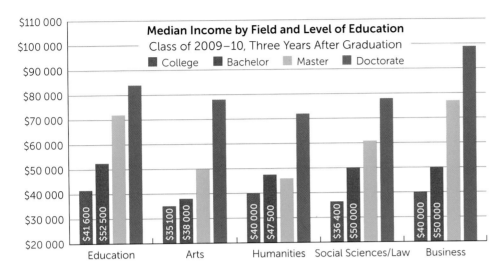

Median Income by Field and Level of Education
Class of 2009–10, Three Years After Graduation
■ College   ■ Bachelor   ■ Master   ■ Doctorate

Education: $41 600, $52 500
Arts: $35 100, $38 000
Humanities: $40 000, $47 500
Social Sciences/Law: $36 400, $50 000
Business: $40 000, $50 000

X-axis The horizontal line along the bottom, which may contain categories or numbers (usually the known data).

Y-axis The vertical line up the side, usually containing numbers (the measured or unknown data).

1. What type of graph is this?
   a) bar graph
   b) line graph
   c) pie chart

2. What is the topic of the graph?

   _____

3. What is measured on the X-axis and on the Y-axis?

   a) X-axis _____

   b) Y-axis _____

4. Decide if the following statements are true or false. If the answer is *False* write the correct answer in the space provided.
   a) College business graduates earn more than college humanities graduates.   ❏ True   ❏ False

   _____

   b) Social science graduates with a bachelor's degree earn about 25 percent more than college graduates.   ❏ True   ❏ False

   _____

   c) Graduates with a bachelor's degree earn more than graduates with a master's degree in all fields.   ❏ True   ❏ False

   _____

5. Write two more *True/False* statements relating to the bar graph and ask another student to find the answers.

1. Pie chart

Shows how a whole is divided into different parts. You might, for example, want to show proportions of students in each college program.

2. Bar graph

Shows numbers that are independent of each other. For example, you could show the number of students in each program, according to their age groups.

3. Line graph

Usually shows trends over time or how variables (data) relate to one another. For example, average grades over a two- or three-year program.

Pronunciation

-ed past tense endings

There are three ways to pronounce the final -ed endings of regular past tense verbs.

The pronunciation is determined by the final sound of the verb in its base form (infinitive). For example, consider the different sounds of *exercised* versus *wanted*.

/ t /	/ d /	/ id /
verbs ending with voiceless sounds such as / p /, / f /, / s /, / k /, / x /, / ch /, / sh /	verbs ending with verb sounds and voiced sounds such as / b /, / g /, / v /, / z /, / r /, / y /	verbs ending with a / t / or / d / sound.
walked, worked, passed	*skimmed, pulled, smiled*	*wanted, visited, added*

1. Read the sentence below out loud and highlight the -ed verbs. How do the sounds of the words differ? Exaggerate and over-articulate as you read the sentences to feel how sounds can be different in English.

   EXAMPLE   Felix wanted to go skiing, but skimmed his books and decided against it. He worked hard and passed his courses.

2. Say each word out loud and circle the correct -ed pronunciation.

   a) helped   / t /   / d /   / id /

   b) laughed   / t /   / d /   / id /

   c) hugged   / t /   / d /   / id /

   d) ended   / t /   / d /   / id /

   e) stayed   / t /   / d /   / id /

   When a word ending in a consonant is followed by a word beginning with a vowel sound we can hear the -ed endings very clearly.

3. Say the following sentences out loud. Identify which -ed sound each has and listen to the rhythm of the sentence.

   a) Mr. Gray stopped aging and never looked any older. _____

   b) Sally worked all week and wanted extra pay. _____

   c) Jasmine helped the students and laughed at their nervousness.

      _____

   d) The band waved at the audience and then stayed and performed another song. _____

   e) We travelled to the city and watched the show. _____

Revising and Editing

1. Correct the nine verb tense errors in the sentences.

   Wilder Penfield is born in 1891. He is revolutionize our understanding of the human brain. He study at Princeton University and he obtain his medical degree from Johns Hopkins University while he studying neuropathology. In 1928, Penfield come to Montreal to teach at McGill University. He establish The Montreal Neurological Institute. The Institute do research and patient care related to the human brain. Penfield dying in 1976.

2. Put the sentences in a logical order to create a well-structured paragraph.
   a) In this way, practising mindfulness can help reduce stress and anxiety and help people to live more fully in the present.
   b) This is a process of observing thoughts, emotions, and sensations as they come and go, with an attitude of curiosity and acceptance.
   c) Several studies indicate that even a 10-minute daily practice yields rewards.
   d) Mindfulness is about paying attention each moment to things as they are, developing compassion, and cultivating a nonjudgmental attitude.
   e) Mindfulness can be applied to experiencing everyday activities such as eating and walking.

Wrap Up

Field-Specific Practice

 Field-specific activity

Who is a leader, innovator, or creative thinker in your field?

1. Research the achievements of a key contributor in your field, take notes in your own words, and write a paragraph (100–150 words).

2. Begin the text with a topic sentence clearly identifying the person and the contribution. Describe the person's origins and education, past achievements, and current work and projects.

3. Check your grammar to make sure that you use the verb tenses appropriately.

4. Share your work with other students in your field and explain why you chose that person for the subject of your paragraph.

Writing

Write a short text explaining the benefits of mindfulness and neuroplasticity in one of the following environments:

- college
- the workplace
- your home life

Incorporate some of the subjects and ideas discussed in this unit such as self-awareness, multitasking, brain plasticity, mindfulness, etc.

Be sure to include a topic sentence that expresses the main idea and provide two or three sentences that provide supporting details. Make sure that your concluding sentence links back to the topic sentence.

For more information about giving oral presentations, see Speaking Strategies, page 168.

Speaking

Do you believe personality tests are accurate assessment tools? Go online and research information about the accuracy and usefulness of personality tests. Present your findings in an oral presentation (2–3 minutes).

Consider the following questions when conducting your research.

- What factors affect the accuracy of a personality test?
- What are the limitations of what a personality test can tell you?
- Can personality tests tell if you are telling the truth?
- Do the results or categories used by a personality test describe a wide range of personalities or behaviours?

Vocabulary

Write the correct word in the space before its definition.

behaviour   clarity   disclose   distinctive   focus   integrity   mindful

1. _____ a strong sense of honesty and morality

2. _____ serving to set apart or mark as particular or unusual

3. _____ to concentrate your attention on something

4. _____ being consciously aware and attentive

5. _____ to make known; reveal

6. _____ the state or quality of being clearly understandable or precise

7. _____ the way a person acts or behaves

When you're finished changing, you're finished.

—Benjamin Franklin

Workplaces are changing. Evolving technology, economic factors, and attitudes drive organizations in all fields to find alternative ways to manage their businesses. Employees are also driving change. By 2020, Generation Z will make up 20 percent of the workforce, and they will bring new ideas and expectations with them. What are you looking for in a job? What skills and qualities will you bring to the workforce? In this unit, we will examine new work trends, the role of different generations in the workplace, and the tools you will need to get a job in your field in these interesting times.

Warm Up

1. Look at the following list of factors related to job satisfaction. Rank the items in terms of their importance to you (from 1 to 12, where 1 is the most important factor and 12 is the least important factor) in choosing a career.

	Rank
• job security	_____
• interesting work	_____
• being appreciated for your work	_____
• good relationship with your colleagues	_____
• salary	_____
• flexible work schedule	_____
• unlimited vacation time	_____
• good work–life balance	_____
• opportunity for career advancement	_____
• ability to make a difference	_____
• challenging work	_____
• ability to work from home	_____

2. Compare your ranking with a partner's ranking and discuss these questions.
   a) Why did you make your first choice?
   b) Which one of these factors do you think will be easiest to achieve in your field of study or future career? Which will be the most difficult? Explain.
   c) What other factors not on this list are important for you in choosing a career?

Field-specific activity

3. With a partner, read the descriptions below and, in the chart, circle the letter that matches the generation that best fits the description. Check your answers on page 44.
   a) Baby Boomers: born between 1946 and 1964
   b) Generation X: born between 1964 and 1980
   c) Generation Y or Millennials: born between 1980 and 1995
   d) Generation Z: born between 1995 and 2007

Description/World events			
• born after World War II • hippie generation • first modern counter-culture • space exploration a b c d	• housing market crash • digital globalization • Internet use starts in childhood a b c d	• experienced the Vietnam War • rise of mass media • end of the Cold War • exposed to daycare and divorce a b c d	• rise of the information age • Iraq War • reality TV • rising gas and food prices a b c d
At work			
• comfortable with digital technology • enjoy teamwork • most educated generation of workers • value freedom/flexibility a b c d	• entrepreneurial spirit • question authority • loyal to profession, not employer • created the concept of work–life balance a b c d	• generation known for valuing work over personal life • work long hours • reluctant to retire a b c d	• very comfortable with changing digital technology • multitaskers • value security and stability a b c d

Signature product			
• television a b c d	• 3D printing • wearable technology a b c d	• tablet • smartphone a b c d	• personal computer a b c d
Communication media			
• text message or social media a b c d	• apps on smartphones a b c d	• email and text message a b c d	• telephone a b c d

Reading

The theory that all people in a generation share characteristics is common but controversial. While there are social, political, and environmental forces that shape people of a similar age, our personalities, interests, and backgrounds play a large role in determining who we are in our social lives and in the workplace. Make your own decision about the theory of generations as you read this article about Generation Z.

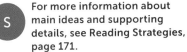

For more information about main ideas and supporting details, see Reading Strategies, page 171.

> ## Reading Strategy
>
> ### Main ideas and supporting details
>
> The main idea describes what the text is about.
>
> Look for clues by reading the introduction, conclusion, and a few words from each paragraph. Note subtitles and bolded words or phrases.
>
> The main idea will be backed up by supporting details. These might include examples, explanations, comparisons, quotes, or data.

Pre-Reading Activity

1. Look for the main idea in the text on on pages 26–27. Which of the following do you think best describes it?
   a) Starting out in the workforce can be challenging for anyone.
   b) People in different generations have different characteristics.
   c) Making the world a better place is the main reason a person in Generation Z goes to work.
   d) Generation Z has unique characteristics in the workplace that managers need to adapt to.

2. Discuss the following questions with a partner.
   a) Do you think your generation is stereotyped?
   b) Do you consider yourself typical of your generation?
   c) How do you think a generation gap might cause problems in the workplace?
   d) Ask your partner your own question about Generation Z.

Vocabulary

Find the following words in the text. Then use the correct word to fill in each blank in the sentences. A synonym or definition has been provided to help you.

challenge (n) (para. 1)   **revealed (v)** (para. 5)

thrive (v) (para. 2)   **mentor (v)** (para. 6)

turmoil (n) (para. 2)   **tech-savvy (adj)** (para. 9)

quest (n) (para. 3)

1. Finding someone to _____ (teach or train) can help you _____ (become successful) in the workplace.

2. I've always been _____ (good with technology), so one of my aspirations has been to get a job with Microsoft.

3. When the director quit, the company was in _____ (a state of great confusion), and it became a _____ (problem) to stay engaged at work.

4. My _____ (long search) _____ (made known) things I never knew about myself.

aspiration (n) ambition to achieve an objective

cohort (n) a group of people with a common characteristic

withstood (v) remained unaffected by

bias (n) a personal, often unreasonable judgment

Making the World a Better Place Tops Generation Z's List for Best Employer

By Tom Turpin, *Financial Post*

1 Twenty years ago when I was starting in the workforce, I was driven, competitive, and engaged—more than anything I'm certain I was a **challenge** to manage.

2 Every generation has its own set of values, **aspirations**, and characteristics. Boomers were driven to build institutions and **thrive** while growing up in the largest **cohort** of human births in the history of the world. Generation X **withstood** economic **turmoil** to innovate with the developing technologies that are driving the world's economy today. Generation Y's innovations and influence are already being felt, as well as their demands for good work, good pay, and great work–life balance.

3 Now, Generation Z is joining the workforce, with their **quest** for making the world a better place and their drive to be their own boss. With all these generations working together come **bias**, stereotypes, and perceptions that can hinder a productive working relationship. But we can make the most of our differences simply by initiating an open dialogue, and the good news is that this is exactly what the younger generation is thirsty for.

4 **Getting to know Gen Z.** Like the generation before them, this fresh young cohort places significant value on companies that are socially responsible and are making a positive contribution to their communities.

5 In a survey conducted by Randstad Canada, 87 percent of respondents **revealed** it was important for them to work for a company that helps the community, with specific focus on creating new jobs locally, rewarding

employees for community service, and closing the gender divide in the workplace.

6 **When it comes to their preferred working styles**, they are looking for their manager to **mentor** them and give feedback regularly, even more so than millennials. It's all about inclusion with the next generation. They are entrepreneurial in nature and see themselves as the drivers in their careers, which is why they prefer an open dialogue with their employers about what's needed to successfully achieve their goals. Multitasking comes extremely easily for this generation because they grew up with at least five screens at all times. Whether it's finding the answer to any question in an instant on their phones, looking for the perfect app or snapchatting with their networks around the world.

7 **As managers, we need to connect with this younger generation and keep them stimulated**. The question is, what do leaders and managers get out of teaching these future top performers?

8 **Never stop growing, networking, or working**. Being part of the senior leadership team means managing colleagues and helping them grow. One of the most rewarding parts of being a leader is watching people progress in their careers. At the same time, it is a leader's responsibility to grow, learn new skills, take new risks, and not only stay competitive but inspiring as well. Challenging the **status quo** and remaining flexible can open up possibilities for innovation and growth, both for the company and development as a leader.

status quo (n) the way things currently are

9 **Social skills are their strength**. There are multiple great skills Generation Z has to offer. They are collaborative, **tech-savvy** and socially engaged. By mentoring this new group and sharing best practices, you can also learn a new skill set. They bring a fresh perspective on how to connect with younger audiences, and also **shed light** on tools they use on a daily basis that could possibly simplify everyday processes.

shed light (exp) to make clear

10 **Always share insights**. You'd think this generation would prefer communication via email or text but, according to the study, 45 percent of Gen Zs believe the most effective way to communicate is in person. They are looking for meaning and purpose in everything they do and will appreciate hearing about different directions they can take. It's a positive situation when you can match experience and insight with energy and creativity.

insights (n) deep understanding

11 **Help people who show interest in themselves**. Generation Zs are comfortable observing and learning but they still have a strong interest in doing the work themselves. If their **entry-level job** requires repetition of less interesting duties, show them your company is interested in what they have to say. Share examples of people whose creative ideas or thoughtful approaches helped them move up, but be sincere about possibilities for advancement.

entry-level job (n) the first job a new graduate or trainee gets after finishing school

12 In other words, give them a chance to shine. It will help business, while creating an inclusive and positive work environment. Chances are, it will be a positive experience for everyone involved.   **[726 words]**

Comprehension

Go to Explore Online for additional practice and comprehension questions.

Answer the following questions. With *True/False* questions, if the answer is *False* write the correct answer in the space provided.

1. Read each description and decide if it represents Baby Boomers (B), Generation X (X), or Generation Y (Y), according to the article.

   a) They want a good salary and time to spend with family. _____

   b) They grew up with the largest population in history. _____

   c) They had to live with economic instability. _____

   d) They were motivated to build institutions. _____

   e) We are starting to feel their influence in the workforce today. _____

2. Both Generation Y and Generation Z feel it is important for companies to help the community.　❒ True　❒ False

3. According to a recent Randstad Canada survey, how do Gen Zs want companies to help their community?

4. Which of these statements are true about Gen Zs, according to the article?

   a) They like to work independently and make their own rules.　❒ True　❒ False

   b) They want a lot of feedback at work as well as guidance from superiors.　❒ True　❒ False

   c) They spend a lot of time on social media at work.　❒ True　❒ False

5. What benefits will managers get from working with and mentoring younger workers?

6. How does Generation Z prefer to communicate?
   a) via email　　b) via text　　c) in person

7. Who is the intended audience for this article? Explain your answer.
   a) Baby Boomers　b) Generation Z　c) Generation X　d) managers

8. How is the main idea supported in the article? Circle all that apply.

examples   explanations   comparisons   quotes   data

Give two examples of supporting details from the article.

_____

_____

Speaking

Do you agree with the characterization of Generation Z in this article? Do you think it is fair or useful to characterize people by generations? In a group of four, have two people think of arguments for why it is fair or useful to use the idea of generations to categorize people. Have the other two people think of arguments for why it is not fair or useful.

Take turns sharing your arguments with the other group. Which arguments do you think are strongest and why? Try to come to an agreement as a group.

Interpreting Data

Look at the infographic about Generation Z, and answer the following questions. With *True/False* questions, if the answer is *False* write the correct answer in the space provided.

1. They expect to have several jobs during their career.   ☐ True ☐ False

   _____

   _____

2. Most of them say their parents are involved in their career choice.   ☐ True ☐ False

   _____

   _____

3. Most of them would take a salary reduction if the company had a mission they feel strongly about.   ☐ True ☐ False

   _____

   _____

4. Most of them prefer working at home as part of a virtual team.   ☐ True ☐ False

   _____

   _____

5. Face-to-face communication is very important for them.   ☐ True ☐ False

   _____

   _____

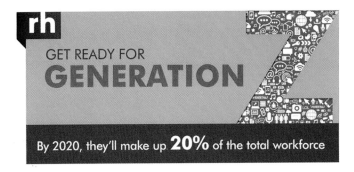

GET READY FOR

GENERATION Z

By 2020, they'll make up **20%** of the total workforce

WORKPLACE EXPECTATIONS

77% EXPECT TO **WORK HARDER** THAN PREVIOUS GENERATIONS

$46,799 MEAN SALARY EXPECTATION PER YEAR FOR THEIR FIRST JOB AFTER COLLEGE

5 YEARS AFTER COLLEGE THEY'D LIKE TO BE:

20% Entrepreneurs   24% Working their way up the corporate ladder   32% Managing employees

4 AVERAGE NUMBER OF ORGANIZATIONS **THEY EXPECT TO WORK FOR** THROUGHOUT THEIR CAREERS

CAREER ATTITUDES

82% SAY THEIR PARENTS WILL HELP INFLUENCE THEIR CAREER DECISIONS

30% WOULD TAKE A 10-20% PAY CUT TO WORK FOR A COMPANY WITH A MISSION THEY DEEPLY CARE ABOUT

TOP 7 JOB SEARCH PRIORITIES
① Growth opportunities
② Generous pay
③ Making a positive impact
④ Job security
⑤ Healthcare benefits
⑥ Flexible hours
⑦ Manager to learn from

50% WOULD LIKE TO RETIRE BEFORE AGE 60

54% EXPECT TO WORK UNTIL THEY'RE 61-70 YEARS OLD

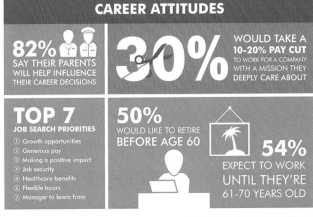

WORKING WITH GEN Z

ATTITUDES TOWARD COWORKERS

52% FEEL IT WILL BE EASY TO WORK WITH GENERATION X[1]

27% FEEL THE SAME ABOUT THE BABY BOOMER GENERATION[2]

WORK ENVIRONMENT
PREFERRED: COLLABORATING WITH A SMALL GROUP IN AN OFFICE SETTING
LEAST IDEAL: WORKING OFF-SITE AS PART OF A VIRTUAL TEAM

74% PREFER TO COMMUNICATE **FACE-TO-FACE** WITH COLLEAGUES

QUALITIES VALUED IN A MANAGER
38% Honesty/integrity   22% Mentoring ability

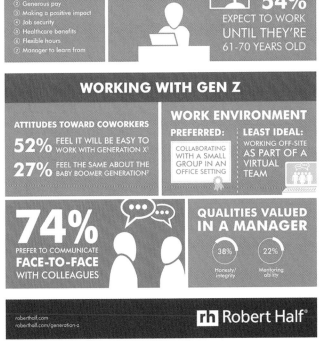

roberthalf.com
roberthalf.com/generation-z

rh Robert Half®

6. Most say that it will be easy to work with Baby Boomers. ☐ True ☐ False

7. A manager's ability to mentor is as important as honesty. ☐ True ☐ False

8. What was one piece of information that surprised you most in this infographic?

9. Aside from honesty and integrity, what qualities do you value in a manager?

Pronunciation

The pronunciation of three-syllable words

In English, stressed syllables are emphasized more and are longer than unstressed syllables. Stress placement in three-syllable words can be on the first, second, or third syllable. When you learn a word, it is helpful to learn its stress pattern as well.

1. Listen to the pronunciation of the following words. Pay attention to the stress pattern.

Stress on the first syllable	Stress on the second syllable	Stress on the third syllable
candidate	department	volunteer
graduate	description	recommend
company	employer	engineer
comfortable	effective	understand

2. Now, listen to the pronunciation of the following words related to work. Put them in the correct column according to their stress pattern.

interview   develop   employee   confident
conference   consider   guarantee   profession
leadership   vacation   pioneer

Stress on the first syllable	Stress on the second syllable	Stress on the third syllable

3. Listen to the following sentences and pay attention to the stress pattern of the words in bold. Then, with a partner, take turns reading the sentences out loud.
   a) The **employer** will **interview** the **candidate**.
   b) We will **consider** her application because she has the necessary **leadership** skills to work in our **department**.
   c) She is **comfortable** speaking in public at the **conference**.
   d) Did you read the job **description** that the **company** posted?
   e) He **recommends** students do **volunteer** work before they **graduate**.
   f) He is **confident** that he will **develop** his skills working in his **profession**.

Listening

Companies spend a lot of time and money developing their brand to set themselves apart from the competition. Developing a personal brand can also help you set yourself apart as you enter the workforce. This audio clip presents some simple tips for selling your unique skills and experiences to employers in your field.

Vocabulary

The following words are used in the audio. Study the definitions before you listen.

Word or phrase	Definition
cutesy (adj)	pleasant in a childish way
screening tool (exp)	way to select for something
target audience (exp)	a group that something is aimed at
call to action (exp)	an instruction to the audience to do something
brand (n)	the symbol, logo, name, and/or words used to represent a company and set it apart from its competition
credentials (n)	qualifications, achievements, and personal qualities
buzzword (n)	a word or phrase that is a popular term in a particular profession or field of study

Listen to the first segment of the talk and answer questions 1–3 that follow. Then take notes on the second segment of the talk, and answer questions 4–8.

Selling Yourself:
The Art of Personal Branding [7:00] 🔊

CBC, *Under the Influence*

Comprehension

Answer the following questions.

1. Emily works at the CBC, but she is applying to work at the *National Post*. According to the speaker, which email address is appropriate on her resumé?
    a) emily_matthews@cbc.ca
    c) emilyliveshere@gmail.com
    b) emily_matthews@gmail.com
    d) hiremenationalpost@yahoo.ca

2. Why don't recruiters like quirky email addresses?

    _____

3. What do employers think when someone sends a resumé from a work-related email address?

    _____

Go to Explore Online for additional practice and comprehension questions.

A CV or *curriculum vitae* is the same thing as a resumé.

4. A smart CV is like a smart _____ _____

Take notes as you listen to how to create a CV.

Question	Notes
Who is your target audience?	
What is your unique selling proposition?	
What do you want your target audience to feel after reading your resumé?	
What's the call to action?	

5. Why does the speaker say "If you're talking to everyone, you're talking to no one"?

    _____

6. What does the speaker call "the heart of your CV"?
    a) your unique selling proposition
    b) your cover letter
    c) your credentials and experience

7. What separates smart brands from other brands?

    _____

8. Why do you think it is important to put a call to action in your resumé?

    _____

Writing

Find a short job advertisement for a job that interests you and relates to your field of study or future career.

Start by underlining the key words in the job ad. Then make a list of job requirements (i.e., responsibilities and qualifications) in the left column and write down your relevant skills and experience in the right column.

Job requirements	My relevant skills and experience

Finally, using the cover letter model in the Professional Writing Strategies on page 158, write a cover letter using what you have learned in this unit about personal branding.

Field-Specific Practice

To get a job in your field, you need to develop your unique selling proposition. What skills and experience do you have that will set you apart from the competition? Make a list of skills you have and skills you will need to develop to work in your field. Go to college and university websites or look up job ads to get ideas.

Skills I have	Skills I will need to develop
EXAMPLE good colour sense and good at drawing (interior design)	**EXAMPLE** technical drawing and Autocad (interior design)

Speaking

Choose three of your skills and with a partner take turns answering the following questions.

1. Where did you learn these skills?

2. In what contexts will these skills be useful when working in your field?

3. Give a specific example of a time when you used these skills in the past.

Speaking

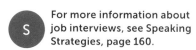
For more information about job interviews, see Speaking Strategies, page 160.

Speaking Strategy

Job interviews

During a job interview, what you say is important, but so is how you say it.

- Speak slowly and not too softly or too loudly.
- Keep a positive expression on your face.
- Prepare, so you know key facts about the company and the job that you are applying for.
- Don't apologize or speak poorly of yourself or your experiences.
- Focus on a few simple ideas and stick to them.

Field-specific activity

In a job interview, not only will you need to sell your technical abilities and your knowledge of your field, you will also need to show that you can work well with others. These are called soft skills. In groups of four, practise answering the following questions that test your soft skills. Be sure to prepare your answers in advance.

1. Talk about a time that a co-worker or another student got angry with you. What did you do?

2. Talk about a tough decision you had to make. How did you choose what to do?

3. Talk about a time you made a mistake. What did you do to fix it?

4. How would other people describe you?

5. Talk about a time you disagreed with someone. What did you do?

6. How do you stay organized?

Watching

One of the ways in which workplaces are changing is an increase in the level of automation, that is, the amount of work done by machines, robots, or computers. For some fields, such as manufacturing and agriculture, these changes have been taking place for a while. For others, they are just beginning. This video discusses the opportunities and the challenges that automation will create for the next generation of workers.

Pre-Watching Activity

Before watching the report, discuss the following questions with a partner.

1. What examples can you give of automation, where computers or machines have started to do the work that used to be done by people?

2. What do you think are some of the advantages of automation?

3. What might be the disadvantages of automation?

4. What is an example of a task or job that is currently automated in your field of study or future career?

5. What is an example of something that might be automated in the future in your field of study or future career?

 Field-specific activity

Vocabulary

The following words and expressions are used in the report. Read the sentences and then match each word with its definition.

1. When I wanted my mom to make pancakes, I found an **ally** in my sister, who wanted them too.

2. My new blender is considered **cutting-edge** kitchen technology.

3. The construction company fixed the road in the middle of the night to avoid **disruption**.

4. If we don't make enough sales, the manager will have to **lay off** some workers.

5. I used to do **manual labour**, but now I work in an office.

6. My old computer has become completely **obsolete**.

7. **White-collar jobs** are being automated.

Word or phrase	Letter	Definition
1. **ally (n)**		a) newest and most advanced
2. **cutting-edge (adj)**		b) no longer used or useful
3. **disruption (n)**		c) to stop employing someone
4. **lay off (v)**		d) someone who assists or supports
5. **manual labour (n)**		e) physical work, mostly done by humans
6. **obsolete (adj)**		f) work done in an office or other professional environment
7. **white-collar jobs (n)**		g) an interruption of the normal course of things

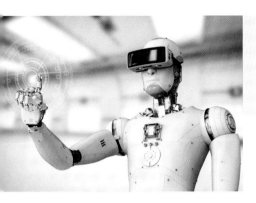

Automation Entering White-Collar Work [11:03] ▶

CBC, *The National*

Go to Explore Online for additional practice and comprehension questions.

Comprehension

1. What are some of the advantages listed of using Bruno to make pizzas?

    _____

2. Why does Alex Garden call the pizza parlour a "co-bot environment"?

    _____

3. According to Sunil Johan, why are white-collar jobs (jobs that require highly educated people) now being automated?
    a) because companies are trying to cut costs
    b) because of the rise of artificial intelligence
    c) because people don't want to work at these jobs

4. Why did Tory Shoreman leave her job at the bank?

    _____

5. How much of Tory's department was laid off due to automation?
    a) 20 percent   b) 40 percent   c) 60 percent   d) 100 percent

6. In one sentence, describe what Benjamin Alarie's legal software does.

    _____

    _____

7. How does Benjamin Alarie say law students can prepare for automation?

    _____

8. What will be the effect of automation on education, according to the video?

    _____

9. Why do you think people decided to learn how to code to deal with automation?

    _____

10. What is the main idea of the report?
    a) Automation is taking manual labour jobs and workers will need to adapt.
    b) Automation will take over many office and professional jobs and workers will need to adapt.
    c) Automation will take over many jobs; workers will need more education.

Field-specific activity

Writing

Write a paragraph (150 words) about what impact you think automation will have on your field of study or future career. In it, discuss the following points:

*   How important is automation in your field? Provide an example.
*   How much has automation changed or increased in your field in the last few years? (Use the past tense in your answer.)
*   What tasks or jobs could be automated in the future?
*   Give an example of a pro and a con of having more automation in your field.
*   Conclude by stating the impact you think automation will have in the future.

Reading

Most jobs today allow employees to take two or three weeks off a year, but a few companies have started to try something different: giving their employees as much time off as they want or need. Sound crazy? In this article, the author makes the case for why unlimited vacation time might be the way of the future.

Pre-Reading Activity

Discuss the following questions with a partner.

1. Do you think it is a good idea for companies to let employees decide how much vacation time they can take? Why or why not?

2. If you could choose, how much vacation time would you like to have at work?

3. How else could a company help its employees have a good work–life balance?

Vocabulary

Use context clues to match the word or phrase in the text with the definition.

Word or phrase	Letter	Definition
1. **open-ended (adj)** (para. 2)		a) becoming less
2. **steer clear (exp)** (para. 3)		b) expresses something indirectly
3. **diminishing (adj)** (para. 3)		c) unrestricted or without limits
4. **relied on (phr v)** (para. 5)		d) puts in place
5. **undergo (v)** (para. 7)		e) to avoid or stay away from
6. **implies (v)** (para. 9)		f) to experience (something unpleasant)
7. **implements (v)** (para. 11)		g) depended on

Does Unlimited Vacation Really Work?

By Aaron Skonnard, Inc.

1   Imagine everyone coming into work when it works for them—and not when it doesn't. In such a scenario, employees at all levels could decide whether they felt like taking a few hours off each day, or taking an entire month (or more) off depending on what's happening in their lives. Is this vision **utopian**, or the wave of the future?

2   The answer may be the latter, judging by the recent announcement of Richard Branson, founder and chairman of the Virgin Group, of a "non-policy" for paid time off (PTO). This decision means that all of Branson's employees in the company's main offices in the US and the UK now have **open-ended** access to **vacation** time.

3   The news from Branson has caused an explosion of interest from the media and social networks, revealing the not-so-hidden truth that nearly everyone is looking for ways to improve work–life balance. An article last month in *Forbes*

utopian (adj) having ideal conditions

vacation (n) a period of time spent away from home or work

clock in/clock out (v) to record the time you arrive and leave work

recharge (v) to restore energy; to make new, or return to normal

run out of (exp) to use up

breeds (v) causes; brings about

blank cheque (n) complete freedom

burden (n) a weight or responsibility

abuse (v) to take advantage of

reported that, contrary to common perception, the majority of Americans actually don't aspire to leadership positions. A recent study conducted by the Harris Poll found that one-third of respondents decided to **steer clear** of the leadership track to avoid further **diminishing** their personal time.

4 Since having time for life outside the office is an increasingly high priority to workers in every industry, other company founders would be wise to take a page from the vacation non-policy book of Branson and other pioneers of this approach (which according to *Businessweek* comprise only around 1 percent of all companies).

5 I'm proud to say that at Pluralsight, we too have this same non-policy as part of our culture. While we previously **relied on** a traditional PTO policy, we killed it because we felt it was awkward and unnecessary for employees to have to ask a manager for permission to take time off. We don't **clock people in and out** each day, so why should we track their days off? Like the other non-policy 1 percenters, all we ask is that each person coordinate his or her chosen days off with team members so that the group can continue to move forward when someone is out.

6 Here are three reasons why we think people actually get more done when they have open-ended access to vacation time:

7 It makes employees less anxious. We feel that taking too little time off is just as damaging as taking too much. We all need to occasionally **recharge** and reconnect with loved ones, and sometimes a difficult event in a person's life doesn't fit within a two-week vacation. One of our employees recently got very ill and had to **undergo** major surgery. Having an open-ended PTO policy eliminated his stress and anxiety about using all of his "vacation time" for an illness, and allowed him to focus on getting better.

8 Special circumstances like these emphasize the point that the right amount of days off for each person will vary from year to year based on circumstances. An open policy makes it possible to accommodate individual needs as they arise. Periodically, too, we should all be able to relax and take a well-deserved break for no good reason—even (or sometimes especially) if we've **run out of** our fixed number of vacation days.

9 It **implies** trust, which **breeds** responsibility. We've been talking about our open-ended PTO policy for a while, and whenever we do, the same questions arise: Don't employees take advantage of the company by taking too much time off, damaging business results? How do we keep people in the office if they have a **blank cheque** to stay home or vacation as much as they want?

10 The answers to these questions may surprise you, but they make sense. If you hire the right people and trust them to manage their own calendars, they won't abuse the non-policy. In fact, most will likely take less time off than if you had a formal policy that provided a limited amount of PTO. With freedom comes great responsibility, and our employees are living proof of this principle. We actually believe that encouraging everyone to take enough vacation is more of a **burden** on leadership than worrying about people taking too much.

11 It makes people happier and want to work harder. Our faith that people won't **abuse** the policy if a company **implements** it goes back to our culture, which includes only two basic rules. Rule 1 is to be respectful, considerate,

and kind even when you disagree. Rule 2 is to always act in Pluralsight's best interests. With a company-wide commitment to Rule 2, we have no need to **monitor** vacation days. Since employees are committed to doing right by the company, we've found that our non-policy actually increases productivity. This is because in addition to being very thoughtful about their workload versus vacation time, when employees do decide to take time off, they work even harder before to make sure that they're not leaving team members with extra work.

monitor (v) to observe; check

12 While the organization as a whole certainly benefits from these realities, we didn't stop tracking time off to reduce the amount of leave people take. On the contrary, we feel it's critically important to everyone's health and well-being to take enough time off to truly **disconnect**, do what they want to do, and take care of important matters in their lives outside of the workplace. The simple truth is that when we let go of managing this function corporately, our open PTO policy creates happier workers who find more inspiration for their jobs, and who truly want to do what's best for the company over time. **[928 words]**

disconnect (v) stop thinking about work

Comprehension

Answer the following questions. With *True/False* questions, if the answer is *False* write the correct answer in the space provided.

Go to Explore Online for additional practice and comprehension questions.

1. Why do many workers choose not to pursue a leadership position?

   _____

2. Most companies have adopted a policy of unlimited vacation time.　　☐ True　☐ False

   _____

3. At the company Pluralsight, they have adopted a vacation non-policy. However, what do they ask employees to do before going on vacation?

   _____

4. What are two reasons why employees will feel less anxious with an unlimited vacation time policy?

   _____

   _____

5. Does the author believe that employees will take advantage of an unlimited vacation time policy?　☐ Yes　☐ No Explain your answer.

   _____

   _____

6. Explain how an unlimited vacation policy might make people work harder.

   _____

   _____

7. What are the benefits for companies when they stop managing vacation time?

   _____

   _____

8. Do you think unlimited vacation time would work for all professions? Explain your answer using an example.

_____

_____

9. Which of the following summarizes the main idea of the text?
   a) Companies with a policy of unlimited vacation time make more money.
   b) Unlimited vacation time can work if employees don't take advantage of it.
   c) Unlimited paid time off is good for employees and good for companies.

Writing

Write a short paragraph explaining whether an unlimited vacation policy would work for a job in your field of study or future career. State your opinion in the topic sentence, then back up your opinion with supporting details.

 **Field-specific activity**

 For more information about topic sentences and supporting details, see Writing Strategies, page 136.

 Go to Explore Online for additional practice using the future tense and modals.

GG **For more information about the future tense, see Grammar Guide, page 210.**

For more information about modals, see Grammar Guide, page 223.

Grammar

Future tense and modals

Future tense

We use the future tense to talk about events that will occur at a time later than now. There are two ways to form the future:

will + verb	_be going to_ + verb
I will take my vacation next week.	I am going to go on a cruise.

Modal auxiliaries

Modal auxiliary (or helping) verbs are used to indicate functions, attitude, or mood such as ability, making requests, expressing possibility, asking or giving permission, giving advice, expressing obligation (something you have to do), etc. A modal auxiliary verb is always used with a main verb. Common modals include _can_, _could_, _may_, _might_, _must_, _should_, and _would_.

EXAMPLES

I could/may/might stop by your house after work. (possibility)

She can work my shift on Monday. (ability)

I would like to go on vacation. (desire)

You should send a thank-you note. (advice)

You must bring a gift to the party. (obligation)

Modal verbs do not change form depending on the verb tense.

1. Circle examples of the future tense in paragraphs 10–12 on page 27.

2. Circle examples of modals in paragraphs 4 and 5 on page 38.

3. Fill in the blanks with _will_ or the correct modal.

   a) The manager says my interview _____ definitely take place on Friday.

   b) My teacher says that I _____ bring an extra copy of my resumé to the interview.

   c) I asked to get off work early so I _____ study for the test.

4. Describe the differences in meaning between these four sentences.
   a) I will go for an interview on Monday.
   b) I can go for an interview on Monday.
   c) I am going to go for an interview on Monday.
   d) I would like to go for an interview on Monday.

   _____

   _____

   _____

   _____

Revising and Editing

Look at the following cover letter. There are many ways it can be improved. There are grammar errors and formality errors. Review the cover letter dos and don'ts in Professional Writing Strategies, page 157, and read the example cover letter. Then write an improved letter.

There are four vocabulary errors. You will need to replace the wrong word with one of these English words: *attached*, *available*, *internship*, *studies*.

Vincent Legault
Partyboyl998@hotmail.com

October 12, 2018

ABC Clothing Inc.

To whom it may concern:

My name is Vincent Legault. I am writing to ask you for a job. I am totally qualified and you would be crazy not to hire me. I recently graduate from Dawson College with a diploma in administration. I search employment in sales. I do not yet have experience in this field, but I believe you are find me to be hard-working and a quick learner.

Through my employment and scholar, I have develop excellent communication, teamwork and organizational skills. I am motivated, and hard worker. I can to multitask. I did extracurricular and volunteer activities during both my high school and college career. I also completed a stage at a bank last month.

I have joined my resumé with this letter. I will greatly appreciate the opportunity to meet with you for an interview when you are disponible. I believe I can make a valuable contribution to your store and you will find me a great addition to your team. Get back to me soon or you will miss out!

Keep it real,
Vincent Legault

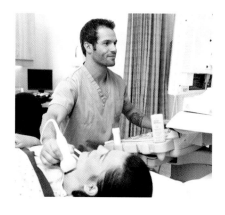

Action verbs help to show your skills and achievements to employers.

analyzed	launched
coordinated	negotiated
demonstrated	organized
designed	planned
developed	simplified
established	trained
improved	transformed

Wrap Up

Field-Specific Practice

Find an English job advertisement in your field of study to respond to. Write a cover letter applying for that position. Be sure to consider the following questions when writing your letter:

- Who is your target audience?
- What is your unique selling proposition?
- What do you want your audience to feel?
- What is the call to action?

Choose an ad from one of the following websites: jobboom.com, careerclick.ca, monster.ca, workopolis.ca or Indeed.com. Review the cover letter dos and don'ts and refer to the cover letter example in Professional Writing Strategies, page 158. Remember to use action verbs.

Writing

Match the leader with his or her generation.

Leader	Letter	Generation
1. **Mark Zuckerberg** An American computer programmer, Internet entrepreneur, and philanthropist. He is the co-founder of the social networking website Facebook.		a) Baby Boomer
2. **Barack Obama** The 44th President of the United States. He is the first African American to hold the office.		b) Generation X
3. **Malala Yousafzai** A Pakistani activist for female education and the youngest-ever Nobel Prize laureate.		c) Generation Y (Millennials)
4. **Larry Page** An American computer scientist and Internet entrepreneur who co-founded Google with Sergey Brin.		d) Generation Z

Now, choose one of these people and write a paragraph about him or her. Based on what you've learned about the different generations in this unit, do you think the person is an example of their generation? Before you write your paragraph, you will need to research the person to develop your supporting points and explain whether you think this person represents his or her generation.

Speaking

Choose a job advertised online in your field of study. Print the ad and prepare to be interviewed for this job by two students. Role-play job interviews in groups of three. Two students can be the interviewers, and one student can be the interviewee. The interviewers should ask five of the job interview questions suggested in Professional Writing Strategies, page 161 and make up five more questions to ask.

The interviewers should evaluate the interviewees based on the following criteria:

Element	1 Needs significant improvement	2 Needs some improvement	3 Good	4 Very good	5 Excellent
Voice					
Eye contact					
Non-verbal expressions					
Clarity of ideas					
Vocabulary					
Content					

Total score: /30

What were two things the interviewee did well?

1. _____

_____

_____

2. _____

_____

_____

What are two ways the interviewee could improve?

1. _____

_____

_____

2. _____

_____

_____

Vocabulary

ally (n)	cutting-edge (adj)	diminishing (v)	open-ended (adj)
revealed (v)	thrive (v)	turmoil (n)	

Which of the above vocabulary words from this unit is an antonym (means the opposite) of the bold word in the sentence? Write the correct answer on the line after the sentence.

1. My schedule is **limited** for the next week. _____

2. After the difficult co-worker left, **peace** returned to the office. _____

3. Poor customer service can cause business to **decrease**. _____

4. In most action movies, there is an **enemy** that the main character must defeat.
   _____

5. Company profits have been **increasing** thanks to sales of the new product.
   _____

6. In the interview, he **hid** the truth about why he left his previous position.
   _____

7. The printing press is an example of an **old** technology. _____

Answer Key for Warm Up question 3 (page 24)

Description/world events: a, d, b, c

At work: c, b, a, d

Signature product: a, d, c, b

Communication media: c, d, b, a

There is an artist imprisoned in each one of us.
Let him loose to spread joy everywhere.

—Bertrand Russell

Leaders agree that creativity is the most important skill of the 21st century and one of the biggest priorities of companies and organizations all over the world. The great news is that Generation Z, the biggest workforce in the world, is also one of the most innovative and creative generations so far.

In this unit, you will have many opportunities to demonstrate your own creativity and entrepreneurship in your specific field of study or future career.

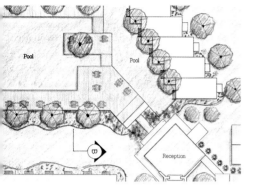

Warm Up

Writing

In a single short sentence, define creativity in your own words. Compare your definition with a partner's.

Speaking

Working in groups of three to four, discuss the following questions.

1. Brainstorm five words you associate with creativity.

2. What does the quotation on page 45 mean? Rephrase it in your own words.

3. How are you creative? In what way is creativity an essential human quality?

4. What jobs do you think involve high or low levels of creativity?

5. What examples of creative inventions or creative processes occur in your field of study or future career?

Field-specific activity

Reading

Can anyone learn how to be creative? Is creativity a mysterious gift for a handful of entrepreneurs and artists or is it about learning and applying well-known creative processes and habits? In this text, Elizabeth Gilbert examines what is involved in creating and offers advice for anyone who wants to be more creative every day.

S For more information about skimming and scanning, see Reading Strategies, pages 173 and 174.

Reading Strategy

Skimming

Skimming is a useful reading strategy to understand the main ideas of a text. The main ideas are usually found in the first and last paragraphs as well as the first sentence of each paragraph.

Scanning

Scanning is a reading strategy used to find specific information such as a number or a word. When you scan, you look rapidly over many lines of print at a time to find a specific piece of information. When you find the word or idea you are looking for, you should then read the entire sentence.

Pre-Reading Activity

Skim the text on page 47 and answer the following question.

What is the text about? _____

Look at the following questions, and then scan the article to find the answers.

1. Name two of Gilbert's books. _____

2. What is the one thing that stops people from pursuing a passion? _____

3. What is one daily habit worth adopting? _____

Vocabulary

Match the vocabulary from the text with the most appropriate meanings. Then find each word in the paragraph to check that you understand how the word is used in context. Use a dictionary to check the answers and the pronunciation.

Word	Letter	Definition
1. **incredibly (adv)** (para. 2)		a) care; take the time to do something
2. **articulate (adj)** (para. 3)		b) recognize
3. **hint (n)** (para. 4)		c) tests; defies or dares
4. **unworthiness (n)** (para. 6)		d) clear and coherent
5. **bother (v)** (para. 6)		e) results; consequences
6. **outcomes (n)** (para. 7)		f) feeling of not deserving respect or attention
7. **acknowledge (v)** (para. 8)		g) clue
8. **quitting (v)** (para. 11)		h) to load; weigh down
9. **burden (v)** (para. 12)		i) very; extremely
10. **challenges (v)** (para. 14)		j) resigning; abandoning or leaving, usually permanently

Tips on How to Be Creative Every Day

By Rachel Nania, WTOP

1 WASHINGTON—If you've ever had the desire to pen a poem, pick up a paintbrush, or try your hand at piano, you're not alone.

2 Elizabeth Gilbert, best-selling author of *Eat Pray Love*, has travelled all over the world to speak at **seminars** and events. She says she's met many people along the way who are doing **incredibly** interesting things in their lives, but most often, she meets those who aren't, but want to be.

3 "Often they have inspiration, they've got ideas, they have little bits of curiosity that they want to follow," Gilbert says. "And when you ask them why they aren't doing it, the answers are usually very **articulate** reasons, material-world reasons about why it's impossible for them right now."

4 **Drawing on** her own experience, Gilbert has advice for those who want to be more creative in their everyday lives, but don't know where or how to start. In her latest book, *Big Magic*, Gilbert explores what it is that stops people from being creative and discusses how to go about pursuing artistic projects in a realistic way. (Here's a **hint**: Don't quit your job to write that first novel.)

5 In a recent interview with WTOP, Gilbert offered up her best advice for breaking out of the shell and tapping into the ingenious within: it's time to face your fear. If there's one thing that stops people from pursuing a passion, it's fear, Gilbert says.

seminar (n) conference or meeting for discussion or training

draw on/draw from (v) make use of; use experience/knowledge

realms (n) areas of activity, interest, or knowledge

6   "There's always some deep fear underneath, some sense of **unworthiness**, some sense that they don't have the right training, that they don't have the right permission, that maybe they won't be able to make a living out of this so why **bother**."

7   There's no need to fully defeat fear or become completely fearless, Gilbert says. Simply learning to navigate around your fear is all it takes. When fear bubbles up—"which it always will because creativity asks you to enter into **realms** that have uncertain outcomes, and your fear hates uncertain **outcomes**," Gilbert says—face it head-on and talk through those hesitations out loud.

8   **Acknowledge** that those fears might be trying to save you from failure, embarrassment, or wasted time, and rationalize with those explanations. "Say, 'I know you're just trying to protect me, but all I'm trying to do is write a poem; nobody's going to die,'" Gilbert advises. Putting curiosity ahead of fear is the first step to unleashing creativity.

9   "My really great saving grace in life is that I'm about 1 percent more curious about the world than I am afraid of it. All it takes is to just be 1 percent more curious," Gilbert says.

It doesn't need to be a full-time job

10   Another reason that people don't engage with a hidden talent or interest is because they think it's not something that will support them. Gilbert says she meets people on both sides of the spectrum when it comes to balancing creative pursuits with life's everyday obligations.

11   Some say they don't have time to create art because they have a demanding job. Others go to dramatic extremes, such as **quitting** their day jobs to write that novel they've always wanted to publish. "That's something I often beg people not to do," says Gilbert, who adds that she didn't quit any of her waitressing, bartending, or au pair jobs until she had already written and published four books.

12   "For me, I love creativity so much, that I never wanted to **burden** it with the responsibility of paying for my life. . . . And I know that it's too weird of a pursuit to count on," she says. Plus, there's no need to set aside eight hours a day for "creative time." Gilbert says even an hour or 20 minutes "will bring forth amazing things within you."

muse (n) a person or personified force who is the source of inspiration for a creative artist

13   "That's the real world that we live in," she says. "I believe in magic and mystery and mysticism and **muses** and inspiration and all that stuff; I also believe that you need a roof over your head." So schedule in some time—as much as you can afford—and get to it.

Don't give up too soon

throw in the towel (exp) to abandon or stop doing something

14   If you don't sell your first painting or your new novel doesn't make the best-sellers list, there's no need to **throw in the towel**. "I think sometimes I watch people murder their creativity because they have this weird insistence that if their creativity is not paying the bills, then it's not real," Gilbert says. But that is not the case. If it **challenges** you, makes you happy, and makes you feel whole, it's worth holding onto.

Interview yourself every day

15 If there's one daily habit worth adopting, Gilbert says it's to check in with yourself each day and tune in "to the most important guide within you." If you want to follow a passion, but are unsure what that passion is, Gilbert says to have patience. You'll soon find what it is you want to do.

16 "We're all looking for the tower of flame and the lightning strike, when really it's a **trail of breadcrumbs**," says Gilbert, adding that those breadcrumbs of curiosity will lead you to something you want to follow. "Ask yourself, 'Is there anything in the world—no matter how random—that I am a tiny bit curious about?' Turn your head a quarter of an inch, look a little closer and start to follow that trail. And that's going to take you there." **[892 words]**

> **trail of breadcrumbs (exp)** series of connected pieces of information, evidence, or ideas. The expression comes from the fairy tale of Hansel and Gretel, who left a trail of breadcrumbs so that they could retrace their route through the forest.

Comprehension

Answer the following questions. With *True/False* questions, if the answer is *False* write the correct answer in the space provided.

Go to Explore Online for additional practice and comprehension questions.

1. Which three reasons does Gilbert say stop people from being more creative?
   a) they are not creative enough, they don't have enough time, they don't try hard enough
   b) their fear, the worry that it won't provide enough (revenue) to support them, they give up too quickly
   c) their family commitments, their fear, their lack of money

2. What is the central idea of *Big Magic*? Why do you think she chose this title?
   _____
   _____

3. What advice does Gilbert offer to people wanting to start a creative venture?
   _____
   _____

4. What does Gilbert claim is the biggest obstacle preventing people from following creative passions?
   _____

5. According to Gilbert, what is the crucial 1 percent in the creativity process?
   _____

6. How often does Gilbert suggest people reflect on their pursuits?
   _____

7. Indicate whether the following statements are true or false.

   a) Gilbert recommends that people resign from dull jobs so that they can focus on creative work.   ☐ True   ☐ False
   _____

   b) A person needs to devote at least six to eight hours daily to creative time.   ☐ True   ☐ False
   _____

c) A creative project can be considered successful
if it leads to financial success. ☐ True ☐ False

d) Gilbert recommends that aspiring writers change
fields rapidly if their first books are not successes. ☐ True ☐ False

e) Creativity involves the development of patience
as well as passion. ☐ True ☐ False

8. Use your own words to describe three pieces of advice for developing
creativity that can be found in the text.

Field-specific activity

start-up (n) a newly formed business, usually offering an innovative new product, solution, or service

pitch (v) to present an idea, solution, project, etc.

make a pitch (exp) try to sell; try to persuade

For examples of how to pitch to investors, check out YouTube videos of popular start-up television shows such as *Shark Tank* and CBC's *Dragon's Den*.

Field-Specific Practice

The Montreal Startupfest is a three-day annual event in which entrepreneurs have a few minutes to pitch their creative ideas, products, and solutions to investors, advisors, and judges. The entrepreneur who makes the best pitch wins a $100 000 investment award.

1. Working in a small group, make suggestions for innovative solutions, tools, products, or services related to your field of study or future career. Explain your idea clearly to your teammates, including the problem it solves or the need it meets.

2. Agree on a single idea that your team will pitch to the rest of the class in a pitch (3 minutes). Include the following information in your pitch:
   a) an attention-getting opening statement
   b) a brief description of your idea and the problem it solves or need it meets
   c) how much investment and time is required to bring your idea to creation

Listening

In this episode of the CBC's *The Current*, "How to Fly a Horse," author Kevin Ashton makes a case that creative genius and the "aha" moment are myths. He argues that creativity is a step-by-step process in which everyone can contribute in some way or another.

Vocabulary

Before listening read the definitions of the following words.

Word	Definition
akin (adj)	essentially similar or related
coined (v)	created a new word or phrase then used by others
cringe (v)	to show discomfort or distaste through your expression or body movements
inspire (v)	to motivate someone to do something
emerge (v)	to appear/become apparent
innately (adv)	naturally/intrinsically
instantaneous (adj)	immediate

How to Fly a Horse [7:29] ◀))

CBC, *The Current*

Comprehension

Answer the following questions. With *True/False* questions, if the answer is *False* write the correct answer in the space provided.

1. What is the term that Ashton coined (created)?

   _____

2. Complete the title of his book: *How to Fly a Horse, the Secret History of*

   _____, _____, and _____

3. Does Ashton believe there is a creative "aha" or "eureka" moment? Explain.

   _____

   _____

4. According to Ashton, what is the source of inspiration for new inventions?

   _____

   _____

5. Human creations emerge from a series of incremental steps. ☐ True ☐ False

   _____

6. According to Ashton, where does the myth that creativity is magical and beyond the reach of most people come from?

   _____

   _____

   _____

Go to Explore Online for additional practice and comprehension questions.

7. Ashton describes the mythical way creativity was seen in the past as a three-legged stool incorporating

a) _____

b) _____

c) _____

8. Not everyone has a creative contribution to make.   ☐ True   ☐ False

_____

_____

9. What does Ashton mean when he says "creation is a chain reaction"?

_____

_____

10. What is the main idea of this listening?
    a) Only people who are creative geniuses can be innovative.
    b) Creativity is usually a collaborative process.
    c) Creativity is a step-by-step process that everyone can contribute to.

Speaking

In the audio clip, Kevin Ashton argues convincingly that everyone is capable of being creative, and he gives examples of what kind of things inspire creativity.

In groups of three or four students, discuss the following questions.

- What kinds of things inspire you to be creative and inventive? Is it other inventions, the challenge of finding a solution to problems, the people you work with, or something else?
- Give an example when you have been creative and explain what it was and how it happened.

Reading

In the following text we look at how Laura Siegel, a Toronto-born fashion designer, has created a successful fashion business based on ethical development by employing artisans from rural villages all over the world to sustain traditional cultures and crafts.

> ## Reading Strategy
>
> ### Note-taking
>
> The goal of note-taking is to capture the main ideas and supporting details in concise notes.
>
> Note-taking helps you understand and remember what you are reading, watching, or listening to. It also provides a reliable reference when revising for homework and tests. Here is an example of the Cornell note-taking method.

sustainable development (n) economic development that doesn't exhaust natural resources

ethical development (n) ensuring ethical working conditions and living wages are provided to employees and collaborators

 For more information about note-taking, see Reading Strategies, page 176.

1. Draw a line down the left side that divides your page into one-third and two-thirds.

2. At the top of your page write the bibliographic information: author, title, date, source, etc.

   - In the left column, write the main idea in one or two key words, or possibly as a question.
   - The right column is for taking notes of the supporting details: very short bullet points that summarize the supporting details.

Use these note-taking strategies and the notepad on page 55 (Reading Comprehension) while reading the "Creative Design—Ethical Fashion" text. Make notes of the supporting ideas. The main ideas have already been entered in the left column.

Author
- Title of Article
Date

Main idea 1	• Supporting details

Main idea 2	• Supporting details

Main idea 3	• Supporting details

Vocabulary

Match the vocabulary from the text with the most appropriate definition provided. Find each word in the paragraph to check that you understand how the word is used in context. Use a dictionary to check the answers and the pronunciation.

Word	Definition
1. **attend (v)** (para. 1)	a) wait b) go to c) help
2. **irrevocably (adv)** (para. 1)	a) permanently b) happily c) vocally
3. **encounter (v)** (para. 2)	a) see at a distance b) meet c) challenge
4. **traceable (adj)** (para. 6)	a) able to be seen b) able to track or find its origins c) capable of leaving a sign
5. **the disconnect (n)** (para. 6)	a) the dishonesty b) the gap between c) the disappointment
6. **ingrained (adj)** (para. 7)	a) growing up b) deeply rooted c) important
7. **consistent (adj)** (para. 11)	a) changing b) unchanging c) containing
8. **creep (v)** (para. 12)	a) move slowly b) move rapidly c) a detestable person

Creative Design—Ethical Fashion

By Melissa Hank, canada.com

posh (adj) classy, exclusive (in informal language)

scooter (n) moped/small motorcycle

down the road (exp) sometime in the future, later on

artisans (n) people who make crafts using traditional methods

1 Laura Siegel **attended** the **posh** Parsons School of Design in New York City and Central Saint Martins in London. But it was in the rough-hewn landscape of Thailand that the Toronto-born fashion designer's craft was **irrevocably** shaped.

2 "I had **scootered** to visit this old temple or palace in the middle of nowhere, but it was closed," she recalls. "That's when I **encountered** a woman crocheting on the side of the road. She didn't speak English, but somehow I asked if she'd be willing to teach me."

3 Siegel spent the next few days in the woman's home learning the centuries-old art. "I was terrible. I don't think she was impressed with my skills, but I just thought it was so special that she was so good at what she did and she did it every day."

4 "I just felt the need to bring work to these people," she says. "I knew that **down the road** I would be sending designs to manufacturers to make my clothes, and why couldn't I just send them to these people who are so good at what they do, but it's in such a beautiful work environment and it's something that means so much to them."

5 That experience outside of Chiang Mai, part of a year off school between her third and fourth year at Parsons, set Siegel on the road to developing ethically handcrafted collections in collaboration with **artisans** in Asia and Latin America.

6 Siegel is at the centre of the new documentary *Traceable*, which follows her as she visits locations in India to develop her 2013 fall/winter collection. It was written, directed, and produced by Canadian filmmaker Jennifer Sharpe and questions **the disconnect** between the origins of mass-produced garments and the people who create and buy them. For Siegel, it's also a chance to spotlight the craftwork of different cultures.

7 "I saw artisans everywhere I went and it seemed to be **ingrained** in the culture. We connected on a level because of my design background and the craft that they've probably known since they were a kid, and was probably passed down from generation to generation," she says.

extinct (adj) no longer existing

8 "I realized that these people should be used in our industry, especially since in a lot of cases the crafts are on their way to becoming **extinct**. Just in general, things being made by hand are becoming extinct. I saw this as an opportunity to change the way things were done."

bucking a system (exp) going against a system or accepted way of doing things/challenging it

9 True, it isn't easy **bucking a system** that's driven by secrecy, competition, and profit. At one point in *Traceable*, Siegel is in India sorting out logistics for her collection as the date to present it back home looms near, and she debates cancelling it altogether.

10 "I'm not able to be in 10 places at the same time, so we've recently hired a production manager overseas and I work with an organization that manages artisans in different regions. But it's difficult coordinating everything from **sampling** to production in all these different places," she says.

sampling (n) the process of taking samples

11 "And just finding the right artisan groups to work with. You want to be supporting artisans who have dedication and heart and love what they do.

You want to make sure that their working conditions are great, that they're getting paid fairly, that they're able to provide **consistent** quality."

12 But, she says, the challenges are worth it. Especially as the deadly 2013 Bangladesh factory collapse, which killed more than a thousand workers, **creeps** further and further out of the news cycle.

13 "It is something that's so easy to talk about for a moment and then you forget, but I've got to give credit to everybody who's continuing the conversation. I think the challenge is finding out what those solutions are going to be. What's feasible, especially in an industry that's so set in its ways? It's going to be hard to really change unless you can prove that there is another way of doing this and you can still create a viable business." **[661 words]**

Comprehension

Take notes about the main ideas and supporting details in the text using the Cornell note-taking strategy described on page 52.

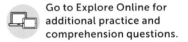

Go to Explore Online for additional practice and comprehension questions.

Siegel: education travel	
motivation for creating ethically handcrafted collection	
Traceable	
problems/ challenges	
value	

Watching

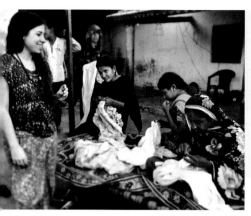

Designer Laura Siegel (left) with artisans in India.

Traceable [3:43] ▶️

Clique Pictures

Traceable follows Laura Siegel as she travels through India meeting artisans to work with on her collections. The documentary is set against the current fashion industry and our startling disconnect with how our clothing is made and who is making it.

Vocabulary

The following words are used in the video. Study the definitions and then use them to fill in the blanks of the sentences below.

Word	Definition
denial (n)	an unwillingness or refusal to accept or see something
diminishing (adj)	becoming less
hubs (n)	centres of activity

1. I was in _____ about how long the assignment would take.

2. Markets act as _____ where artisans come together to sell their products.

3. By buying sustainable fashion, I hope I am _____ the effects of clothing production on the environment.

Comprehension

Go to Explore Online for additional practice and comprehension questions.

Take notes about the main ideas and supporting details in the listening clip using the Cornell note-taking strategy described on page 52.

Siegel's ultimate goal	
community	
craft and culture	

social media	
transparency	

Speaking

Field-specific activity

In groups of three to four discuss the following topics:

1. What organizations, companies, and industries are leading the way in sustainable development and/or ethical development around the world? Explain what you know about them and how they operate.

2. Why don't more companies take sustainable and ethical development into consideration when creating new products, processes, and inventions? Make a list of the top five reasons and then discuss them with your partners. Do you share the same ideas?

3. Are there examples of inventions, ideas, and processes in your field of study that take into consideration sustainable or ethical development? Provide examples and explain how they are sustainable or ethical.

Writing

For more information about writing a summary, see Writing Strategies, page 143.

> **Writing Strategy**
>
> ### Writing a summary
>
> A summary is a shortened, condensed version of a longer text. It expresses the author's main points in your own words.
>
> In the first sentences, write the name of the author and the title or source of the article as well as the purpose of the author and the main idea of the article. Then use your own words to show how the author supports, defines, and illustrates these main ideas.
>
> **EXAMPLE**
>
> In the canada.com article "Creative Design—Ethical Fashion," Melissa Hank outlines Seigel's involvement in the documentary *Traceable*. Hank explains how Seigel first learned traditional crafts while travelling in Thailand. She continues . . .

Using your outline notes from the reading "Creative Design—Ethical Fashion," write a brief summary (6–7 sentences) of the reading text. Use your own words. The first two sentences are provided in the Writing Strategy box.

Go to Explore Online for additional practice using the passive voice.

Grammar

Passive voice

In academic and professional writing, we sometimes use the passive voice when we want to focus on the result rather than the person doing the action.

Look at the highlighted verbs in the text below. How is the passive voice formed? What verb tenses are being used?

> Crocheted fabrics **have been found** in Europe dating back to the 19th century. The word *crochet* **is derived** from the French term *crochet*, meaning "small hook." Crochet hooks **were used** in 17th-century lacemaking. Crochet hooks **are made** of materials such as metal, wood, or plastic and **are manufactured** commercially or **can be produced** in artisan workshops. Wool, yarn, and threads **are used** in both crochet and knitting, but in crochet each stitch is completed before the next one is **begun**, whereas in knitting a large number of stitches **are kept** open at the same time.

Look at the four pairs of sentences below. Which sentences are active and which ones are passive?

1. a) Laura Seigel designs clothes.
    b) Clothes are designed by Seigel.

2. a) A woman in Thailand taught Siegel the art of crocheting.
    b) Laura Siegel was taught how to crochet by a woman in Thailand.

3. a) The collection was produced in India.
    b) Manufacturers in India produced the collection.

4. a) A film has been made about the collection.
    b) A filmmaker has made a film about the collection.

The passive voice is formed by conjugating **be + the past participle** of the main verb.

Active	Laura Seigel designs clothes.
Passive	Clothes are designed by Seigel.
Active	Students are studying grammar.
Passive	Grammar is being studied (by students).

GG For more information about the passive voice, see Grammar Guide, page 236.

Change the following active voice sentences to the passive voice.

1. Elizabeth Gilbert wrote *Eat Pray Love*.

    _____

2. Gilbert has met many people at seminars around the world.

    _____

3. Gilbert told the audience to pursue creative dreams.

    _____

Interpreting Data

1. Look at the figures on the right. Use predicting, previewing, and skimming strategies to answer the following questions.

   a) What is the subject of each figure?

   _____

   _____

   _____

   _____

   b) Identify what type of graph is used in each figure. What is being measured in each axis?

   _____

   _____

   _____

   _____

   _____

   _____

   c) What **trends** can you identify?

   _____

   _____

   _____

   _____

   _____

   _____

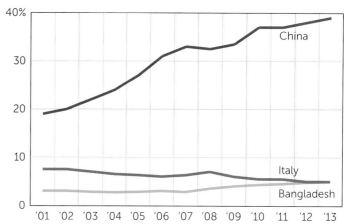

Figure 1: Percentages of world's clothing exports

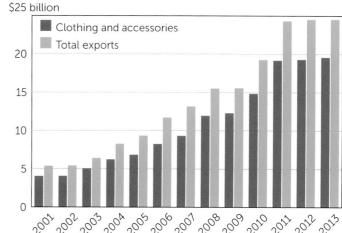

Figure 2: Bangladesh's export growth

2. Look at the data in the figures and decide if the following statements are true or false.

   trend (n) tendency over time

   a) In 2013 China had an almost 40 percent share of the world's clothing exports. ❏ True ❏ False

   b) In 2001 China had 20 percent, Bangladesh 20 percent, and Italy less than 10 percent share of the world's clothing exports. ❏ True ❏ False

   c) China's export share grew rapidly from 2005 to 2007 and then levelled out for the next two years. ❏ True ❏ False

   d) Exports of clothing and accessories were worth almost $25 billion for Bangladesh in 2012. ❏ True ❏ False

   e) Exports of clothing and accessories constitute 50 percent of total exports for Bangladesh. ❏ True ❏ False

   f) Exports of clothing and accessories almost doubled in Bangladesh from 2009 to 2013. ❏ True ❏ False

3. In groups of three to four, discuss the following questions.

   • How equitable and fair to workers is the clothing industry? Find examples to support your answers.
   • How does the treatment of workers compare to your field of study?

 Field-specific activity

Pronunciation

Voiced and silent *h-*

The letter *h-* at the beginning of words sometimes causes pronunciation challenges. *H* is generally pronounced *aitch* when alone, but some English speakers may say *haitch*. The former is more common, but you can use either pronunciation!

At the beginning of a word sometimes the *h-* is **voiced** (spoken), sometimes the *h-* is **silent**. When is *h-* silent and when is it pronounced?

- *H-* is voiced at the beginning of most common words, such as **h**otel, **h**ouse, **h**am
- *H-* is usually silent in words that are of Latin origin, such as *hour, honest, heir,* and *honour.*

1. Listen to the audio recording and sort the following words into **silent** and **pronounced** *h-* sounds.

Silent	Pronounced	

2. With a partner create a tongue-twisting challenge. Prepare a sentence using a combination of pronounced *h-* and silent *h-* words and challenge your classmates and teacher. Say the sentences out loud, paying careful attention to the silent and pronounced sounds.

> **EXAMPLE**   Horrified, Helen announced that I had the honour of a harmless horrible Huntsman spider in my hair.

honest	hair	horrid	hospital
humble	Henry	hour	horn
honour	human	harmless	heart
happy	house	heir	health
Helen	help	hurtful	Harry
huge	hat	humour	herb

Revising and Editing

1. Rewrite the following first sentences of a summary of the first reading text from this unit. Be attentive to verbs, subject–verb agreement, and word choice.

    > In the article about creativity that I read last week the person said lots of things. The article was wrote by Rachel. It is about Elizabeth. She say everyone are creative person. I'm not sure I agree.

2. Rewrite the following paragraph that explains the process of selecting sunglasses. Include transition words and passive voice. Make sure that you have introductory and concluding statements. Be attentive to verbs, subject–verb agreement, and word choice.

    > When you buy new sunglasses you want the most fashionable ones in the store. Selecting sunglasses can be difficult and expensive. Mirrored aviators cannot be considered the best choice for everyone. There are some points to consider like gender and colour of face and eyes and frames. Another is face shape and proportion. Lastly you should think about whether the glasses are better for men or women.

Wrap Up

Field-Specific Practice

Describing a process

In academic and work fields, it is important to be able to explain a process or the sequence/steps in which something is done. For example, in science we describe the process of reproduction; in mechanics, we describe how a motor functions, and in manufacturing we describe the manufacturing process. The passive voice is often used when describing a process.

 Field-specific activity

1. Read this process text on page 62 and answer the following questions.
    a) Underline three examples of the passive voice in the text.
    b) Highlight five transition words in the text.
    c) What is the purpose of the first and last sentences?
    d) Use the information in the text to take notes and write an outline of the five key steps in the creative process.

    > The creative process has been examined by psychologists for many years; although it is not necessarily linear, it is sometimes described as having five stages. These are preparation, incubation, insight, evaluation, and elaboration. Creativity involves going back and forth between each of these different stages. First of all, a lot of information is gathered. Research is done and often the person is completely absorbed by the issue or idea. Then, in the second stage the idea is incubating or gradually developing. It could take years before the creator makes an incremental step forward and has a moment of insight or understanding. After this, the creator needs to be able to reflect and evaluate the idea. Finally, the last stage is elaboration. This consists of the hours and hours of refining, developing, and testing out the idea. In sum, no creation is a simple "eureka" moment.

2. Explain a brief process related to your field of study or future career.

Plan to write approximately 10–12 sentences. Keep it simple—you are not writing an instruction manual. Make sure to include an introductory and concluding statement as well as appropriate transitions.

Speaking

How is creativity important in your field of study or future career? Research and think of three ways that creativity is used in your field that you find inspiring. It could relate to an idea, a process, a particular type of job, or a design.

Make a short oral presentation (2–3 minutes) on the role creativity plays in your field.

• include images if possible
• describe
   • the three ways creativity is used
   • the purpose of using creativity in these ways: how it is used, the problem it solves, its benefits
   • the reason why you chose these three examples of creativity

Writing

Use your outline notes from the *Traceable* video on page 56 to write a summary in which you identify the source, purpose, and main idea of the video report.

Vocabulary

Choose 12 of the new words from this unit and create a short definition for each word. When you have finished, exchange your definitions with another student and try to guess which word is being defined.

acknowledge	challenges	diminishing	ingrained	outcomes
akin	coined	emerge	innately	quitting
articulate	consistent	encounter	inspire	the disconnect
attend	creep	hint	instantaneous	traceable
bother	cringe	hubs	irrevocably	unworthiness
burden	denial	incredibly		

We cannot solve our problems with the same thinking we used when we created them.

—Albert Einstein

We are living in a time of great innovation. New ideas, products, and solutions are emerging daily and affecting the way we live, work, and play. What innovations have had an effect on your life? Do you think they have changed your life for the better? Do you think some innovations have made your life worse? In this unit, we will learn about new innovations, their potential effects on us, and how they connect to different fields of study.

Warm Up

Work with a partner and match each innovation with the correct description. The first one has already been completed.

1. In 1953, James Watson and Francis Crick discovered the molecular structure that encodes the genetic instructions used in the development and functioning of all known living organisms.	a) mobile phone
2. In 1973, Motorola created the first device of this kind. It weighed more than 1 kg and people could use it to talk to each other for only 30 minutes. The battery took 10 hours to charge.	b) airplane
3. Orville and Wilbur Wright invented this flying machine in 1903.	c) penicillium
4. In 1896 Ernest Duchesne, a French medical student, discovered the antibiotic properties of this fungus which was developed into a common antibiotic that is still used worldwide.	d) DNA
5. In 1592, Dutch eyeglasses makers Zacharias and Hans Jansen discovered that objects were magnified when looking through a specially shaped lens. This invention led to innovations in many fields, including science and medicine.	e) bar code
6. In 1600, English scientist William Gilbert gave a name, which originated from the Greek word for *amber*, to this discovery. Later, in 1752, Ben Franklin showed that lightning and sparks produced by amber were the same phenomenon.	f) the television
7. John Logie Baird gave the first public demonstration of images in motion, at Selfridges department store in London in 1925. Today, this invention can be found in most people's living room.	g) the printing press
8. German inventor Johannes Gutenberg invented this machine in 1450. This invention made it possible for the mass production of books and the rapid spread of knowledge throughout Europe.	h) electricity
9. These black and white lines found on almost all products help inventory managers and stores keep track of their products and prices.	i) the microscope

Speaking

In a group of three or four, discuss the following questions. Before you begin your discussion, make notes of your opinions. In your discussion, support your opinions with reasons, facts, and examples.

1. Which three innovations or inventions in the last 100 years are the most important and why?

2. What inventions have had the most positive impact on society?

3. What inventions have had the most negative impact on society?

4. What inventions or innovations have been most important in your field of
    study or future career and why?

 Field-specific activity

Reading

3D printing is a revolutionary innovation that is transforming a wide range of
industries such as medicine, manufacturing, and engineering. It has been used to
produce such diverse products as artificial limbs, manufacturing components, car
parts, jewellery, toys, coffee makers, and even food. How do you think it might
transform your field of study or future career? What impact do you think this
innovation will have on our society as it becomes more popular and convenient?

Pre-Reading Activity

Discuss the following questions with a partner. If you do not know the answer,
make a guess and explain your choice to your partner. Take notes and be prepared
to share your answers with the class.

1. What do you know about how 3D printing works?

2. How expensive do you think a 3D printer is?

3. What are some possible dangers associated with the use of this innovation?

Decide if the following statements are true or false.

4. A house can be built using 3D printed pieces.   ❏ True ❏ False

5. There is only one type of 3D printer.   ❏ True ❏ False

6. A small 3D printer can be purchased for around $1000. ❏ True ❏ False

7. 3D printing is easy and inexpensive.   ❏ True ❏ False

8. Guns have been made from 3D printed materials.   ❏ True ❏ False

9. There is a 3D printer at the La Grande Bibliothèque
    in Montreal.   ❏ True ❏ False

Vocabulary

Find the following words and phrases in the text, read the whole sentence
surrounding the bolded word or phrase, and choose the best meaning from the
two choices below.

Word or phrase	Meaning 1	Meaning 2
1. **hype** (para. 2)	excitement surrounding something new	information given over the news
2. **production line** (para. 5)	a manufacturing process that includes a series of steps	a process for printing documents at home
3. **layer** (para. 7)	material that covers a surface or another layer	the piece of paper upon which ink is printed
4. **stack up** (para. 13)	place on top	compare
5. **sceptical** (para. 15)	doubting	curious

3D Printing for Dummies: How Do 3D Printers Work?

By Andrew Walker, *The Independent*

1 You've heard the hype about 3D printing, but how does it actually work? Andrew Walker explains how it works.

2 It seems like everyone from the White House to Amazon.com is talking about 3D printing these days, but what exactly is it? Here's a quick guide to what all the **hype** is about . . .

What is a 3D printer?

3 3D printers are a new generation of machines that can make everyday things. They're remarkable because they can produce different kinds of objects, in different materials, all from the same machine.

4 A 3D printer can make pretty much anything from ceramic cups to plastic toys, metal machine parts, stoneware vases, fancy chocolate cakes or even (one day soon) human body parts.

5 They replace traditional factory **production lines** with a single machine, just like home inkjet printers replaced bottles of ink, a printing press, hot metal type, and a drying rack.

Why is it called printing?

6 If you look closely (with a microscope) at a page of text from your home printer, you'll see the letters don't just stain the paper, they're actually sitting slightly on top of the surface of the page.

7 In theory, if you printed over that same page a few thousand times, eventually the ink would build up enough **layers** on top of each other to create a solid 3D model of each letter. That idea of building a physical form out of tiny layers is how the first 3D printers worked.

How do 3D printers work?

PC (n) personal computer

8 You start by designing a 3D object on an ordinary home **PC**, connect it to a 3D printer, press "print" and then sit back and watch. The process is a bit like making a loaf of sliced bread, but in reverse. Imagine baking each individual slice of bread and then **gluing** them together into a whole loaf (as opposed to making a whole loaf and then **slicing** it, like a baker does). That's basically what a 3D printer does.

gluing (v) sticking

slicing (v) cutting

slice (n) a thin piece

9 The 3D printing process turns a whole object into thousands of tiny little **slices**, then makes it from the bottom up, slice by slice. Those tiny layers stick together to form a solid object. Each layer can be very complex, meaning 3D printers can create moving parts like **hinges** and wheels as part of the same object. You could print a whole bike—handlebars, saddle, frame, wheels, brakes, pedals and chain—ready assembled, without using any tools. It's just a question of leaving gaps in the right places.

hinge (n) the moveable part on a door, gate, etc. that allows it to open and close

What are the opportunities?

10 Have you ever broken something, only to find it's no longer sold and you can't replace it? 3D printing means you can simply print a new one. That world,

where you can make almost anything at home, is very different from the one we live in today. It's a world that doesn't need **lorries** to deliver goods or **warehouses** to store them in, where nothing is ever out of stock and where there is less waste, packaging, and pollution.

lorries (n) trucks (in Britain)

warehouses (n) buildings where large quantities of goods are stored

11 It's also a world where everyday items are made to measure, to your requirements. That means furniture made to fit your home, shoes made to fit your feet, door handles made to fit your hand, meals printed to your tastes at the touch of a button. Even medicines, bones, organs, and skin made to treat your **injuries**.

injuries (n) hurt or damage to the body

12 You can get some of those things now if you're wealthy, but 3D printing brings affordable, **bespoke** manufacturing to the masses. If that sounds like pure fantasy, try googling "personalized 3D printed products" and see for yourself. After all, the notion of doing your supermarket shopping on an iPad was like something out of *Star Trek* 20 years ago.

bespoke (adj) made specifically to the needs of an individual customer

What are the limitations?

13 Although buying a 3D printer is much cheaper than setting up a factory, the cost per item you produce is higher, so the economics of 3D printing don't **stack up** against traditional mass production yet. It also can't match the smooth finish of industrial machines, nor offer the variety of materials or range of sizes available through industrial processes. But, like so many household technologies, the prices will come down and 3D printer capabilities will improve over time.

Is it the next big thing?

14 Yes, if you're a product designer or engineer, but for most people, no.

15 Like all new technologies, the industry hype is a few years ahead of the consumer reality. It's an emerging technology, which means, like home computers or mobile phones, most people will remain **sceptical** about needing one until everyone has got one . . . and then we'll all wonder how we ever managed without them.   **[765 words]**

Comprehension

Answer the following questions using your own words.

Go to **Explore Online** for additional practice and comprehension questions.

1. What makes 3D printers so exceptional?

   _____

   _____

2. How did the first 3D printers work?

   _____

3. In your own words, explain why the process of 3D printing is like making a loaf of sliced bread in reverse.

   _____

   _____

4. What are three advantages to having access to a 3D printer?

_____

_____

_____

5. Give three specific examples of items that can be produced using 3D printers.

_____

6. What will no longer be needed when 3D printers become widespread?

_____

7. What are two weaknesses of 3D printers?

_____

_____

8. What does the author believe is the future of 3D printing?

_____

Speaking

With a partner, discuss the following questions.

1. How do you think 3D printing will change our society?

2. What products would you find most useful to print using a 3D printer?

3. Can you think of any ethical issues related to 3D printing?

Field-specific activity

4. How do you think 3D printing will affect your field of study or future career? Explain how it might be used in your field of study or future career.

Listening

When you study for a test or exam, do you have trouble concentrating? Do you constantly check your phone or computer? In this PBS *NewsHour* interview, Nicholas Carr, author of the book *The Shallows: What the Internet Is Doing to Our Brains*, claims that the Internet has a negative impact on us. Listen to the interview and decide if you agree with him.

Pre-Listening Activity

Working with a partner, discuss the following questions. Answer with as much detail as you can.

1. How much time do you spend on average using the Internet every day?

2. How much time do you spend every day reading print books, magazines, or newspapers?

3. Do you think people are more or less intelligent today because of the Internet? Explain.

4. What do you think the long-term effects of the Internet will be on the way we think?

Vocabulary

The following words are used in the audio. Read the sentences and then use context clues to match the bold words with their definitions.

1. There was a huge **backlash** when the school tried to stop students from using their phones in the classroom.

2. How much screen time to give children is a **conundrum** for most parents.

3. Children's brains are particularly **malleable** and this helps them learn quickly.

4. The **plasticity** of the brain helps us learn new things and forget things that are not useful to us anymore.

5. One of the hot topics in **neuroscience** is the effect of meditation on the brain.

6. It can be hard to find time for quiet **contemplation** in today's busy world.

Word	Letter	Definition
1. **backlash** (n)		a) the quality of being easily shaped
2. **conundrum** (n)		b) easily influenced or changed
3. **malleable** (adj)		c) deep reflective thought
4. **plasticity** (n)		d) the study of the brain and the nervous system
5. **neuroscience** (n)		e) a difficult problem
6. **contemplation** (n)		f) a negative reaction

Is the Internet Changing the Way We Think? [5:13]

Nicholas Carr, PBS *NewsHour*

Comprehension

Answer the following questions. With *True/False* questions, if the answer is *False* write the correct answer in the space provided.

1. What is the main idea of the interview?
   a) Nicholas Carr believes that people should read more books and use the Internet less.
   b) Nicholas Carr has done research in neuroscience and discovered that prolonged Internet use is changing our brains in a negative way.
   c) Nicholas Carr argues that although Internet use has some benefits, extended use has a negative effect on our deeper thinking skills such as long-term memory and critical analysis.

2. What happened when the original article by Nicholas Carr on this topic was published?

   _____

3. Why did Nicholas Carr become interested in this topic?

   _____

Go to Explore Online for additional practice and comprehension questions.

4. The more you do something, the more your brain will change to become better at that task. ☐ True ☐ False

_____

5. According to Nicholas Carr, what parts of the brain are strengthened by long periods of Internet use?

_____

6. What abilities are weakened by long periods of Internet use? Choose one or more answers.
   a) deep concentration
   b) reflection
   c) multitasking
   d) focus shifting
   e) attentiveness
   f) consideration for others

7. What are we losing when we use the Internet for long periods of time?
   a) our ability to show empathy
   b) our short-term memory
   c) our ability to focus for a long period of time
   d) our ability to focus on many things at one time

8. Why is the process of paying deep attention important?

_____

_____

9. Does Nicholas Carr think that new technologies will promote deeper concentration? Why or why not?

_____

_____

Writing

In an article, Nicholas Carr asked the question "Is Google making us stupid?" Write a paragraph in which you answer that question. Provide two supporting details to support your opinion.

Reading

Today we increasingly rely on the Internet for information, entertainment, and personal connection. Scientists in the fields of neuroscience and psychology have been studying what effects all this screen time might be having on us. This article discusses five facts about Internet use that may surprise you.

S For more information about objective and subjective writing, see Reading Strategies, page 172.

Reading Strategy

Objective and subjective writing

Objective writing

Objective writing is writing that can be backed up with evidence rather than the author's opinion. The language is neutral and uses facts, statistics, and research. This type of writing is used when the writer wants to present unbiased information and let the reader determine his or her own opinion. Newspapers and school textbooks often use objective writing.

Subjective writing

Subjective writing is writing that cannot be backed up with evidence. Subjective writing might express feelings, opinions, and judgments. This approach could be used for writing a personal essay or an opinion column for a newspaper, but should not be used when the goal is simply to inform the audience.

Fact versus opinion

The difference between fact and opinion is not always clear.

Fact: A fact is something that you know has happened or is true. Facts can be checked and backed up with evidence. Statements that contain statistics tend to be facts.

Opinion: An opinion is what you think or believe about someone or something. You can agree or disagree with an opinion, but you cannot state that it is true or false.

Writers often use facts to support their opinions.

Working with a partner, read the following sentences and decide which are facts and which are opinions.

1. The majority of young adults use social networking sites on a regular basis. _____

2. The Internet is the most useful invention in history. _____

3. The modern Internet was invented in 1989. _____

4. The Internet has made people's lives easier. _____

Vocabulary

The following words are found in the text on page 72. Find the word in the paragraph and read the sentence to help you understand the meaning. Then match the word with its definition. The first example has been completed for you.

Word or phrase	Letter	Definition
1. **rewiring (v)** (title)	e	a) remove
2. **freaky (adj)** (para. 3)		b) to increase something in number, value, or strength
3. **craving (n)** (para. 4)		c) to cause something to start or happen
4. **unplugging (v)** (para. 4)		d) a strong desire for something
5. **withdrawal symptoms (n)** (para. 4)		e) changing the connections between neurons
6. **trigger (v)** (para. 6)		g) disconnecting
7. **filter out (v)** (para. 11)		h) signs someone has stopped using a drug
8. **boost (v)** (para. 12)		i) strange

mates (n) people we want to date or marry

The Internet is an interruption system. It seizes our attention only to scramble it The Internet gets our attention but also makes us lose focus of other things.

addict (n) someone who obsessively wants and is dependent on something

disregard (v) to pay no attention to; ignore

heighten (v) to increase

teens (n) short for *teenagers*; people aged 13–19, also called adolescents

This Is How the Internet Is Rewiring Your Brain

By Jacqueline Howard, *The Huffington Post*

1   We email. We tweet. We facebook. We google. In this incredible age of technology, our computers sometimes seem to have taken control over our everyday lives—from how we buy groceries to how we find **mates**. How is all this screen time affecting our brains?

2   In his provocative book *The Shallows: What the Internet Is Doing to Our Brain*, author Nicholas Carr wrote, "**The Internet is an interruption system. It seizes our attention only to scramble it**."

3   That doesn't sound good. Or, is it possible the online world simply helps us adapt to become better multitaskers, all while we still maintain critical thinking skills? After all, the brain is plastic, meaning it changes based on our behaviour and experiences. So then when it comes to technology, what behaviour are we practising—and how does *that* affect our minds? Here are five **freaky** facts.

4   **Fact #1: The Internet may give you an addict's brain.** MRI research has shown that the brains of Internet users who have trouble controlling their **craving** to be constantly plugged in exhibit changes similar to those seen in people addicted to drugs and alcohol. A 2011 study showed that **unplugging** from technology for one day gave some users physical and mental **withdrawal symptoms**, *The Telegraph* reported.

5   "The majority of people we see with serious Internet addiction are gamers— people who spend long hours in roles in various games that cause them to **disregard** their obligations," Dr. Henrietta Bowden Jones, an Imperial College, London psychiatrist who runs a clinic for Internet addicts and problem gamblers, told *The Independent*.

6   **Fact #2: You may feel more lonely and jealous.** Social media may make it easier to connect with others, but recent research by German scientists suggests that constantly viewing images of others' vacation photos, personal achievements, etc., can **trigger** strong feelings of envy, even sadness. Researchers have even described the phenomenon as "Facebook depression."

7   "We were surprised by how many people have a negative experience from Facebook with envy leaving them feeling lonely, frustrated, or angry," Hanna Krasnova, a researcher at Berlin's Humboldt University, told Reuters.

8   **Fact #3: Internet use may heighten suicide risk in certain teens.** After conducting a review of previous research on studies on teens' Internet use, researchers at the University of Oxford in England concluded that online time is linked to an increased risk of suicide and self-harm among vulnerable adolescents. Their paper was published online on October 30 in the journal *PLOS ONE*.

9   "We are not saying that all young people who go on the Internet increase their risk of suicide or self-harm," one of the researchers, Dr. Paul Montgomery, professor of psycho-social intervention at the university, said in a written statement. "We are talking about vulnerable young people who are going online specifically to find out more about harming themselves or because

they are considering suicide already. The question is whether the online content triggers a response so that they self-harm or take their own lives and we have found that there is a link."

10 **Fact #4: Memory problems may be more likely.** Even a rather typical session of social media browsing can lead to information **overload** and make it harder to file away information in your memory, according to Dr. Erik Fransén, professor of computer science at Sweden's KTH Royal Institute of Technology. A 2009 study from Stanford University suggests that the brains of people who are constantly bombarded with several streams of electronic information—from instant messaging to blogs—may find it difficult to pay attention and **switch** from one job to another efficiently.

overload (n) an excessive amount of something

switch (v) to change from one thing to another

11 "When they're in situations where there are multiple sources of information coming from the external world or emerging out of memory, they're not able to **filter out** what's not relevant to their current goal," Dr. Anthony Wagner, an associate professor of psychology at Stanford, said in a written statement. "That failure to filter means they're slowed down by that irrelevant information."

12 **Fact #5: But it's not all bad—in moderation, the Internet can actually boost brain function.** A 2008 study suggests that use of Internet search engines can stimulate neural activation patterns and potentially **enhance** brain function in older adults.

enhance (v) to improve something or make it better

13 "The study results are encouraging, that emerging computerized technologies may have physiological effects and potential benefits for middle-aged and older adults," the study's principal investigator, Dr. Gary Small, professor of neuroscience and human behaviour at UCLA, said in a written statement. "Internet searching engages complicated brain activity, which may help exercise and improve brain function." **[788 words]**

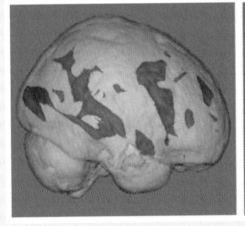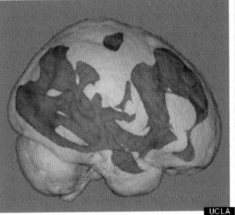

Functional MRI brain scans show how searching the Internet dramatically engages brain neural networks (in red). The image on the left displays brain activity while reading a book; the image on the right displays activity while engaging in an Internet search.

Comprehension

Go to Explore Online for additional practice and comprehension questions.

Answer the following questions using your own words. With *True/False* questions, if the answer is *False* write the correct answer in the space provided.

1. Which of the following statements about the brain is true?
    a) The brain is more stimulated when reading a book than when searching the Internet.
    b) Overall, technology has very little impact on the brain.
    c) When faced with a lot of information, the brain easily filters out what is not important.
    d) The brain is always adapting based on what we do and learn.

2. In your own words, explain how Internet addiction is similar to other types of addictions.

    _____

    _____

3. What is Facebook depression?

    _____

4. Internet use increases the risk of suicide among
    all adolescents.   ❒ True   ❒ False

    _____

5. What happens to people when they are bombarded with a lot of online information at the same time?

    _____

6. How is Internet use helpful for older adults?

    _____

7. Why do you think Nicholas Carr's book might be called *The Shallows*?

    _____

    _____

8. In one sentence, summarize the main idea of the text.

    _____

    _____

9. Is the article subjective or objective? Explain your answer.

    _____

    _____

10. The author presents five facts about how the Internet is affecting our brains. Do you agree that these are really facts? Why or why not? How are they supported?

    _____

    _____

    _____

    _____

Writing

Go online and find two articles about the impact of the Internet on some aspect of society: one should be an objective text and the other should be a subjective text. Write a paragraph comparing the approaches in the two articles. For the objective article, explain why you believe it to be objective. For the subjective article, explain why you believe it is subjective, what argument the writer is making, and whether or not it is convincing and why. If you were writing a paper, which article would you use as a reference and why?

Speaking

The Internet has had wide-ranging impacts on all industries. How has it changed your field of study or future career? Think of the effects it has had on research, employment, and collaboration.

Prepare a presentation (2 minutes) on the role of the Internet in your field of study.

In your introduction, explain what effect the Internet has had on your field or the key ways it is used in your field. This will be your main idea.

In your body section, give two examples of ways that the Internet has affected—or the key ways it is used in—your field.

In your conclusion, give a concise summary of your main idea.

 For more information about giving presentations, see Speaking Strategies, page 168.

 Field-specific activity

Grammar

Present perfect and simple past

One use of the present perfect is to talk about an action that occurred at an unspecified time in the past. The present perfect is formed with the auxiliary *have/has* + **past participle** of a verb.

> EXAMPLE   Scientists **have studied** the effects of long-term Internet use on our brains.

If the specific time in the past is known, the simple past is used. The simple past is formed with the base **verb + -ed** (or the simple past form of an irregular verb).

> EXAMPLE   Last year researchers **concluded** that our brains are malleable.

Look at the following examples of present perfect and simple past taken from the text:

> **Present perfect:** MRI research **has shown** that the brains of Internet users who have trouble controlling their craving to be constantly plugged in exhibit changes similar to those seen in people addicted to drugs and alcohol.

> **Simple past:** A 2011 study **showed** that unplugging from technology for one day **gave** some users physical and mental withdrawal symptoms.

1. Go back to the text "This Is How the Internet Is Rewiring Your Brain" and find two more examples where the present perfect is used.

 Go to Explore Online for additional practice using the present perfect and the simple past.

For more information on the present perfect tense, see Grammar Guide, page 215.

For more information on the simple past tense, see Grammar Guide, page 200.

2. Choose whether the blanks should be filled with the present perfect (unspecified past time) or simple past (specific past time) option.

   a) In a study published two years ago, researchers found/have found that playing video games leads to faster decision making.

   b) The scientist discovered/has discovered a new vaccine.

   c) The student spent/has spent hours on the Internet researching his topic.

   d) The Internet has/has had a negative impact on my reading skills.

   e) In 1973, Motorola created/has created the first mobile phone.

Field-specific activity

Field-Specific Practice

Make a short list of examples of modern technology (machines, equipment, processes) that are important in your field of study or future career. Provide a brief (one- to two-sentence) description of each one and then explain how it is used (its applications) in your field.

Watching

Drones are remote-controlled flying machines. They were originally associated with the military. In recent years they have increasingly been used in a variety of fields for such diverse purposes as search and rescue, traffic monitoring, firefighting, and photography. Today, prices have dropped and people everywhere now own their own drone. This video clip explores the "age of the drone."

Vocabulary

Review the following words before watching the video clip.

Word or phrase	Definition
array (n)	variety
Big Brother (n)	a person or organization exercising total control over people's lives
customized (adj)	built to individual requirements
nuisance (n)	a person, thing, or situation that annoys you or causes you trouble
start-up (n)	a new business
trade show (n)	an event at which many different companies show and sell their products

The Age of the Drone [10:38]

Zoot Pictures and CBC

Comprehension

As you watch part of the documentary *The Age of the Drone*, answer the following questions.

1. What reputation do drones have?

    _____

2. According to the report, how many drones will be in the air in North America by 2020?
    a) 2000   b) 20 000   c) 30 000   d) 25 000

3. What are two examples of commercial fields that are starting to use drones?

    _____

4. According to Chris Anderson, what qualities make a drone?

    _____

5. Why did drones come down in price so drastically?

    _____

6. How much does it cost to build your own drone?
    a) $300   b) $500   c) $750   d) $1500

7. What was the idea behind the pocket drone?

    _____

    _____

8. What are some concerns the video mentions about drone use?

    _____

    _____

    _____

Go to Explore Online for additional practice and comprehension questions.

Speaking

With a partner, discuss the following questions. Be prepared to support your opinions with reasons, facts, and examples.

1. Would you purchase a drone? If you answer *yes*, for what purposes? If you answer *no*, why not?

2. What do you think are the most important benefits of using drones in society?

3. What are some of the dangers of drone use that concern you?

4. How could drones be applied to your field of study or future career?

5. Should drone use be regulated? Explain.

 Field-specific activity

Interpreting Data

Using drones to do tasks that were previously done by humans is an example of an innovation a company might make. This chart shows the most common **obstacles** to innovation for North American companies.

obstacle (n) something that gets in the way of progress or action

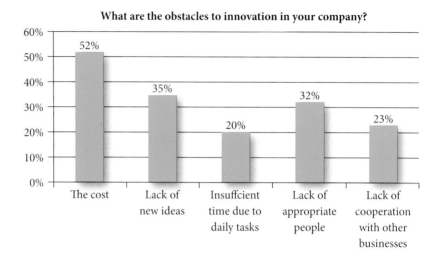

What are the obstacles to innovation in your company?

Comprehension

Go to Explore Online for additional practice and comprehension questions.

Look at the data in the chart and decide if the following statements are true or false. If the answer is *False* write the correct answer in the space provided.

1. The biggest obstacle to innovation is lack of new ideas.   ❏ True   ❏ False

   _____

2. Lack of cooperation with other businesses is one of the smallest obstacles.   ❏ True   ❏ False

   _____

3. Insufficient time and money are obstacles to innovation.   ❏ True   ❏ False

   _____

4. Twenty-three percent say that they lack the appropriate people.   ❏ True   ❏ False

   _____

5. The cost of innovation is the biggest obstacle.   ❏ True   ❏ False

   _____

6. Lack of new ideas is the second biggest obstacle.   ❏ True   ❏ False

   _____

7. Government regulations is an obstacle to innovation.   ❏ True   ❏ False

   _____

When you have answered all of the questions, compare and verify your answers with a partner.

Speaking

With your partner, think of three ideas that might help solve these obstacles to innovation. Share your ideas with another group.

Writing

> ## Writing Strategy
>
> ### Essay writing
>
> An essay consists of an introduction with a strong thesis statement (your opinion), two or three body paragraphs that begin with topic sentences, and a conclusion.
>
> **Thesis statement:** This is the main purpose of your essay or your main argument. Each of your body paragraphs will be developed to directly link to and support your thesis. Your thesis statement should be an opinion and not a fact. It should be interesting and persuasive.
>
> Your thesis statement must not be a question or a topic announcement ("In this essay I will . . ."). When you write a thesis statement, avoid the words *I*, *we*, and *you*. Your thesis statement should be the last sentence of the introduction.
>
> **Topic sentences:** Each body paragraph should begin with an interesting and persuasive topic sentence that states the main idea/argument of the paragraph. Each topic sentence will offer a unique support for the thesis statement. The topic sentence is more specific than the essay's thesis statement and it can be described as a "mini" thesis statement for the paragraph. Your topic sentences should also be interesting and persuasive.

 For more information about writing an essay, see Writing Strategies, page 138.

 Field-specific activity

Think of what might be the greatest obstacle to innovation in your field of study or future career. Now write an **essay outline** about how to overcome this obstacle to innovation. Your introduction should outline the problem (there is an obstacle to innovation). Your thesis statement should give your opinion on how it can be addressed. Each of your two topic sentences should give one solution to the problem. Use the brainstorming you did with your partner for ideas.

For more information about writing essay outlines, see Writing Strategies, page 139.

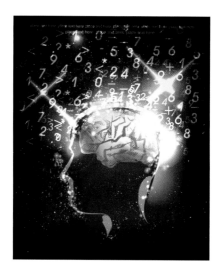

Pronunciation

The pronunciation of two-syllable nouns and verbs

The pronunciation of some two-syllable words changes depending on whether they are used as nouns or verbs.

1. Look at the following examples:
   a) The amount of time I spend online im**pacts** my ability to concentrate.
   b) The amount of time I spend online has a negative **im**pact on my reading skills.

   > In example a, *impact* is used as a verb and stress is placed on the second syllable (im**pact**).

   > In example b, *impact* is used as a noun and the stress is placed on the first syllable (**im**pact).

2. Listen carefully to the recording. Working with a partner, practise pronouncing the following words. Pay attention to placing the stress on the first syllable (nouns) or second syllable (verbs).

Noun	Verb
effect	af**fect**
conduct	con**duct**
conflict	con**flict**
contrast	con**trast**
decrease	de**crease**
impact	im**pact**
object	ob**ject**
project	pro**ject**
progress	pro**gress**

3. With a partner, take turns to read the following sentences out loud and decide if the word in bold is a noun or verb. Be careful to pronounce the words with the correct stress pattern.
   a) His reading skills have **decreased** in the last few years.
   b) We **project** that more and more people will be using drones for personal reasons.
   c) There has been a lot of **progress** in the field of nanotechnology in recent years.
   d) Some people are worried that using drones will have an **impact** on safety.
   e) A drone is an **object** that flies on its own.
   f) Scientists will **conduct** research in how the brain is **affected** by Internet use.
   g) There is a **contrast** in Internet use among young adults and older adults.

Then listen to the recording, paying attention to the stressed syllable.

Revising and Editing

 For more information about sentence types, see Grammar Guide, page 264.

Writing Strategy

Sentence types

One way to make your writing more interesting when you are revising it is to use different sentence types.

A **simple sentence** is the most basic sentence; it contains a subject and a verb and is a complete thought. It is also called an independent clause.

> **EXAMPLE**   A 3D printer can make almost anything.

A **compound sentence** contains two independent clauses joined by a coordinating conjunction. The coordinating conjunctions are *for*, *and*, *nor*, *but*, *or*, *yet*, and *so* (the acronym FANBOYS will help you remember them).

> **EXAMPLE**   The price of 3D printers will come down, and 3D printer capabilities will improve over time.

A **complex sentence** contains an independent clause and a dependent clause joined by a subordinating conjunction. The most common subordinating conjunctions are *after*, *before*, *when*, *while*, *although*, *as*, *because*, *if*, *since*, *where*, and *while*.

> **EXAMPLE**   3D printers are remarkable because they can produce different kinds of objects in different materials.

Tip: Do not begin a sentence with *And* or *But*. However, you can begin a sentence with a subordinating conjunction such as *Although*.

---

1. Combine the following simple sentences to make either a compound or a complex sentence.

   a) 3D printing is a new technology. It can be useful in many different fields. (compound)

   _____

   b) 3D printers are amazing. They can produce a variety of everyday objects. (complex)

   _____

   _____

   c) 3D printers are very expensive. Most people cannot afford to buy one. (complex)

   _____

   _____

   d) Social media makes it easier to connect with others. Studies have shown that viewing other people's vacation photos can cause sadness. (complex)

   _____

   _____

e) Drones were first used with the military. Recently, they have been used in many different fields. (compound)

_____

_____

2. Fill in the blanks with either the past tense or the present perfect of the word provided.

Scientists _____ (invent) drones for military use. The US military _____ (use) drones extensively in recent years. The first recorded killing by a drone _____ (occur) in 2001. Between 2009 and 2015, US military drones _____ (kill) approximately 2500 people. Some people _____ (speculate) that this has been damaging to the US's influence in the world.

Wrap Up

Field-specific activity

Field-Specific Practice

When doing online research, it is important to use credible articles and websites that include information that is factual and unbiased. Review "Evaluating Online Sources" in Research Strategies, page 165, and then pick a topic related to your field of study or future career. Find two articles or websites on this topic from a variety of sources (newspapers/magazines, scholarly journals, government websites, blogs, company websites, personal websites). For each article/website, write a paragraph in which you evaluate its credibility.

Consider the following questions.

- Is the article subjective or objective?
- Does it contain facts, opinions, or a mixture of both?
- Is the author biased?
- Is there evidence of advertising, and how might this affect the quality of information?
- Is the information up to date?
- Would you use this article/website as a reference for an essay you write? Why or why not?

Writing

Write a four-paragraph opinion essay (350 words) on one of the topics below. Use the information from the readings, listening, and discussions in the unit to support your opinions.

A. **General essay topics**

1. Choose an innovation that interests you and give your opinion on how it has affected society positively or negatively.

2. Discuss the benefits and risks of 3D printing.

3. Choose a cutting-edge innovation and discuss its impact on society.

B. **Field of study essay topics**

Field-specific activity

1. Write an essay about the importance of technology in your field of study.

2. Choose a recent innovation/invention and discuss how it is beneficial to your field of study or future career.

3. Choose a recent innovation/invention and explain how it has changed your field of study or future career.

Speaking

Field-specific activity

Research and choose two articles (500–800 words) that discuss an important innovation in your field of study or future career and prepare a presentation (5 minutes) describing the innovation. If you find longer articles that are relevant, you could use part of the articles for your presentation.

S For more information about essay writing and to see a sample essay, see Writing Strategies, page 138.

Include the following elements in your presentation:

- When was it invented or developed?
- Who invented it?
- How has it improved your field of study or future career?
- What are the disadvantages to this invention?
- What are the future implications of this innovation?

1. Research and choose your two articles. When you have found articles that interest you, evaluate the sources using the website evaluation (ABCD) criteria in Research Strategies, page 165.

2. Scan the titles and subtitles to get a general idea of the articles, and then read each article in detail and highlight any important information. In the margin, make notes of the information you want to use in your presentation. In your presentation, include the answers to the questions above.

S For more information about doing research, see Research Strategies, page 163.

3. a) On a separate sheet of paper, make notes of the information that you want to use in your presentation. Make sure you use your own words.
   b) Structure your presentation into main sections: introduction, body, and conclusion.
   c) Prepare cue cards with key words only (no sentences).

4. Follow these tips to help you prepare a successful oral presentation:
   a) Practise your presentation and time yourself to make sure it is approximately five minutes long.
   b) Begin with an attention grabber (interesting fact, quotation, or statistic) that will get the audience interested in your presentation.
   c) Speak clearly and be sure to maintain eye contact with the class.

Vocabulary

Review the new words you studied in this unit. Circle the ones you know well. Underline any words you do not understand and review their meanings. Choose 10 words and write a sentence for each word that demonstrates the meaning in context.

array	drone	multitasking	start-up
backlash	enhance	neuroscience	switch
Big Brother	freaky	nuisance	trade show
boost	hype	overload	trigger
conundrum	injuries	plasticity	unplugging
customized	lack	rewire	withdrawal
disregard	malleable	seize	symptoms

_____

_____

_____

_____

_____

_____

_____

_____

_____

_____

_____

Excellence is never an accident. It is always the result of high intention, sincere effort, and intelligent execution; it represents the wise choice of many alternatives— choice, not chance, determines your destiny.

—Aristotle

There are many factors that contribute to how we make decisions. Our personality and background, and our particular circumstances in any one moment, play a role but, whether we realize it or not, there may be other forces at work. This unit looks at the way human behaviour can be influenced via the fields of design, criminology, marketing, economics, and psychology.

Warm Up

Speaking

The following words all relate to the topic of this unit.

Word	Definition	Example sentence
allude (v)	to make indirect reference to	In her speech, the CEO will allude to a new focus for next year.
appeal (v)	to be attractive or of interest	The television show features older characters to appeal to the Baby Boomers.
elicit (v)	to draw out a feeling, emotion, or response from someone	The new study recommending a four-day workweek elicited great excitement.
manipulate (v)	to cause someone to change their actions or beliefs	My friend is good at manipulating situations to his advantage.
persuade (v)	to convince someone	The salesperson persuaded me to get the two-for-one deal.
subconscious (n)	the part of the human mind that influences behaviour without a person's full awareness	What we really want is hidden in the subconscious.

In groups of three or four, discuss the following questions.

- Do advertising and marketing **manipulate** us? How? Explain your answer and give examples.
- Think of your favourite advertisement. How and why does it appeal to you? What kind of response does it elicit?
- In what circumstances might you want to **allude** to something, rather than say it directly?
- When was the last time you tried to **persuade** someone to do something?
- What role do you think your **subconscious** plays in your decision-making?
- Do you agree with the quotation on page 85 from Aristotle? Is choice more important than chance in determining what happens to you? Why or why not?

Writing

Cognates

The words in bold in the discussion questions above are examples of cognates, words that look and mean the same thing in French and English.

1. Review the words, definitions, and sample sentences.

2. Write another sentence for each of the words. Share them with a partner and correct each other's grammar, spelling, and word use.

3. False cognates are words that look the same or similar in English and French, but have different meanings. Work with your partner to add five more false cognates to the table below. Have you come across any false cognates in your field of study? Add them to the list.

S For more information about false cognates, see Vocabulary Strategies, page 178 and Appendix 7, page 284.

False cognate	English word and its French equivalent	French word and its English equivalent
a) attend/attendre	attend: assister	attendre: wait
b) remark/remarquer	remark: un commentaire	remarquer: to notice
c) quit/quitter	quit: démissionner	quitter: to leave
d)		
e)		
f)		
g)		
h)		

Reading

Are you aware of when you are being influenced? This text explores a technique increasingly being used by governments, businesses, and non-profit organizations to encourage people to make "good" decisions, often without realizing it. Choice architecture, or "nudging," is a way of influencing human behaviour using psychology, design, and a deep understanding of the decision-making process.

Pre-Reading Activity

Answer the following questions.

1. Think of a time when you had to make an important decision. What was the decision?

   _____

   _____

2. List three factors that contributed to the decision you made.

   _____

   _____

   _____

3. Did someone or something influence your decision? If not, who or what might have had the power to influence your decision in different circumstances?

   _____

   _____

4. If you had to make the decision again, would you make the same choice? Explain.

   _____

   _____

Vocabulary

Find each word in the text and then, using context, match it with the correct definition.

Word	Letter	Definition
steer (v) (para. 1)		a) discovered something unexpectedly
eliminating (v) (para. 1)		b) constant
undertake (v) (para. 2)		c) removing
stumbled upon (v) (para. 3)		d) to begin doing something
soared (v) (para. 4)		e) to guide or direct
persistent (adj) (para. 5)		f) not planned; unexpected
unintended (adj) (para. 8)		g) increased a lot

thereby (adv) consequently, in that way

insulate (v) to add material to prevent loss of heat

attic (n) a room or space just below the roof of a building

monetary incentives (n) money-based rewards

junk (n) useless or unwanted items

Nudge: The Persuasive Power of Whispers

CBC, Under the Influence

1   Schools, marketers and even governments are now using small nudges to gently **steer** people toward making more positive decisions in their lives. Those nudges include sending people a handwritten note when they are behind on their taxes because a handwritten note gets their attention, or putting the image of a housefly in urinals so men had something to aim at, **thereby eliminating** overspray by 80 percent. Or the simple act of getting high school kids to fill out a college application before they graduated was the nudge that changed the course of their lives. It's called "nudging"—and it's the study of giving people a subtle *nudge* to influence their decisions and to steer them to positive outcomes.

2   It's a fascinating area of persuasion, and it can generate huge results. The art of the nudge has been adopted by schools, charities, marketers . . . and even governments. The field of behavioural economics is a relatively new area of study. While influencing behaviour has been intensely studied by the advertising industry for decades, the subtle motivation now being employed has taken a big leap forward. The classic definition of behavioural economics is to gently steer people toward decisions that improve their lives—while still leaving them free to choose. It is to get them to take a little step in order to **undertake** a bigger one.

3   In Britain, the government tried to encourage homeowners to **insulate** their **attics** to save energy costs and prevent heat loss. As part of that campaign, the government made compelling economic arguments to persuade the public to insulate. On top of that, generous **monetary incentives** and subsidies were offered. Yet, nothing seemed to work. The public appeared to have no interest in insulating their attics and saving money on heating costs. This surprised the government, but when it investigated, it **stumbled upon** the reason for the resistance. Apparently, UK homeowners simply didn't want to clear the **junk** out of their attics. In the UK, attics are storage spaces. And just the thought of having to clear out their attics was enough for people to forgo the energy savings of insulating.

4   Once the government had isolated that reason, it got to work on an interesting solution. It teamed up with a local home improvement company and offered *an attic-cleaning service*. With that, the number of people who insulated **soared**. The attic-cleaning offer was the "nudge" to get people to do the bigger thing—which was to insulate.

5   The airport in Amsterdam, Holland, wanted to solve a **persistent** problem in the men's washrooms. So they **etched** the image of a housefly into the urinals near the drain. Overspray was reduced by 80 percent. The housefly was a nudge—because men just love to aim at things.

etched (v) cut writing or images into a hard material

6   Recently, several retailers and some New York City cabs have added a digital tipping feature to their tablet and mobile apps. Calculating a tip is frustrating for many people. And research has shown that if you can lessen the amount of mental effort required to calculate a tip—the greater the chance of giving one. So many companies are giving customers three digital options:

The first is called "Basic" and leaves 15 percent.

The second is called "Better" and leaves an automatic 18 percent.

The third is called "Best" and leaves a nice, fat 20 percent tip.

The presence of those three nudges has not only resulted in more people giving tips—but the resulting amounts have been greater.

7   One of the critical aspects of nudging has to do with getting the wording or imagery just right. In Richard Thaler and Cass Sunstein's book, *Nudge*, they tell the story of a city in California that gave its residents an accurate reading on the average energy **consumption** of households in their neighbourhood. The hope was that when people saw they were using more energy than their neighbours, they would scale back.

consumption (n) amount used

8   It worked—except an **unintended** problem appeared. The above-average energy users dramatically *decreased* their energy consumption, but the below-average energy users significantly increased their energy use to come up to the average!

9   The solution was to use emoticons instead of numerical averages. So if you used more than an average amount of energy, you got a *frowning* emoticon ☹. If you used an average amount of energy—or if you used less than average—you received a *smiling* emoticon ☺. As a result, the big energy users reduced their energy consumption, but even more importantly, the problem of below-average users **bumping up** their consumption disappeared *completely*. The smiling/frowning emoticons were the perfect nudge.

bumping up (exp) increasing

10 There is a lot to be said for the power of a nudge. While there are many supporters of nudging, there are critics, too. Many are against the practice, saying they are uneasy when the government influences any decisions with an invisible hand. They ask: When does a nudge become a **shove**? **Proponents** of choice architecture point out that a nudge is a gentle push, and people still have the freedom to choose in the end.

shove (n) pushing someone very hard
proponents (n) people in support of something

11 One thing is for certain—nudges are everywhere, even if we don't see them. So, the next time you're faced with a big decision, it might be a good idea to sniff out the nudge . . . when you're under the influence.   [865 words]

Go to Explore Online for additional practice and comprehension questions.

Comprehension

Answer the following questions. With *True/False* questions, if the answer is *False* write the correct answer in the space provided.

1. In your own words, define what a nudge is.

   _____

   _____

2. The study of behavioural economics has been around a long time and is well established. ☐ True ☐ False

   _____

3. People in Britain wouldn't insulate their attics because it didn't make financial sense. ☐ True ☐ False

   _____

4. Why did showing people their energy consumption compared to other people initially not result in the desired response of reducing overall energy consumption?

   _____

5. Complete the missing information in chart below to describe the nudge campaigns in the text.

Location	Goal	Solution	Result
a) UK	to get people to insulate their attics		The number of people who insulated their attics soared
b) Holland		etching a housefly near the drain	
c) New York City			More people are leaving tips, and the tips are bigger.
d) California	to get people to reduce the amount of energy they use		

6. What is a problem with nudges, according to some people?

   _____

7. Do you think nudge campaigns limit people's choice and freedom? Why or why not?

   _____

   _____

8. Why do you think the article suggests that you should be aware of nudges when making big decisions?

   _____

   _____

Speaking

How might nudging be useful in your field of study or future career? Brainstorm with a partner to make a list of common problems or issues that could be addressed with nudging. Choose one and think of a simple nudging idea that might help to solve it. Share your idea with another group.

Speaking

In groups of three or four, look at the following pictures that depict nudges and discuss these questions. Be ready to share your ideas with the class.

1. What is the message? Describe the intention in one sentence.

2. Explain how the nudge works. What behaviour is being encouraged or prevented?

3. Do you think this nudge will be successful? Why or why not?

4. Can you think of some other examples of nudges?

Writing

Writing Strategy

Writing a proposal

A proposal is a formal way of asking for support for an idea or a plan of action. It includes

- an introduction explaining the background, issue, and situation or problem
- a body in which you propose a solution
- a conclusion restating the need for a solution

In your proposal, provide concrete details about how you will accomplish your plan. Include method, timeline, and budget, if possible, and use persuasive language.

 For more information about writing a proposal and to see a sample proposal, see Writing Strategies, page 155.

Write a short email to propose a new social awareness program in your workplace, college, or town.

Use one of the nudges on page 91 or another you are aware of, and follow this format:

1. Introduce yourself.

2. Explain the problem or behaviour that needs modifying.

3. Describe the nudge you propose.

4. Explain how the nudge will work.

5. Provide supporting evidence.

For example:

Make sure to use a professional-sounding email address.

Indicate the date and subject matter of your correspondence.

Use Ms or Mr. and the surname of the person or *Dear Sir or Madam* if you do not know the name.

Keep the message brief and to the point.

Use a formal sign-off such as *sincerely, regards, respectfully*.

To: Cityplanners@city.com

From: Myworkemail@office.com

Date: May 19, 2016

Subject: Campaign to increase residents' physical fitness

Dear Ms Paradis/Dear Sir or Madam

My name is Emilia Antrobus and I am a student in the health sciences program at Édouard Montpetit. I am very concerned about the impending health crisis in Canada. According to Statistics Canada, over half the population is now both overweight and sedentary. This means that they are at risk for numerous chronic health conditions such as diabetes, stroke, and high blood pressure.

People need to be encouraged to make healthy choices. One project that could be tested would be to persuade citizens to take the stairs. This could be achieved simply by painting the stairs different colours. Various health benefits could be painted on each step making the stairs the fun option.

This would not be an expensive project to implement, but would shift people's attention towards physical activity and steer them towards making better health choices.

Thank you for considering these ideas.

Yours sincerely,

Emilia Antrobus

Watching

How do workplaces influence the behaviour and productivity of their employees? In this audio clip, CBS News explores how Google uses perks, workplace design, and even nudges to create a unique corporate culture and get the most out of its employees.

Vocabulary

Familiarize yourself with the following terms before you watch the video.

Word or phrase	Definition
analytics (n)	relating to data and statistics
data mining (n)	the process of examining large amounts of data to generate new information
perk (n)	an extra advantage or benefit on top of regular pay

Inside Google Workplaces, from Perks to Nap Pods [5:06]

CBS News

Comprehension

Answer the following questions.

1. What award did Google win four years in a row?

   _____

2. How many people send resumés to Google each year? _____

3. What example does Laszlo Bock give to show that behaviour can affect productivity?

   _____

   _____

4. Why does David Radcliffe call the Google offices "a living laboratory"?

   _____

   _____

5. What is Radcliffe's goal when designing the Google environments?

   _____

6. Give three examples of perks provided for Google employees.

   _____

7. What problem caused Google to try nudging?

   _____

Go to Explore Online for additional practice and comprehension questions.

8. Give three examples of nudges used to deal with the problem.

_____

_____

9. In a seven-week period, how many fewer calories of M&Ms were consumed after nudging?
   a) 10 percent   b) 15 percent   c) 2.5 million   d) 3 million

Speaking

With a partner, discuss your ideal workplace. Is it an office building, a store, your home, or an outdoor space? What does the environment look like? What perks would you most want? As in the case of Google, sometimes things that are great about a workplace can cause issues. Think about a potential issue that might arise in your field-of-study workplace.

Field-Specific Practice

1. Research a company or organization in your field that you might want to work for. Look at the company's website and any other information you can find online. Write notes on the following:

   - name
   - location(s)
   - description of business
   - company/organization size (number of employees)
   - company vision, values or mission statement
   - company history
   - recent company news
   - any other interesting information

2. Use your notes to write a paragraph summarizing your research called "A Company Profile." Your topic sentence should introduce the company and describe what field it is associated with. Alternatively, make a short oral presentation of your notes to the class.

Go to Explore Online for additional practice using the comparative and the superlative.

Grammar

The comparative and the superlative

The comparative form of an adjective or adverb is used to compare two people, places, or things.

> **EXAMPLE**   This exam is **harder than/more difficult than** the last one.

The superlative is used to compare three or more people, places, or things—to compare one person, place, or thing with all other members of the same group.

> **EXAMPLE**   This is **the greatest/the best/the most rewarding** job ever.

	Comparative	Superlative
short adjectives *cold* *small* *young*	add *-er* to the adjective *colder* *smaller* *younger*	add *the + -est* to the adjective *the coldest* *the smallest* *the youngest*
long adjectives or adverbs *intelligent, beautiful, slowly*	add *more* before the adjective and *than* after *more intelligent than*	add *the most* before the adjective *the most intelligent*
two-syllable adjectives ending in -y *happy* *easy*	change the *-y* to *-ier* *happier* *easier*	change *-y* to *-iest* *happiest* *easiest*
irregular adjectives *good* *bad* *little* *far*	*better* *worse* *less* *farther/further*	*the best* *the worst* *the least* *the farthest/the furthest*

 For more information on comparatives and superlatives, see Grammar Guide, pages 259, 260, and 262.

1. Fill in the blanks with the correct comparative form of the word provided.

    a) A push is _____ (strong) than a nudge.

    b) Some decisions are _____ (important) than others.

    c) Behavioural economics is _____ (new) than most other scientific fields.

    d) Using nudging is _____ (easy) than telling people to do things differently.

2. Fill in the blanks with the correct superlative form of the word provided.

    a) Some people think perks are _____ (good) way to motivate employees.

    b) Google is one of the _____ (well-known) tech companies in the world.

    c) Taking the stairs is one of the _____ (simple) ways to get more exercise.

    d) The _____ (bad) companies do not support their employees.

3. Choose between the comparative and superlative to complete the following sentences.

    a) Giving people three tipping options made them _____ (generous).

    b) It is _____ (hard) to get a job in my field than in your field.

    c) A museum would be _____ (exciting) place to work.

    d) I am _____ (young) person at my company.

Interpreting Data

Researchers have studied whether lunchroom design could make people eat healthier by putting certain foods in more strategic places; for example, making the vegetables easier to find than the junk food (less healthy food). The results of some of these studies are described in the paragraph and the graph below.

1. Underline the comparative and superlative forms in the following description of different studies.

   In one study, one of two lunch lines was arranged to better display healthier foods. In the healthier line, sales of more nutritiously rich food increased by 18 percent and the amount of less wholesome food consumed decreased by 28 percent. Another study found similar results when researchers made food harder to reach or changed the serving utensil. The researchers discovered that even small changes reduced intake of unhealthy food by 8–16 percent. If the healthiest choices are more prominent, they become the most popular.

2. Answer the following questions using the information in the paragraph above.

   a) How much less unhealthy food was eaten when placed in the healthier line?

   _____

   _____

   b) If the healthier choices are put in the most accessible places, they become the most consumed. ❏ True ❏ False

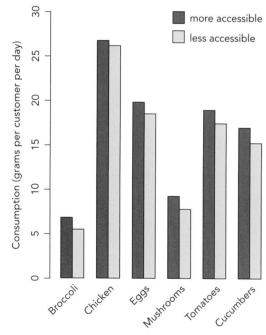

3. Use the data in the graph to answer the following questions.

   a) The most popular food in the lunchroom is _____.

   b) Consumption of all items decreased when they were made less accessible. ❏ True ❏ False

   c) Broccoli is the least popular food in the study. ❏ True ❏ False

   d) Mushrooms are consumed <u>more/less</u> than eggs in the lunchroom.

   e) Cucumbers are eaten <u>more/less</u> than broccoli.

4. Use the comparative or the superlative to create two more sentences that describe information in the eating habits studies.

   _____

   _____

   _____

   _____

   _____

   _____

   _____

Reading

The ability to influence people's behaviour through nudging has wide-ranging implications. In this text, two doctoral candidates propose it could be used to reduce shoplifting. What other areas do you think nudging might be applied to?

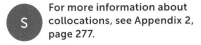

For more information about collocations, see Appendix 2, page 277.

Vocabulary Strategy

Collocations

A collocation is two or more words that are often used together. For example, *dinner party* (not *dinner event*), *health benefits* (not *health advantages*), *heavy workload* (not *big workload*).

The following collocations are taken from the text:

> *low cost* rather than *small cost* or *less cost*
>
> *tackling crime* rather than *attacking crime* or *dealing with crime*
>
> *contribute to society* rather than *help to society* or *contribute for society*

1. Working with a partner, find the following words in the text on page 98 and write the missing part of the collocation.

   a) *appeal* (para. 3) _____

   b) *crime* (paras. 2 & 13) _____

   c) *element* (paras. 3 & 12) _____

2. Go online to use the *Online Oxford Collocation Dictionary of English*. Type in a word related to your field of study or future career, e.g., *nurse* or *nursing*, and make a list of collocations related to that word. Be prepared to share your word list with the class.

Field-specific activity

Vocabulary

Find the following words in the text and then use them to fill in the blanks in the sentences.

perceived (v) (para. 1)   **potential (adj)** (para. 3)

consumers (n) (para. 1)   **unconscious (adj)** (para. 3)

range (n) (para. 2)   **imply (v)** (para 6)

maximize (v) (para. 2)   **conventional (adj)** (para. 13)

1. The shoplifter gained access to the building after hours to _____ the amount of time he had in the store.

2. Every day we are exposed to nudges, but we are usually _____ of them.

3. Google employed a _____ of techniques to help employees lose weight.

4. When I asked you when you were coming home, I didn't mean to _____ you were late.

5. Weekends are often _____ as a time to relax, but not when you work in retail!

6. The company's ad campaign was aimed at wealthy _____.

7. Starting your own company is not the _____ way to get your first job.

Shopping Mall Design Could Nudge Shoplifters into Doing the Right Thing

The Conversation

1   **Shoplifting** is a serious problem. Although it is often **perceived** as an "ordinary crime" due to its supposed **victimless** nature, in fact it costs the UK's retail industry £335m a year. Part of this cost is passed on to **consumers** in the form of higher prices.

2   The way buildings and streets are designed can help reduce shoplifting, and architects, city planners, and law enforcement teams have a **range** of techniques to help them do this. For example, Crime Prevention Through Environmental Design (CPTED) strategies try to **maximize** opportunities for official **surveillance** and restrict people's access to certain areas while directing them to others.

3   Such techniques appeal to rational thought in **potential** shoplifters by trying to make the costs or risks of crime **outweigh** the benefits. But other elements of retail design appeal to **unconscious** decision making, encouraging you to do things without realizing, in order to increase the chances of you making a purchase. We believe the same ideas can be used to **deter** shoplifters.

4   A retail environment can be described as "a bundle of cues, messages, and suggestions that communicate to shoppers." This has an ability to manipulate people's behaviour and make them more likely to buy something.

5   Have you ever wondered why you have to walk all the way to the far end of a shopping mall to access the next set of stairs or escalators? While dictating the flow of visitors around the shopping centre, it also ensures people are exposed to the maximum number of stores and products, increasing the chance of an **impulse buy**.

6   Because "all buildings **imply** at least some form of social activity," the arrangement of wall partitions, doors, and other features can affect, amplify, or **curtail** social interaction. For instance, a designer can create specific areas such as access lanes where people can come into contact with each other. It is this ability of a retail environment to influence choices that is at the heart of our proposition to tackle high-street crime.

Nudge theory

7   The nudge theory is the idea that people make most decisions unconsciously and non-rationally and so people can be encouraged to do things without having to convince them logically.

8   Under this idea, we believe potential shoplifters can be encouraged to do the right thing using environmental signals that target the non-rational parts of their brains. Nudging provides an interesting **antithesis** to conventional

shoplifting (n) the act of stealing from a store

victimless (adj) a crime in which no one gets hurt

surveillance (n) the act of closely watching someone or something

outweigh (v) to give more importance to something over something else

deter (v) to discourage

impulse buy (exp) buying something you didn't plan to buy

curtail (v) to limit

A high street is traditionally the main street of a town—typically the centre of retail activity.

antithesis (n) the opposite of something

approaches because it is not dependent on a rational judgment by the criminal (for example, deciding security cameras make a theft too risky).

9 We believe that nudges can either be developed to target shoplifters specifically or to **foster** an environment that affects everyone in it by **enhancing** natural surveillance. For example, we can imagine a store that gives a certain amount each year for charitable work and another amount as shoplifting costs. What if the store displayed signs indicating that money saved by reduced shoplifting would be donated to charity?

foster (v) to encourage

enhancing (v) increasing

10 By presenting this cue we are not threatening **prosecution**. We are offering a choice that allows a potential criminal to contribute to society by not stealing from the store.

prosecution (n) the act of convicting someone of a crime

11 We are enhancing the benefits of not committing crime as an alternative to enhancing the cost of doing so. Although this approach still relies on some rational thinking on the part of the criminal, it is inspired by nudge theory because it alters the way choices are presented to criminals in order to encourage them to do the right thing.

12 The more non-rational elements of nudging could also be employed to produce playful environments that encourage natural surveillance. If people want to interact with their space, for example if it includes art installations or technology, they may be encouraged to unconsciously watch their immediate environment. Such playful interactions with goods or other customers in a retail environment (if designed correctly) would present a harder target for criminals and at relatively low cost.

13 We want to encourage a shift from **conventional** approaches from punishment to prevention when tackling high-street crime. To do this, we think designers and architects should experiment with nudge theory to produce innovative thinking in this space, **augmenting** conventional crime prevention methods such as CPTED. We have already tried **incarceration** for centuries and people are still found shoplifting. Perhaps alternative ideas could help reduce crime.   **[710 words]**

augmenting (v) adding to

incarceration (n) the act of locking people up for their crimes

Comprehension

Answer the following questions. With *True/False* questions, if the answer is *False* write the correct answer in the space provided.

 Go to Explore Online for additional practice and comprehension questions.

1. According to the article, who are the victims of shoplifting? Choose all that apply.
    a) the stores   b) the police   c) the government   d) consumers

2. What techniques are currently employed to reduce shoplifting?

    _____

    _____

3. How do these conventional techniques encourage people not to shoplift?

    _____

4. In your own words, describe the main idea of the text.

    _____

5. How is nudging different from the conventional approaches the authors describe?

_____

_____

6. What do you think the meaning of *natural surveillance* is in the article?

_____

_____

7. Describe, in your own words, why a "playful environment" might prevent shoplifting.

_____

_____

8. The authors recommend using nudging instead of
   the conventional techniques to stop shoplifting.　　❏ True　❏ False

_____

_____

Speaking

In groups of three or four, brainstorm to complete the table; then share your ideas with the class.

Advantages of nudging being used in shopping mall design	Disadvantages of nudging being used in shopping mall design
•	•
•	•
•	•

Pronunciation

Silent letters

In English, like French, not all letters of a word are pronounced. Knowing which letters are silent will help you be understood in English.

1. Listen to the pronunciation of the following words.

2. Then practise saying the sentences with a partner. Check each other's pronunciation.

	Letter	Example	Sentence
1.	a	romantic**a**lly	I am not romantically involved with anyone.
2.	b	clim**b**	It was a long climb up the mountain.
3.	c	s**c**issors	Never run with scissors.
4.	d	We**d**nesday	The job starts on Wednesday.
5.	e	blu**e**	Blue is my favourite colour.
6.	g	si**g**n	Snow is a sign of winter.
7.	gh	dau**gh**ter	Her daughter is four years old.
8.	h	**h**our	Most people get an hour for lunch at work.
9.	i	bus**i**ness	Daniel is studying business.
10.	k	**k**now	I know how to get there.
11.	l	sa**l**mon	We had salmon for dinner.
12.	m	**m**nemonic	A mnemonic is a learning device.
13.	n	autum**n**	The leaves change colour in autumn.
14.	o	pe**o**ple	People can be influenced.
15.	p	**p**sychology	Psychology is a fascinating subject.
16.	r	Feb**r**uary	We'll take a vacation in February.
17.	s	i**s**land	The trip was to Vancouver Island.
18.	t	cas**t**le	The castle sat on top of the hill.
19.	u	g**u**ess	When people don't know the answer, they guess.
20.	w	ans**w**er	She gave the correct answer.
21.	x	fau**x** pas	It's a faux pas to wear your backpack on the subway.
22.	y	ma**y**or	Our mayor is coming to the event.
23.	z	rende**z**vous	The rendezvous was set for 6 PM.

Listening

How do you feel when you walk down a city street? Do you feel differently when you walk through a park? In this CBC *Spark* interview, a cognitive neuroscientist describes a project in which he measures people's responses to different types of buildings and urban spaces. Using research from the fields of urban design, architecture, neuroscience, and environmental psychology, he points out another way we may be influenced without realizing it.

Pre-Listening Activity

With a partner, discuss the following questions.

1. How often do you function on "auto-pilot" and not notice your surroundings? Can you think of an example when it got you in trouble?

2. In your field of study, what would be an example of a time when being on auto-pilot could cause problems?

 Field-specific activity

3. Think of a building or place that you associate with a positive feeling. Describe it and how it makes you feel. Do you think there is a connection between how it looks and how you feel?

4. Now think of a building or place that you don't like. Is there a connection between its physical appearance and how you feel about it?

Vocabulary

Read each sentence and then choose the correct definition for the word in bold.

Sentence	Meaning 1	Meaning 2
1. I've had **chronic** back pain my whole life.	long-time	brief
2. The surface of the planet Mars is very **bleak**.	quiet and calm on most days	miserable/not interesting
3. Some people say the use of smartphones has eliminated **boredom**.	monotony/lethargy	a state of excitement about an upcoming event
4. More people now live in **urban** settings than in the country.	related to the city	related to the modern day
5. My **ancestors** came from Kenya, but none of my family lives there now.	family members of an earlier generation	family members who live in a different country
6. When I get stressed out, I find going out with friends can be **restorative**.	soothing or healing	exciting or thrilling

Can a Building Make You Sad? [8:00]

CBC, *Spark*

Comprehension

Take notes as you listen to the interview, and then answer the following questions. With *True/False* questions, if the answer is *False* write the correct answer in the space provided.

Go to Explore Online for additional practice and comprehension questions.

1. "Smart cities" are usually designed to maximize people's sense of well-being.　　☐ True　☐ False

    _____

2. How does Colin Ellard gather data about people's reactions to different buildings and spaces?

    _____

    _____

3. What are the two purposes of Ellard's experiment?

    a) _____

    b) _____

4. Name three effects that an unbroken, closed façade of a building can have on a pedestrian.

    _____

    _____

5. Scientists now know how much time a person needs in a green space to contribute to their well-being.　　☐ True　☐ False

    _____

6. What is one of the biggest differences between us and our ancestors in terms of how we live, according to Ellard?

    _____

    _____

7. According to Ellard, why do people like to stand at the edge of public spaces?

    _____

8. What is Ellard's advice for people, based on his research?

    _____

    _____

    _____

Speaking

You are conducting your own "psychology on the street" project. With a partner, create a questionnaire (five questions) to measure reactions or feelings towards a building in your area. Either visit the building or show a picture of the building to five other students and give them the questionnaire. Work with your partner to analyze your findings.

Write a paragraph describing the building and the responses it inspired. How might it affect the well-being of the people who walk by it? Would you recommend more buildings like this be built? Why or why not?

Revising and Editing

Correct the mistakes in spelling, verb tense, and comparative and superlative forms in the following paragraphs. There are 10 errors.

One of the most power tools of persuasion are a well-timed and strongly delivered speech. In fact, some have made the argument that words can be the most powerful than action. The most famous speeches occurred at key moment in history and worked to sway people to a particular point of view or strengthen their belief in a course of action.

For example, in his "Their Finest Hour" speech during World War II, Winston Churchill encouraged the people of England to stay strong and keeps fighting after France had been invaded by the Germany. Martin Luther King's "I Have a Dream" speech calling for the end of racism and became a defining moment for the civil rights movement.

People have debated what makes a great speech. Is the content, the delivery, the audience, or the timing the most importance factor? Most people agree it is a combination. The audience must be ready to be persuade and not set on a different point of view. The content must speak to both the particular moment in history and capture larger, universal themes. Finally, the speaker must be passionate, speak the truth, and inspiring confidence at a moment when the audience, perhaps even the world, is looking for leadership. Then a speech takes on the power to change lives and the course of history.

Wrap Up

Field-Specific Practice

In your field of study or future career, what problems or issues would benefit from nudges or the insights of choice architecture?

1. Identify a problem or issue in your field (e.g., if you are in an early childhood education program you might choose the issue of handwashing in daycare centres).

2. Create a questionnaire to gather information about the problem from different key people involved (e.g., early childhood educators, parents, cleaners). Use the facts collected to support your proposal (e.g., the majority of parents want to increase hygiene in daycares).

3. Propose a nudge (e.g., a poster showing ways to calculate the number of bacteria on your hands).

4. Explain how the nudge will work and the expected outcomes (e.g., "This will personalize the problem to each person involved and people will feel more responsible for their surroundings.").

5. Outline how you will measure the results and evaluate the nudge.

6. Prepare a PowerPoint presentation of 10 slides to present the problem and the proposed nudge to the class in a persuasive presentation (2 minutes).

Writing

Write an opinion essay (4 paragraphs) about the ethics of nudging. Decide if you think nudging is or is not ethical and then write an essay providing reasons to support your position. Your thesis statement should state your opinion and your body paragraphs should provide reasons and evidence to support your thesis.

S For more information about writing thesis statements, see Writing Strategies, page 138.

Speaking

Using the key words "famous speeches," find a recorded speech online that interests you. Pay particular attention to the tone and language of the speaker. Now write and deliver a powerful speech (3 minutes) about a topic that you are passionate about related to your field of study. It could be an idea, a person, or your opinion about a controversial topic. Your speech should use persuasive language and have a clear introduction and conclusion that uses persuasive language.

 Field-specific activity

Vocabulary

Fill in the following chart with different forms of the same word. The first one has been done for you. Provide the meaning of the verb or noun.

Noun	Verb	Adjective	Adverb	Meaning
manipulation	manipulate	manipulative	manipulatively	to change someone or something for one's purposes
		persistent		
		restorative		
	perceive			
	persuade			to convince someone of something

Fill in the blank with the appropriate form of one of the words from the chart.

1. Marketing companies spend a lot of time trying to understand how people
   _____ value.

2. The salesperson came around every week and eventually wore me down with
   his _____.

3. At the meeting, the employees argued _____ for healthier food in
   the cafeteria, which led to a change of menu.

4. I find using nudges to be _____ and would prefer if governments
   and companies did not use them.

5. After the new product failed, the CEO had to work hard to _____
   confidence in the company.

It is a modern day, and these times need modern solutions to modern problems.

—Corin Nemec

Change offers new opportunities . . . and new challenges. In this unit, we look at some innovative solutions to problems in fields like transportation, urban design, health, safety, and agriculture, and give you the opportunity to use your knowledge and skills in your own field of study or future career to solve a pressing problem.

Warm Up

Speaking

1. Working with a partner, look at the following list of modern problems. Discuss and answer the questions that follow.

   - youth unemployment
   - poverty
   - refugees
   - population growth
   - obesity
   - drug abuse

   - climate change
   - war and terrorism
   - food production
   - traffic accidents
   - gun violence
   - access to health care for people in remote areas

   a) Which problem do you think is most serious? Why?

   _____

   b) Which problem do you think is least serious? Why?

   _____

   c) Choose one of these problems and describe a possible innovative solution to address it.

   Solution: _____

   _____

   _____

   d) Show your problem/solution to another pair of students. Explain your reason for choosing that specific problem and your innovative solution to it. Do those students have any suggestions to improve your solution? Do you have any suggestions to improve the solution to the problem they chose?

   _____

2. Look at the following solutions and label them with the problem they are addressing. Then, with your partner, discuss whether you think this solution could work.

   a) making certain types of bullets very expensive _____

   b) using driverless cars _____

   c) having young workers start off at 80 percent of the workload

   _____

   d) inventing a pill that gives the same results as exercise _____

   e) using drones to deliver medication _____

   f) using urban farms _____

Field-specific activity

3. Work with a partner in the same (or a similar) program as you. Brainstorm a list of problems specific to your field of study. Then discuss some possible solutions.

   Write a short paragraph explaining your field-specific problem and solution.

Watching

Driverless cars are no longer a vision of the future; they are being used and tested around the world today. This report from CBC's *The National* explores the benefits of driverless technology and the impact it will have on our cities, affecting not just transportation but architecture, urban planning, economics, and human behaviour.

Pre-Watching Activity

Before watching the report, discuss the following questions with a partner.

1. What do you know about driverless cars?

2. Would you consider using a driverless car?

3. What do you think might be the potential benefits of driverless technology?

4. What are the potential drawbacks of driverless technology?

Vocabulary

The following words and expressions are used in the report. Study the definitions and then use the words to fill in the blanks in the sentences below.

Word or phrase	Definition
fleet (n)	a large group of vehicles
hit the brakes (exp)	stop a vehicle by activating the braking system
narrow (adj)	having a small width
tipping point (exp)	the moment when a series of small changes cause a larger, more important change
trend (n)	tendency
urban landscape (n)	the physical aspects of a city

1. The _____ is changing due a growing focus on pedestrian-friendly streets.

2. The taxi company had a _____ providing service to the west side of the city.

3. We have not yet reached the _____ where driverless cars are common on the roads.

4. Another _____ that is changing transportation is the move toward using electric vehicles.

5. Autonomous vehicles _____ when they sense an obstacle in their path.

6. If the roads are _____, there will be more public space.

How Driverless Cars Will Change Cities [8:22]

CBC, *The National*

Go to Explore Online for
additional practice and
comprehension questions.

Comprehension

Answer the following questions. With *True/False* questions, if the answer is *False* write the correct answer in the space provided.

1. In the past, what was associated with car ownership? Circle all answers that apply.

    status   fun   money   freedom   friendship   adventure

2. In what three areas will there be a shift due to driverless technology?

    _____

3. According to urban planner Jennifer Keesmaat, what are two of the effects driverless technology will have on the urban landscape?

    _____

4. What are the two mega-trends that Barry Kirk describes?

    _____

5. What will be the result of the two trends converging?
    a) more cars on the road   b) driverless taxis
    c) more public transportation   d) more public spaces

6. What percentage of road accidents today are the result of human error?
    a) 80 percent   b) 90 percent   c) 93 percent   d) 73 percent

7. Driverless cars will effectively end deaths by
    car accident.   ❏ True ❏ False

    _____

8. What are experts most worried about regarding the future of driverless cars?
    a) An increase in road accidents.
    b) The malfunctioning of driverless cars.
    c) Human drivers sharing the road with computer drivers.
    d) Society's lack of trust of driverless cars.

9. What percentage of time is the average car in use? _____

10. Is the report favourable to driverless technology?   ❏ Yes ❏ No

    Explain your answer.

    _____
    _____
    _____
    _____
    _____

Speaking

1. With a partner, think of three modern problems that driverless technology could solve.

   1. _____

   2. _____

   3. _____

2. Now think of three problems it might create.

   1. _____

   2. _____

   3. _____

3. Overall, do you think driverless technology will benefit society or not? Why?

Reading

One of the most compelling arguments for the use of driverless cars is that they are safer. In this article, research, data, and examples are used to show the benefits of driverless technology.

<table>
<tr><td>

Reading Strategy

The author's purpose

The purpose of a text is the author's main goal. Why did he or she write the text? Most texts you will read in college, university, or the workplace fall under two main purposes:
- to inform
- to persuade

Some other purposes are
- to entertain
- to describe
- to recommend
- to explain
- to encourage

As you read the following text, think about what effect the author wants to have on you, the reader, to find its purpose.

</td></tr>
</table>

S For more information about purpose, see Reading Strategies, page 171.

Pre-Reading Activity

 Field-specific activity

New technologies, such as driverless cars, have effects on many industries. Think of a technology invented in the last 50 years that has affected your field of study or future career, and then take turns answering these questions with a partner.

1. What is the technology?

2. In what ways did it change your field of study or future career?

3. What other industries do you think were affected by this technology?

Vocabulary

Compound adjectives are two or more words that together make an adjective. They contain a hyphen when they are placed directly before a noun. Understanding each word individually will help you guess the meaning of the compound adjective. For example, a "five-page document" is a document that is five pages long.

1. Find five compound adjective + noun combinations in the article "Self-Driving Cars Could Save 300 000 Lives per Decade in America." Then provide a simple definition.

Term	Definition
self-driving	can drive itself

2. Find each word in the corresponding paragraph and then try to match each word with its definition.

Word	Letter	Definition
1. **realm (n)** (para. 3)		a) careful examination looking for problems
2. **efficacy (n)** (para. 5)		b) something that must be overcome
3. **widespread (adj)** (para. 8)		c) a field or domain where something occurs
4. **hurdle (n)** (para. 8)		d) found over a large area
5. **scrutiny (n)** (para. 10)		e) the power to produce a desired result

vast (adj) large

Self-Driving Cars Could Save 300 000 Lives per Decade in America

By Adrienne LaFrance, *The Atlantic*

Automation on the roads could be the great public-health achievement of the 21st century

1   If driverless cars deliver on their promise to eliminate the **vast** majority of fatal traffic accidents, the technology will rank among the most transformative public-health initiatives in human history. But how many lives, realistically, will be saved?

2   By the end of this century, there's good reason to believe that tens of millions of traffic fatalities will be prevented around the world.

3   This is not merely theoretical. There's already some **precedent** for change of this magnitude in the **realms** of car culture and automotive safety. In 1970, about 60 000 people died in traffic accidents in the United States. A dramatic **shift** toward safety—including required seat belts and **ubiquitous** airbags—helped vastly improve a person's chance of surviving the American roadways in the decades that followed. By 2013, 32 719 people died in traffic crashes, a historic low.

precedent (n) an earlier event that is considered to be an example

shift (n) a change

ubiquitous (adj) found everywhere

4   Researchers estimate that driverless cars could, by midcentury, reduce traffic fatalities by up to 90 percent. Which means that, using the number of fatalities in 2013 as a **baseline**, self-driving cars could save 29 447 lives a year. In the United States alone, that's nearly 300 000 fatalities prevented over the course of a decade, and 1.5 million lives saved in a half-century. For context: Anti-smoking efforts saved 8 million lives in the United States over a 50-year period.

baseline (n) a measure against which something else is compared

5   The life-saving estimates for driverless cars are **on par** with the **efficacy** of modern **vaccines**, which save 42 000 lives for each US birth cohort, according to the Centers for Disease Control.

on par (exp) equal to

vaccines (n) medicine given to prevent getting a disease

6   Globally, there are about 1.2 million traffic fatalities annually, according to the World Health Organization. Which means driverless cars are likely to save 10 million lives per decade—and 50 million lives around the world in half a century.

7   "By midcentury, the penetration of [autonomous vehicles] and other [advanced driver-assistance systems] could ultimately cause vehicle crashes in the United States to fall from second to ninth place in terms of their **lethality** ranking among accident types," wrote Michele Bertoncello and Dominik Wee in a paper for the consulting firm McKinsey & Company. Bertoncello and Wee further estimate that better road safety will save as much as $190 billion a year in health-care costs associated with accidents.

lethality (n) capability of causing death

8   Of course, all this relies on **widespread** adoption of driverless cars, which is as much a cultural **hurdle** as a technological one. As Andrew Moore, the computer science dean at Carnegie Mellon recently told me, "No one is going to want to realize autonomous driving into the world until there's proof that it's much safer, like a factor of 100 safer, than having a human drive."

9   And even then, there are complex questions to consider. People are still establishing **frameworks** for how to think about responsibility in a driverless world. Even with cars that are a factor of 100 safer than their manned **predecessors**, fatal accidents will happen.

frameworks (n) systems; structures

predecessor (n) something or someone who came before

10   "There will be situations where a car knows that it's about to crash and will be planning how it crashes," Moore said. "There will be incredible **scrutiny** on the engineers who wrote the code to deal with the crash. Was it trying to save its occupant? Was it trying to save someone else?"

11   Moore suggests the driverless car revolution will hit a **snag**—setting it back at least a few years—after the first high-profile fatalities. Others have made similar predictions. It may be during the transition to wider-spread driverless adoption that autonomous vehicles are least trusted and roads are most dangerous.

snag (n) difficulty

12   "During the transition period when conventional and self-driving vehicles would share the road, safety might actually worsen, at least for the conventional vehicles," wrote Michael Sivak and Brandon Schoettle, transportation researchers at the University of Michigan, in a paper earlier this year.

sterling (adj) highest standard

13 After all, even a machine with a **sterling** driving record can't account entirely for human error. Google's fleet of self-driving cars has learned this lesson first-hand. Its cars have driven in autonomous mode for more than 1 million miles since 2009. In all that time, they've been involved in 16 accidents through August—none of which were caused by the self-driving car.

14 All this suggests that, despite the growing pains ahead, the promise of driverless cars remains enormous—and **within reach**.   [723 words]

within reach (exp) possible

Comprehension

Go to Explore Online for additional practice and comprehension questions.

Answer the following questions.

1. According to the first two paragraphs of the article, what is the most important potential benefit of driverless technology?

   _____

2. What two safety features introduced after the 1970s have reduced the number of deaths on the roads?

   _____   _____

3. What modern invention is comparable to driverless technology in terms of the number of lives it will save? _____

4. In one year, how many lives could driverless technology save in the US?

   _____

5. According to Andrew Moore, when will people be ready to adopt driverless technology?
   a) when they have proof it is safe
   b) when the cost is reduced
   c) when it is culturally acceptable
   d) when it is more technologically advanced

6. According to Moore, what could set driverless technology back a few years?

   _____

7. What is the risk when driverless cars share the road with conventional cars?

   _____

8. How many accidents have Google's driverless cars been involved in since 2009? _____. How many accidents did self-driving cars cause? _____

9. Is this article objective or subjective? _____

   Explain your answer.

   _____

   _____

   _____

10. What is the purpose of the article? Explain your answer.
    a) to inform   b) to persuade

    _____

    _____

Make a list of five fields that will be affected by driverless technology. Beside each field, give a brief description of what potential effects it will have. Include both positive and negative effects. An example is shown below.

Trucking Industry

positive effects of driverless technology	• increases efficiency: trucks can drive 24 hours a day
	• saves companies money: no paid drivers
negative effects of driverless technology	• job loss: truck drivers would lose their jobs
	• pollution: trucks on the road longer each day

Be prepared to share your ideas with the class.

Writing

> **Writing Strategy**
>
> ## Recognizing organizational patterns
>
> Authors develop their ideas in many ways depending on the topic and the purpose. Effective readers are able to recognize the organizational pattern in a text.
>
> Some common organizational patterns are explained below, along with key transitional words or phrases.
>
> 1. **Compare and contrast:** In this pattern two people, places, items, or concepts are compared and/or contrasted. The purpose is to show how the elements being compared or contrasted are either similar or different, or better or worse.
>
>   **Transitional words and phrases**
>
>   **Compare:** *likewise, similarly, also, in the same way*
>
>   **Contrast:** *although, but, however, on the other hand, conversely, in contrast*
>
> 2. **Cause and effect:** In this pattern, the reasons for and the result or outcome of something are discussed.
>
>   **Transitional words and phrases:** *accordingly, as a result, because, consequently, thus, therefore*
>
> 3. **Process:** In this pattern, the method of how to do something or how something works is explained.
>
>   **Transitional words:** *first, second, third, then, next*
>
> 4. **Problem–solution:** In this pattern, a problem is described and a solution is proposed.
>
>   **Transitional words and phrases:** *therefore, if . . . then, to solve*

S For more information about organizational patterns, types of essays, and writing styles, see Writing Strategies, page 138.

1. Look at the following writing topics and decide which organizational pattern should be used.

   a) The reasons for global warming are described. _____

   b) There are many steps involved in using a 3D printer. _____

   c) There are several solutions to youth unemployment. _____

   d) There are many differences between the human brain and a computer. _____

2. Look at the article "Self-Driving Cars Could Save 300 000 Lives per Decade in America." What is the organizational pattern of the article?

   _____

   Explain your answer.

   _____

   _____

3. Write a topic sentence for a paragraph related to driverless technology, based on each of the four organizational patterns. The first one is done for you.

   Compare and contrast: **There are more advantages than disadvantages to adopting driverless technology in Canada.**

   Cause and effect: _____

   Process: _____

   Problem—solution: _____

4. Use one of the topic sentences you created above to write a paragraph that includes supporting details and a concluding statement.

Interpreting Data

emerging market (exp) market that is developing/growing rapidly

The following infographic makes the case that people want to buy driverless cars. Look at the graph, and then answer the following questions with a partner.

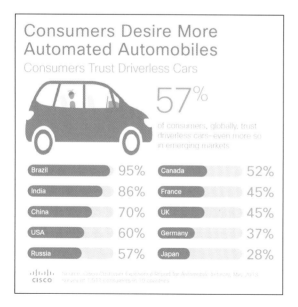

Consumers Desire More Automated Automobiles
Consumers Trust Driverless Cars

57% of consumers, globally, trust driverless cars—even more so in emerging markets

Brazil	95%	Canada	52%
India	86%	France	45%
China	70%	UK	45%
USA	60%	Germany	37%
Russia	57%	Japan	28%

1. Based on the data provided, which countries do you think count as **emerging markets**?

   _____

2. According to the survey, which two countries have the fewest respondents who trust driverless cars?

   _____

3. How do Canadians feel about driverless cars compared to consumers in other countries?

   _____

4. In which two countries are consumers' attitudes the most different?

   _____

5. Which two countries trust driverless cars equally?

_____

6. How does Russians' trust of driverless cars compare to the average trust around the world?

_____

7. Provide two reasons why people from some countries might trust driverless cars much more than people from other countries.

_____

_____

_____

_____

Listening

In this report we learn about a promising solution to a growing problem: the number of overweight people in the world. Scientists and pharmaceutical (drug) companies are looking for ways to develop a pill that will prevent obesity and help people lose weight. Imagine a future where we get all the benefits of exercise while sitting on our couches. Does it seem too good to be true? Listen to the report and find out.

Pre-Listening Activity

1. Before listening to the report, discuss the following questions with a partner.
   a) Do you think obesity is a serious problem in Canada?
   b) Do you believe there could be a **magic bullet** to cure obesity?
   c) What advice would you give to someone who wants to lose weight?
   d) If you could take a pill to replace exercising, would you stop exercising?
   e) Do you think the number of obese people is increasing or decreasing?
   f) What are the dangers of leading a sedentary lifestyle?

magic bullet (n) a medicine or other remedy, especially an undiscovered or hypothetical one, with miraculous properties

2. Look at the following statistics about obesity in Canada, and decide if they are true or false. If the answer is *False* write the correct answer in the space provided.

   a) Almost 25 percent of adult Canadians are obese.　☐ True　☐ False

   _____

   b) More women in Canada are obese than men.　☐ True　☐ False

   _____

   c) One in ten children are obese.　☐ True　☐ False

   _____

   d) Fifty percent of men in Canada are overweight or obese.　☐ True　☐ False

   _____

   e) Obesity rates are lower in Quebec and British Columbia than in the rest of Canada.　☐ True　☐ False

   _____

Vocabulary

Study the following definitions before you watch the report.

Word or phrase	Definition
epidemic (n)	something that affects a large number of people within a group or community
jump on the bandwagon (exp)	join others in doing something that will probably succeed
metabolism (n)	the process by which the body burns energy
spawned (v)	started
side effects (exp)	secondary effects (often negative) of a drug or treatment

Exercise Pill [6:26] ◀))

ABC TV *Catalyst*

Comprehension

As you watch the report, answer the following questions. For *True/False* questions, if the answer is *False* write the correct answer in the space provided.

1. Why are pharmaceutical companies spending money to develop drugs that address obesity?

   _____

2. How did Adro Sarnelli lose weight?

   _____

3. According to Dr. Boyd Swinburn, what is the problem with using drugs that affect a person's appetite?

   _____

4. What have researchers done to deal with the problem of using human growth hormone to cause weight loss?

   _____

5. Human trials using human growth hormone have shown promise.   ☐ True ☐ False

   _____

6. How soon will this new drug using human growth hormone become available?

   _____

7. How does the drug being developed in Melbourne, Australia, work?

   _____

8. Did the obese mice lose weight using this new drug?   ☐ Yes ☐ No

Go to Explore Online for additional practice and comprehension questions.

9. What other advantage of exercise is mentioned in the report, other than weight loss?

_____

10. Overall, is this report
    a) in favour of an exercise pill?
    b) against an exercise pill?
    c) neutral about an exercise pill?

    Explain your answer.

_____
_____
_____
_____

Speaking

What is your opinion about people "popping" a pill to lose weight? Are you in favour of or against the "exercise pill"? Explain your point of view.

Think of two reasons for both sides of the argument. Share your reasons with a partner and debate your points. See whether you come to the same or different conclusions.

Field-Specific Practice

Find an article in your field of study that describes a solution to a problem. It could be recommending a new way of doing something, explaining something that was unknown or misunderstood, or describing a recent discovery in the field. Highlight five words in the article that are new to you and use a dictionary to define them below.

Word (part of speech)	Definition
1.	
2.	
3.	
4.	
5.	

Writing

Write a summary of your article (250 words). Include in your summary a description of the problem and the solution proposed in the article. If your article is long, summarize a section of about 1000 words. Begin your summary with a sentence that describes the main idea of the article.

For more information about writing summaries, see Writing Strategies, page 143.

Pronunciation

The schwa vowel sound

The schwa (ə) is the most common vowel sound in English. It can be used with any vowel. It is a short, neutral sound that is used in longer words because it can be said more quickly. The closest vowel sound to it is the short *u* (as in *cut*).

Listen to the following examples and underline the schwa vowel sound. Then practise saying each word out loud.

1. amazing
2. about
3. professional
4. develop
5. continue
6. occur
7. support
8. solution

Many multiple syllable words use the schwa. It is often used in unstressed syllables. For example, in the word *professional*, the second syllable is stressed—pronounced slightly louder and longer: **pro·FE·ssion·al**. Notice the schwa (underlined) in the first syllable.

Listen to the following words from this textbook. Listen to a partner repeat each word out loud, paying attention to how the stressed syllable affects the other vowel sounds.

1. tech·no·lo·gy
2. i·nno·va·tion
3. or·gan·i·za·tion
4. op·por·tu·ni·ty
5. o·be·si·ty
6. au·to·no·mous
7. au·to·ma·tion
8. sus·tain·able
9. de·vel·op·ment
10. ex·pe·ri·ence
11. i·ni·tia·tive
12. con·ven·tio·nal

Working with a partner, say each of the following words out loud. Underline the schwa sounds.

1. majority
2. designer
3. metabolism
4. community
5. selection
6. condition
7. autonomous
8. responsible
9. materials

Then listen to the recording and repeat each word out loud, paying attention to the stressed syllable.

Reading

More than half the world's population now lives in towns or cities, where there is very little arable land. This means that food needs to travel great distances at great expense for a large portion of the population. This text explores the possibility of bringing agriculture into the city with the new industry of rooftop farming.

Vocabulary

Compound nouns contain two or more words that join together to make a single noun. They are very common in English. They are either written as one word, hyphenated, or written separately.

Compound nouns often have different meanings depending on how they are written. For example:

greenhouse: a place where plants grow

green house: a house that is painted green

1. Scan the article below and list five compound nouns.

   _____

2. Look at the following definitions and try to find a word or phrase that has the same meaning in the corresponding paragraph.

   a) _____ (phrase; para. 1) practical; realistic

   b) _____ (noun; para. 3) a lack

   c) _____ (compound noun; para. 6) the total area covered by something

   d) _____ (verb; para. 9) the first to be developed

   e) _____ (noun; para. 10) a direction in which something is developing

   f) _____ (noun; para. 12) plants grown as food

   g) _____ (adjective; para. 13) normal

   h) _____ (noun; para. 15) small insects that suck liquid from plants

Rooftop Farming Gains High Ground in Montreal

By Wallace Immen, *The Globe and Mail*

1 Nothing's more down to earth than farming, but a new urban farm in Montreal is inspiring designers to think of growing in the clouds.

2 Lufa Farms, on the roof of a commercial building near Montreal's Marché Central, is a 32 000-square-foot [2975-square-metre] **hydroponic** greenhouse that's producing more than 453 kilograms of vegetables every day, all year round.

3 With demand growing for local produce and a shortage of open fields in urban areas, the concept is attractive. But Lufa Farms founder Mohamed Hage has found that it is way more complicated to be a rooftop farmer than setting up a glass house and planting seeds.

hydroponic (adj) method of growing plants in sand, gravel, or water

4   It took him five years just to find a suitable building, convince the owner and the city building department to allow it, and to design and build it. And it took an investment of almost $2 million to get it off the ground and into production.

5   But it's an example that is inspiring other rooftop farms, says Aaron Quesnel, founder of Sky Harvest Inc., a start-up in Vancouver that's also planning a rooftop greenhouse farm.

6   While roofs represent as much as 30 per cent of the surface areas of major cities, only about 10 per cent of commercial rooftops in Canada could support the weight of a greenhouse farm, Mr. Quesnel says.

7   In a study of urban farming Mr. Quesnel co-authored while a student at a technical institute in Sweden, he found that even those buildings whose roofs can carry the load are often off limits because they're already built to the maximum height for their **zoning**.

8   But he sees great potential for using what's basically **wasted space** at this point. "In cities where you have **astronomical** real estate costs it makes increasing sense to use this amazing resource," he says. Growing locally is also preferable because of the monetary and environmental costs of shipping food long distances.

9   The rooftop farming movement is being pioneered in Montreal and New York. He knows of groups in Calgary, Boston, New York, and Seattle as well as abroad in London that are looking at rooftop farms.

10   "The costs are still relatively high but as worries grow about the risk of the sustainability of the food-supply chain it will become more of a trend," Mr. Quesnel predicts. Sky Harvest co-owner Dirk Gibbs says he's found there is a great deal of investor interest in funding rooftop farms. That's important because the development costs add up even before a site is chosen.

11   With a farm on the ground, it's relatively easy to begin cultivating. But the costs of doing engineering studies on rooftops, for example, can be astronomical even before you start installing equipment, Mr. Gibbs explains.

12   "There are very few ideal spaces in a city. You need to have a roof built with materials that are designed to carry at least 10 percent more weight, depending on where water and crops are stored." Engineers also have to take "live load" into account; that's the ability to carry the number of people moving around the roof to tend the crops.

13   Construction costs can also go beyond the fabrication and lifting of components onto a roof that may be in a crowded urban area. **Building codes** for

zoning (n) a set of restrictions put in place by a city or region

wasted space (exp) space that is not used

astronomical (adj) very large

building codes (n) city regulations for buildings

workplaces generally require more than one exit, and the tops of commercial buildings are designed for machinery and don't often have elevator access for moving people and equipment to the greenhouse, Mr. Gibbs notes. But he predicts that as greenhouse roofs become more mainstream, new buildings will be engineered to accommodate the trend.

14 One **under-utilized** source of strong roofs is parking structures, which are built to hold the weight of cars and trucks. One community garden in Seattle has set up on the roof of a parking garage, he adds. The urban farm concept is different from existing attempts to grow vegetables on "green roofs," Mr. Hage explains. Being in operation year-round, a hydroponic greenhouse on a roof provides environmental benefits of cooling a building in the summer and holding in heat in the winter.

under-utilized (adj) not used to its full potential

15 The green pluses include being able to grow with natural pest control, such as using ladybugs to eat aphids.

16 Lufa Farms' glass enclosure produces 40 types of vegetables and herbs in a variety of growing media, moisture, and lighting conditions. There are two macro-zones and several micro-zones. Tomatoes, for instance, grow best in the sunny south-facing part of the greenhouse while lettuce does better in the cooler, northern portion of the roof.

17 Crops are harvested each day by six employees who work in the greenhouse. The produce is boxed and taken to pick-up points for customers who have pre-ordered custom selections of vegetables. Lufa Farms employs 30 people, including sales people and logistics staff.

18 So far, demand for the produce is growing faster than supply. Mr. Hage says the company hopes to open two more greenhouses, another in downtown Montreal and one in Laval, Quebec.

19 "This is an idea whose time has come," Mr. Hage says. "Big cities like Montreal, Toronto, and Ottawa are basically **food deserts**; most of the year you can't find locally grown sustainable food and we have to rely on imports." **[857 words]**

food deserts (exp) areas where it is difficult to buy fresh food

Comprehension

Answer the following questions in your own words.

Go to Explore Online for additional practice and comprehension questions.

1. Give two reasons why rooftop farms are becoming popular.

    _____

    _____

2. What obstacles did Lufa Farms founder Mohamed Hage encounter in starting his own business?

    _____

3. What are the benefits of growing food locally?

    _____

4. Why is it so expensive to set up a rooftop farm?

    _____

    _____

5. What type of building is ideal for a rooftop farm?

   _____

6. What is the difference between a green roof and a rooftop farm?

   _____

7. How do we know that Lufa Farms is successful and doing well? Give two reasons.

   _____

8. What is the purpose of this article?
   a) to inform
   b) to persuade
   c) to entertain

   Explain your answer.

   _____

   _____

9. What problem does rooftop farming solve?

   _____

Speaking

Lufa Farms and Sky Harvest are examples of start-ups, new companies that are trying to do something differently. Go online and find a **start-up** company related to your field. What's its name and what does it do? How many people does it employ? How successful is it? Write notes and then share your information with a partner. Take turns asking each other questions about your start-up businesses.

 Field-specific activity

start-up (n) typically a young, innovative company that plans to meet a specific market need or solve a specific problem.

 Go to Explore Online for additional practice using countable and uncountable nouns.

 GG For more information on countable and uncountable nouns, see Grammar Guide, pages 243 and 244.

Grammar

Countable and uncountable nouns

Countable nouns are people, places, or things that can be counted. Uncountable nouns are things or concepts that can be measured but cannot be divided or counted.

Countable nouns have a singular and a plural form. Uncountable nouns only have one form: singular.

1. Find three more examples of countable and uncountable nouns in the article "Rooftop Farming Gains High Ground in Montreal" and write them in the chart below. Include the plural version of the countable nouns.

Countable nouns	Uncountable nouns
designer/designers	farming
cloud/clouds	produce
rooftop/rooftops	time

Singular countable nouns take a singular verb and plural countable nouns take a plural verb in the present tense. Uncountable nouns take a singular verb in the present tense.

2. Fill in the blanks with the correct tense of the verb provided.

a) Green roofs _____ (use) to grow vegetables in the summer.

b) Montreal _____ (be) home to several rooftop farms.

c) People _____ (want) to buy local food.

d) Forty types of vegetables _____ (grow) by Lufa Farms.

e) The zoning _____ (determine) the building's maximum height.

The following table shows which articles and determiners to use for countable and uncountable nouns.

- We use *a/an*, and 0 (nothing) when referring to things in general.
- We use *the* when referring to specific or previously mentioned nouns.

Singular countable nouns	Plural countable nouns	Uncountable nouns
a/an, the	zero (no article), the	zero (no article), the
	many, some	much
	a lot of	a lot of
	a few	a little

3. Fill in the blanks with the correct article (*a/an*, *the*, 0)

a) It took him five years just to find _____ suitable building.

b) The farming company has been doing studies on _____ city buildings.

c) Rooftop farming is _____ interesting concept.

d) _____ rooftop farming is popular in Montreal and New York.

e) This is _____ idea that is very innovative.

f) Lufa Farms is _____ successful company.

Revising and Editing

1. Correct the errors in articles, singular/plural use, and compound words in the following sentences.

a) The roof top farming is a innovative solutions to the problem of lack of green spaces.

_____

b) Green roof are becoming more common in many city in Canada.

_____

c) Good farmlands is disappearing quickly.

_____

d) Lufa Farms built a first rooftop green house in 2011.

_____

e) The obesity is a major problem in the world.

_____

f) Researchers are developing an exercise pills to help people lose weight.

_____

g) Driverless cars will make the road safer.

_____

h) Would you buy driverless car?

_____

2. Rewrite the following sentences using a compound adjective. The first one has been done for you.

a) He is open minded.
    He is an open-minded person.
_____

b) The fatalities were high profile.

_____

c) The room was brightly lit.

_____

d) The movie was three hours long. (remove the _s_ on _hour_)

_____

e) It takes 10 minutes to drive to work. (remove the _s_ on _minute_)

_____

Wrap Up

Field-Specific Practice

Research a problem related to your field of study and different solutions to it. Prepare a persuasive oral presentation (5 minutes). You must cite a minimum of two sources verbally during your presentation and they must be listed in a Works Cited list you hand in.

Structure your presentation as follows:

Introduction

Begin with an interesting question, quotation, fact, or surprising statistic.

*   Describe the problem
*   Discuss the causes of the problem
*   Introduce the solution(s)

Body

- Explain the problem in detail
- Explain why the solution you propose will work

Conclusion

- Summarize your main points (remember, no new information)
- End with a final thought (call to action or prediction)

Include your sources in a Works Cited list in MLA format.

Writing

Research a problem related to your field of study or future career and different solutions to it. Choose one of the organizational patterns (compare–contrast, cause and effect, process, or problem–solution) and write an essay (350 words) about this problem.

For more information about doing research, see Research Strategies, page 163.

> For example:
>
> Explain the problem and compare and contrast different approaches to solving it.
>
> Discuss the positive and negative effects the solution had.
>
> Discuss the process of implementing the solution or how it works.
>
> Discuss the problem and offer your own idea for a solution.

Include your sources in a Works Cited list in MLA format.

Speaking

In the video "How Driverless Cars Will Change Cities," Barry Kirk asks the following question: "If it is proven that computers are safer drivers than humans, is it ethical to allow humans to drive their own cars?"

In teams of four students, think of arguments for and against humans being allowed to drive if computer-driven cars are in fact safer.

Now, in teams of two, conduct a debate on the topic. A debate is a structured conversation in which two groups present arguments on different sides of an issue.

The statement for this debate is: Humans should not be allowed to drive their own cars if computers are safer drivers.

One team of two will support the statement and the other team will oppose it. Your teacher will assign a moderator/timekeeper.

The debate will be structured as follows:

FOR: First speaker makes an argument in favour of the statement (1 minute)

AGAINST: First speaker makes an argument against the statement (1 minute)

Pause: One minute to prepare

FOR: Second speaker addresses opponents' argument (1 minute) and presents another argument (1 minute)

AGAINST: Second speaker addresses opponents' argument (1 minute) and presents another argument (1 minute)

Pause: One minute to prepare

AGAINST: First speaker makes a closing statement (1 minute)

FOR: First speaker makes a closing statement (1 minute)

The audience or moderator will ask questions and decide which team presented the best case.

Vocabulary

The following compound words or phrases appear in the unit. Fill in the blank with the correct one.

urban landscape	tipping point	baseline	widespread	framework
within reach	side effects	mainstream	food desert	under-utilized

1. Many drugs to treat illnesses have a long list of _____; it's hard to know if they will make you feel better or worse!

2. If you live in a _____, you often have to take a long bus ride to get groceries.

3. Driverless cars are _____, but no one yet knows when they will become the norm.

4. A major shift in how we commute to work may affect the _____ and how cities are constructed.

5. Governments are in the process of developing a _____ to guide how rooftop farms are built.

6. Today the refugee crisis is _____, affecting countries all over the globe.

7. Many scientists believe that we have reached the _____ for global warming, and if we don't change our behaviour, we will be unable to reverse its effects.

8. On the whole, privately owned cars are _____, which is why people are becoming increasingly interested in car-sharing programs.

9. Sometimes new ideas are overlooked by _____ culture for many years before they become accepted.

10. Many sales companies give employees a salary as a _____, in addition to a percentage of their sales.

Projects

Project A

Teach Us Something Video

Work with a partner to teach the class about a process in your field of study. You will prepare a video clip six to eight minutes long (3–4 minutes for each partner) showing your classmates how a process works or how to complete a process. You will present your filmed project in class and provide five interactive quiz-style questions for students to answer, to check how well they have understood the explanation. The quiz can be on paper or online with an app such as Kahoot.

Choose one of the following:

1. **Explain how to do something.** Provide detailed step-by-step instructions. For example, explain how to select appropriate glasses, motivate preschoolers, market a new product, make a small room look bigger, provide first aid, or give CPR.

2. **Explain how something happens or happened.** Explain a concept, historical event, or movement so that a college student who is not a specialist in your field of study can understand it. For example, explain a physics phenomenon or scientific principle, events leading to discoveries, or how feminist or civil right movements came about in different places around the world.

Follow these steps to prepare your video:

1. Find a partner in the same or a similar career path. Select a topic to teach.

2. Submit your team's Teach Us Something proposal. This is a text (75–100 words) in which you outline the topic for your presentation and why you believe it is interesting and pertinent for this assignment. Your teacher will provide feedback.

> **(S)** For more information on writing effective proposals, see Professional Writing Strategies, page 155.

Example Proposal

The topic for our presentation is the process of fermentation. Fermentation is the process of converting carbohydrates to alcohol or organic acids using yeasts, bacteria, or other microorganisms—in anaerobic conditions (without air). Fermentation occurs in the manufacture of wine, cider, and beer as well as the leavening of bread and the preservation of sour foods such as sauerkraut and yogourt with the production of lactic acid. Understanding this scientific process allows us to better comprehend how humans around the world have transformed and preserved foods.

---

3. Plan your Teach Us Something video. Make sure the topic is clear; limit your scope to fit the time constraints of the assignment. The plan should include an introduction that previews the information with a clear description of what you are going to teach, a body that develops the information, and a brief conclusion. This plan will help you to develop the script to film your video. Provide a well-organized explanation and define any technical terms you use.

4. Look at some online courses on YouTube, howstuffworks.com, or Lynda.com for examples of instructional and how-to videos.

5. Plan the sequence of your process. You might want to create a storyboard of the different parts of your video. (A storyboard is a series of drawings, including directions and dialogue, that represent the shots planned for a movie or television production.)

> **(S)** For more information on giving effective oral presentations, see Speaking Strategies, page 168.

6. Film the Teach Us Something video. Plan the interactive questions that you will ask the class and prepare your quiz with Kahoot, with PowerPoint, or on paper.

7. Deliver the presentation. You will have one minute to present your team and the topic of the Teach Us Something video. Show the video and give the quiz. Answer any questions and thank the audience for listening.

Project B

Design and Present a Survey Report

The aim of the survey is to find out people's opinions and attitudes about a problem, a solution, or an issue related to your field of study or future career. You will conduct the survey, analyze your findings, interpret the results, and offer recommendations.

Use these guidelines in preparing your survey and your report:

1. Decide what problem or issue will you investigate.
2. Decide on the main goal of your survey (for example, to find out people's opinions about driverless cars).
3. Make some hypotheses about how people will respond.
4. Decide who you will survey: What age group? Gender? Occupation?
5. How many people will you survey? (A minimum of 10 people is recommended.)
6. Prepare your survey questions. You should have 10 questions that are either multiple choice or *Yes/No*. Using *Yes/No* and multiple choice questions makes it easy to compile the results.
7. Administer your survey. You can administer the survey in person or you can use Survey Monkey.
8. Compile the results.
9. Write a report on your findings.

Survey report writing

Write a report (350 words) discussing the results of your survey. Include the following information in your report:

1. Introduction: Describe the general purpose of the survey. What topic did you chose? Why did you choose this topic? What do you know about this topic? What are your opinions about the topic?
2. Hypotheses: Include your predictions of how you thought the respondents would answer before you conducted the survey. What opinions did you think people would have about the topic?
3. Methodology: Describe how you conducted the survey. Who were the respondents (students? teachers? gender? age?) and what was the response rate (i.e., did 50 percent refuse to answer, so you had to find other respondents?)?
4. Results: Use statistics, pie charts, and graphs to show the survey results.
5. Conclusions: Describe your interpretation of the results. How did the respondents answer the questions? What generalizations can you make based on the results? Were your hypotheses confirmed or disproved? How do the results and hypotheses differ? Why? What aspect of your findings is the most important, the most interesting, or even the most surprising? What are some possible interpretations of the results?
6. Recommendations: Based on the results of your survey, what recommendations or solutions to the issue could you suggest? Outline the advantages and disadvantages from different stakeholder perspectives of at least ONE recommendation.
7. Limitations: Reflect on any difficulties you encountered with the project. Do you consider the results to be valid and reliable? Explain why or why not.
8. Works Cited and Appendices: Include a reference list.
9. Attach a copy of the survey to your written report.

To avoid plagiarism, use your own words and always acknowledge where your information came from. For more information about avoiding plagiarism, paraphrasing, and citations, see Research Strategies, page 163.

Go to Explore Online and download a sample survey and survey report from the Resources section.

Example survey questions

Topic: drinking habits among college students

Related fields of study: social science, social service, r

General research question: Is alcohol consumption a p college students?

Gender: a) male b) female

Age: a) 18–22 b) 23–25 c) 26–30 d) over 30

Survey questions

1. Do you drink alcohol? ❏ Yes ❏ No
2. How often do you drink alcohol? a) Every day b) 3 c) once or twice a week d) less than once a week e
3. What type of drinker are you? a) moderate drink c) heavy drinker
4. At what age did you have your first drink? a) 12 o d) 15 e) 16 f) 17 g) 18
5. Where do you drink? a) parties b) bars c) holidays
6. Does alcohol have a negative impact on your stu
7. Why do you drink? a) to relax b) to relieve stress d) to forget about a problem e) other _____
8. Have you ever done something you regret wher ❏ Yes ❏ No
9. What types of drinks do you usually drink? a) b
10. Have you ever driven a car under the influence of a

Predictions: Most students drink alcohol on a re situations. Many students drink in social situation a drinking problem. Binge drinking is common am

Project C

Company Profile

S To avoid plagiarism, use your own words and always acknowledge where your information came from. For more information about avoiding plagiarism, paraphrasing, and citations, see Research Strategies, page 163

The objective of this project is to learn more about a company that relates directly to your field of study or future career—a company you might want to work for after you graduate.

You will research a company and interview someone who works there. Once you have completed the research, you will prepare a written report and an oral presentation.

Part 1—Your written report

Your written report should be two to three pages in length and you must include a Works Cited list of all your sources. Make sure to summarize the information using your own words.

Include this information in your written report:

1. The name of the company, the type of industry (retail, government, not-for-profit), company size, and your reasons for choosing this company.
2. Provide some historical information about the company.
3. What is the company's philosophy and mission?
4. What are some of the company's accomplishments?
5. What are some other interesting facts about the company?
6. What are the company's future projects?
7. What positions are available in the company?
8. What qualifications are needed for a position that is vacant or one that interests you?

Part 2—The interview

1. Choose a person working for the company to interview.
2. Contact the person and make an appointment to conduct the interview in a private setting.
3. Prepare 10 interview questions. Use a variety of question words (*Why, Where, When, How, What*). Do not ask *Yes/No* questions.
4. Have your teacher or someone else review your questions before you conduct the interview.
5. Conduct the interview in person or on the phone and record it. You must ask the interviewee's permission to record the conversation.
6. At the end of the interview thank the person and draw a positive conclusion about what you learned.
7. Listen to the recording of the interview and take notes.
8. Organize the information into separate points with main ideas and supporting ideas.

Part 3—Your oral presentation

S For more information on giving effective oral presentations, see Speaking Strategies, page 168.

1. Give an oral presentation (3–4 minutes) to the class (or a small group).
2. Present your company and summarize the interview.
3. Use PowerPoint as a visual aid and include five to eight slides.

Project D

Design an App

Work with a partner or small group on this project. First, you will describe and review apps that are useful in your field of study and then propose a useful new app. You will write a report (350–400 words) and prepare a presentation (5–6 minutes) about your research and proposed app. Each partner will present for two to three minutes. Identify apps that already exist in this field by describing their features, strengths, and weaknesses; then explain the need for the new app (what, why, for whom), how it will work, and what gaps it will fill (comparing your idea to other apps). You do not need to have the technical knowledge to implement the app, but you could show visual ideas about the design and plan of the app.

Examples of existing apps related to different fields of study:

- budgeting app for business administration
- nutrition app for health sciences
- room creator app for interior design
- learning numbers app for early childhood education

Follow these steps in designing your app:

1. Find a partner (or partners) in the same or a similar career path. Brainstorm ideas for research, organization, or communication tools useful in your field. Look at a variety of apps in different categories such as social media (Instagram), creativity (Snow), learning difficulties (Math Tutor), going out (AroundMe), work (Slack), and stores (Canadian Tire).

2. Create a "literature review" text (approximately 150 words) where you describe at least three existing apps. What are the main features? Who uses these apps? What do you see as the strengths and weaknesses of each app?

3. Describe your idea for a new app (150–200 words).
   a) Explain the need for this new app.
   b) What are its main features?
   c) Who will use the app?
   d) What are its main strengths?
   e) What perceived difficulties in design, marketing, or use can you imagine? How could you attempt to address these?

4. Prepare an interactive oral presentation of your app (4–5 minutes). Be prepared to answer questions from your classmates about the idea's relevance and feasibility. Answer any questions and thank the audience for listening.

For more information on giving effective oral presentations, see Speaking Strategies, page 168.

5. Write your report. Your written report will consist of an introduction (give context and explain why there is a gap in the market or need for such an app); body (include your literature review of existing apps and present your new idea for an app—its features, strengths, possible problems, etc.); and a conclusion (a summary of the main points).

For more information on writing effective reports, see Academic Writing Strategies, page 147.

Learning Strategies

Academic Writing Strategies

All writing—whether it is a paragraph, essay, report, or letter—should be clear, focused, and organized. Writing is a process that includes generating ideas (prewriting), drafting, revising, and editing. When you are asked to write about a topic, start by gathering information, articulate a well-defined main idea, expand upon it, and provide supporting information. Be prepared to return to write a second or third version of your original draft before submitting your work.

Writing a Paragraph

A paragraph has

* a topic sentence. The topic sentence expresses the **topic** and the **controlling idea** (the point that you want to make in the paragraph).

  EXAMPLE   A number of lifestyle factors (**topic**) have an effect on the health of an individual who is dealing with a chronic disease (**controlling idea**).

* supporting details. These sentences are explanations, facts, examples, reasons, or statistics to develop the topic sentence.

  EXAMPLE

  Supporting detail 1: Studies show exercise and social habits affect life expectancy.

  Supporting detail 2: Studies show stress and job choice affect health outcomes.

* a concluding sentence. The concluding sentence unifies the ideas. It often restates the topic sentence in different words and it may link back to the thesis of the essay.

  EXAMPLE   It is essential that health professionals communicate with patients about the risks associated with lifestyle, as lack of knowledge can affect long-term quality of life.

Topic sentence	A number of lifestyle factors have an effect on the health of an individual who is dealing with a chronic disease. First of all, several studies show that exercise and social habits such as diet and alcohol consumption affect life expectancy after diagnoses. Secondly, occupation and stress levels are widely reported to have major impacts on the health outcomes of people with chronic diseases such as heart conditions or diabetes. It is essential that health professionals communicate with patients about the risks associated with lifestyle, as lack of knowledge can affect long-term quality of life.
Supporting details	
Concluding sentence	

Exercise 1

Circle the topic and underline the controlling idea in the following topic sentences.

1. Listening skills and empathy are essential in management.

2. Open-plan work spaces lead to better communication.

3. Many advertising campaigns are informed by psychological theories about behaviour.

4. Creative types prefer to break rules rather than to follow them.

5. The design of shopping malls encourages spending time and money.

Exercise 2

Answer the following questions about the paragraph below.

1. What is the topic sentence? Indicate it by underlining the topic and circling the controlling idea.

   _____

   _____

2. In your own words, what is the paragraph about?

   _____

   _____

3. Look at the development of the main idea and how the topic sentence is supported. List two supporting details.

   a) _____

   b) _____

4. Look at the concluding sentence. What is its role?

   _____

   _____

Assignment essay tasks help students to master their study subject in a number of ways. Firstly, assignment tasks enhance understanding of a subject. Psychologists claim that learning is more effective if students develop an expertise and are involved in research and writing about their field of study. Secondly, research demonstrates that students learn the writing conventions of a subject area while they are researching, reading, and writing in their discipline. In this way, students are learning their subject matter as well as how to write in that field of study by researching and writing assignment essays.

Writing an Essay

Sentences are composed of words; paragraphs are composed of sentences; and essays are composed of paragraphs. An essay consists of an introductory paragraph with a strong thesis statement (your opinion), two or three body paragraphs that contain topic sentences that support the thesis statement, and a concluding paragraph.

Introduction

A rhetorical question is a question that does not require an answer. Sometimes the answer is obvious and the question is asked just to make a point. We use rhetorical questions to make an impact on the reader or listener.

Your introduction should have a hook that gets the reader's attention (a quote, an interesting fact, or a rhetorical question) and then introduce the topic or issue of the essay. The last sentence of the introduction should be a clear thesis statement.

The thesis statement is the most important sentence of the essay. It is a well-formed sentence presenting your topic and your position or opinion about that topic. This is the point that you will develop in the body paragraphs.

Your thesis statement should be an opinion and not a fact. It should be interesting and persuasive. Do not make your thesis statement a question or a topic announcement ("In this essay I will . . ."). Avoid the words *I*, *we*, and *you*.

EXAMPLE

Correct   Everyone should get six weeks of paid vacation a year for economic and social reasons.

Incorrect   I think everyone should get six weeks of paid vacation a year.

What's wrong with everyone getting six weeks of paid vacation a year?

Exercise 3

Identify which of the following are appropriate thesis statements.

1. Creativity leads to a better sense of fulfillment, happiness, and freedom. _____

2. I am going to write about the job application process. _____

3. Job applicants must show an appropriate attitude, aptitude, and ability. _____

4. What is the most important ingredient to success? _____

5. Active leadership involves setting goals, mentoring staff, and allowing workers liberty to take charge of issues. _____

6. This essay will explain active leadership. _____

Body paragraphs

Each body paragraph will include a topic sentence, supporting evidence, and a linking sentence connecting back to the topic sentence, thesis statement, or the next section of the essay.

Conclusion

In the conclusion, restate the thesis statement, summarize the main ideas of the essay, and finish with a concluding comment. The concluding comment might be a prediction, suggestion, or solution.

Never add new ideas or end your essay with a question; the purpose of the conclusion is to sum up and pull everything together.

Essay outline

Before you start writing your essay, it is useful to create an essay outline or plan.

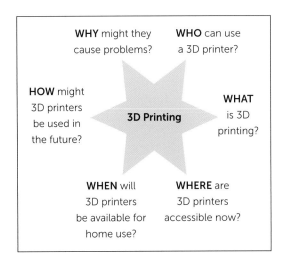

Start by brainstorming ideas about the topic. *Starbursting* is a form of brainstorming where you ask questions about a topic and then answer them; then you ask further questions about the answers to the first questions.

Put the essay question into your own words; use a *starburst* and write down questions about the topic.

Think about the purpose of the essay. Is it to inform or to persuade the reader? Is it to teach a process or to compare and contrast two ideas?

Write down your ideas and then try to group your ideas together logically. Decide which ideas you want for each body paragraph and think about how you can develop and support each topic sentence.

Finally, you should create your thesis statement. This should be an opinion related to the topic. For more on writing thesis statements, see page 138.

Use the template on page 140 to prepare your outline.

Types of essays

There are several different types of essays. Each essay type has a specific purpose. The most common essays types are

- A narrative essay describes and tells a story.
- A compare and contrast essay describes and evaluates similarities and differences of two subjects by analyzing, comparing, and contrasting them.
- A process essay describes the steps of a process or procedure. There are two types of process essay: one describes how something works and the other describes how to do something.
- A persuasive essay presents rational and persuasive arguments to support an opinion and convince the reader to accept the writer's point of view.
- A problem–solution essay identifies a problem or issue and proposes solutions to the problem.
- A cause and effect essay describes the reasons for something and then examines the results or outcome of it.

Essay Outline Template

Introduction

Interesting background/facts (to get the reader's attention)

_____

_____

_____

Thesis statement (your opinion that you will develop in your essay)

_____

_____

_____

Body Paragraph 1

Topic sentence (states the main idea of the paragraph)

_____

_____

_____

Supporting details (examples, reasons, facts)

_____

_____

_____

Body Paragraph 2

Topic sentence (states the main idea of the paragraph)

_____

_____

_____

Supporting details (examples, reasons, facts)

_____

_____

_____

Conclusion

Concluding idea (a prediction, suggestion, or solution)

_____

_____

_____

Writing a Problem–Solution Essay

Problem–solution essays present a well-defined problem in the introduction. The body of the essay presents and argues for specific solutions to the problem, and the conclusion sums up the ideas, evaluates the solutions, and makes a recommendation (or recommendations).

The tone should be reasonable and the solutions proposed should be feasible.

Problem–solution essays are commonly used to test your ability to understand an issue or problem related to your field of study.

Problem–Solution Essay

Obesity and Fitness

The popularity of processed and convenience food with high fat and sugar content along with an overdependence on commuting by car have contributed to an increase in obesity and a decrease in levels of fitness in the Canadian population. According to Statistics Canada, approximately 25 percent of the adult population is obese. This is a significant problem as obesity and poor fitness can lead to chronic disease and decreases in life expectancy. Therefore, it is essential for individuals and governments to collaborate and tackle this issue, so that citizens' diet and fitness levels improve.

A successful strategy to improve this situation is to encourage individuals to make changes to their levels of physical activity. Every day people make small decisions that have a big impact on their health. For example, instead of driving to work, people could choose to walk or bike. Instead of taking the elevator or escalator, they could take the stairs. Making simple changes like these will add up and result in important long-term improvements in Canadians' health and fitness.

Governments can also play a role in improving people's health and fitness by implementing initiatives that help people make healthier choices. Increasing taxes on processed, unhealthy food would make people less likely to buy it. Requiring all restaurants to list the ingredients and calories of their menu items would allow people to be informed about what they are eating. Clear government policy that makes public health a priority will result in improvements regarding the problem of obesity and fitness levels.

In conclusion, the combination of obesity and poor fitness is an important, expensive problem in Canada. Individuals and governments can work together to tackle this problem and improve diet and fitness. Of the solutions suggested, those made by individuals will probably have more immediate impact, but it is clear that government policy prioritizing public health is important for the future. With obesity levels continuing to rise worldwide, solutions should become a priority.

The **introduction** moves from general to specific. It starts by introducing the topic and providing interesting background information. It then establishes the issue of the essay. The last sentence of the introduction is the most important: the thesis statement. The thesis is the backbone of the essay.

Each **body paragraph** contains a topic sentence and support. In the body you answer the essay question by showing your knowledge about the subject, offering evidence to develop your argument, and using relevant examples and sources to support your argument.

Topic sentence

Supporting details

Concluding sentence

The conclusion moves from specific to general. It should restate your thesis statement, summarize the main points, and include a final broad statement about possible future directions or implications.

Restatement of thesis

Summing up ideas presented

Concluding and evaluating

Final recommendation

1. _____

2. _____

3. _____

4. _____

5. _____

6. _____

Public Transportation

Increasing levels of congestion and air pollution in most of the world's cities can be directly linked to the rapidly increasing number of cars on city roads. Although Canadians enjoy the convenience of commuting in their own cars, they should be aware that this behaviour has an environmental impact. Campaigns to improve and promote public transportation should be created to encourage people to leave their vehicles at home and use public transportation.

First of all, it should be made clear that public transportation can benefit people financially. Buying a car is expensive, and then there is the cost of fuel, insurance, and maintenance. According to data from the Canadian Automobile Association and Globe Drive, on average, it costs more than $10 000 a year to own a car. If people knew that using the bus and subway would save them enough money to take a vacation in Mexico each year, many more individuals would be persuaded to travel in this way, which would decrease the number of cars on the road.

Using Cohesive Devices

Cohesion is important in writing; it's how you hold a text together and make it flow successfully. If your writing is cohesive, it will be easy for the reader to understand. One strategy to increase cohesion is to use linking words. Two common types are reference words and transition words.

Reference words

Reference words point to other ideas in the text. By using reference words, you make connections between ideas and information in the text. Common types of reference words are

- pronouns (e.g., *he, she, they*)
- synonyms (e.g., *create, construct, build*)
- variations of the same word (e.g., *educate, education, educator*)

Transition words

Transition words allow you to connect one idea to the next and to signal to the reader the relationship between the ideas. This table shows different types of transition words.

Time/ sequence	Comparison/ contrast	Addition	Reason/ support	Consequence	Clarification	Condition
first of all	compared to	in addition	for example	therefore	in other words	if
initially	in the same	furthermore	for instance	thus	for example	unless
firstly	way	moreover	this is because	as a result	that is to say	provided that
finally	similarly	also	due to	hence		whether
next	equally	as well as	in this way	it follows that		even if
then	likewise	another	such as	in light of this		assuming that
before		too	for this reason			
after	unlike					
since	however					
at the same	on the other					
time	hand					
	in contrast					
	although					
	though					
	nevertheless					
	otherwise					

Exercise 5

Read the "Obesity and Fitness" and "Public Transportation" texts on pages 141 and 142. For each paragraph, circle and label at least two cohesive devices or words.

Writing a Summary

The purpose of writing a summary is to give the reader a clear, objective summary of the original article/text in a very condensed form. A summary restates in your own words the author's main point, purpose, and essential supporting details.

How to write a summary

1. Read actively, highlight, and annotate the text. Highlight the topic sentences and write key words in the margin beside each paragraph.

2. Write down the source (author/publication/title/date/URL, etc.).

3. Take notes and put into your own words the main idea and the important supporting points and/or explanations.

4. Organize these notes into a plan using key words to prioritize the main ideas and supporting points.

5. Write an introductory sentence identifying the author/source and presenting the main idea. For example, "In the article entitled X, the writer Jane Doe explains . . ."

6. To complete the summary, elaborate on the main ideas, focusing on how the writer supports, defines, and/or illustrates the main points. For example, "Doe states that . . ."

7. The summary is in your own words, but it is not your opinion. It should only contain the author's view and your language should be as objective as possible.

8. Use reporting verbs such as *states, shows, explains, argues, claims, describes, reports*.

9. Refer to the author in your summary. You could do this at the end. For example, "The author describes the importance of teamwork in the workplace."

10. Put the ideas in the same order as the original text.

11. Leave out anecdotes, details, and examples.

12. Use transition words and phrases to connect your ideas.

13. You can include one or two direct quotations in your summary.

14. Revise and edit your summary. Reread the original text and ask yourself questions such as: Have I changed the meaning from the original? Have I copied sections from the original? Have I remained objective?

15. How long is a summary? Approximately one-quarter or one-third of the original length is a good guideline unless an assignment specifies a particular word count. In the example summary on page 145, the original text was 915 words and the summary is 211 words.

Exercise 6

1. Read the text "Tips on How to Be Creative Every Day" in Unit 3 (page 47) and annotate the original text and prepare a plan of the key points.

   EXAMPLE   part 1: people with inspiration; not being creative; time; fear

2. Write the first two sentences of the summary, identifying the source and the main idea of the text.

3. Now turn to page 145 and look at the sample annotated summary of the article.

Summary

Summary of Tips on How to be Creative Every Day

In the article by Rachel Nania entitled "Tips on How to Be Creative Every Day," published online by WTOP, the author reports ideas about creativity from author Elizabeth Gilbert. The text explains how fear is often the biggest obstacle preventing people from engaging in creative projects.

The first sentence identifies the source(s) and the main idea.

The second sentence clearly restates the key thesis/main premise of the original text.

Nania writes that Gilbert's book *Big Magic* tells readers to confront, acknowledge, and overcome fear so that they can pursue creative endeavours. The article explains how important it is to be rational while following a passion; creativity must be balanced with other aspects of life. Nania reports Gilbert's advice to make creativity part of living rather than feeling that you should make a living from a creative project. She suggests spending 20 minutes or an hour daily rather than making it a full-time job.

Notice use of writer's surname (not Rachel).

This section elaborates on the main ideas with some detail.

An example about time spent being creative is included.

The article advises readers to be persistent and to keep trying rather than giving up at their first setbacks. Gilbert says to use a schedule to dedicate time to passions. She writes that people need to be patient and to check in regularly to see how they are feeling about projects. According to the article, creativity is about having ideas, being curious, as well as being reflective about what you want to do and what you are doing to achieve that.

The concluding statement restates the main idea and ends with the same idea as the original text.

Writing a Process Essay

The purpose of writing a process essay is to explain a process or procedure, i.e., the sequence or steps in which something is done. There are two types of process essay; one describes how something works and the other describes how to do something. In science, this could be the process of reproduction or photosynthesis; in mechanics, this could be the way the gear box functions or how electricity works.

A process should

- be written in the present tense
- have a clear starting and ending point
- begin with a thesis statement that identifies the process
- use transition words (see the chart on page 146 for common transition words)
- end with a concluding statement that summarizes the process

When you explain a process or sequence, don't assume that the reader knows as much about the topic as you do. It is important to use clear, simple language and avoid jargon. When are you finished writing the process, read over your work carefully to make sure that all the steps are included.

Transition words

Transition words are like road signs; they direct the reader from one point to the next and show relationships between ideas, sentences, and paragraphs. When writing a process, use transition words to indicate the sequence of steps, to describe the relationship between steps in the process, and to provide examples to clarify the process.

to show sequence	*firstly, first, second, etc.; then, next, after, finally*
to add another idea	*in addition, furthermore, moreover, also*
to refer to an example	*for example, for instance, such as*
to compare	*similarly, in the same way, on the one hand*
to contrast	*in contrast, whereas, however, on the other hand*
to summarize	*finally, in conclusion, as a result, consequently, therefore*

Process essay—How something works

A process should start with a thesis statement explaining what the subject is.

Use transition words to guide the reader through the steps.

Finish with a concluding sentence that refers back to the thesis statement.

The Process of Lightning

Lightning is a sudden electrostatic current that occurs during a thunderstorm. First of all, in order for lightning to form, there must be a cloud. When the ground is hot, it heats the air above it. Then this warm air rises, and as it rises, water vapour cools and forms a cloud. Water and ice move around inside the cloud, forced up by warm air currents, down by gravity, and compressed in the cloud. Lighter, positively charged particles move up, and heavier negatively charged particles move down to the bottom of the cloud. Just like rubbing a balloon can create static electricity, the particles in the cloud become charged. Eventually, the whole cloud fills up with electrical charges and then there is a giant spark—lightning, like static electricity between the two charges in the cloud. Positive charge builds up on the ground beneath the cloud, which is attracted to the negative charge in the bottom of the cloud. Finally, the positive charge from the ground connects with the negative charge from the clouds and a spark of lightning strikes. Sparks of lightning are almost 20 000°C, and rapidly heat the air around to create shock waves.

Process essay—How to do something

First Aid CPR

Remembering the steps of CPR and administering them correctly can be a challenge, but it can save a life; the acronym DR'S ABC can help. First of all, check the area around the patient for DANGER. Next, you should check for a RESPONSE from the patient when you speak to or touch him or her. The third step is to SEND for help. Fourth, check that the AIRWAYS are clear and after this, check BREATHING. If there is no breathing, you must start CPR. CPR consists of chest compressions. Press down firmly, rhythmically, and smoothly 30 times, then give two breaths into the mouth and repeat until the person starts breathing, an automated external defibrillator (AED) becomes available, or medical help arrives. Basic knowledge of first aid steps and CPR can be the difference between life and death.

> Here the thesis statement explains what the process is and why it is useful.

> Use transition words to guide the reader through the steps.

> Finish with a concluding sentence that refers back to the thesis.

Writing a Report

A report presents research findings, analysis, and recommendations. Like an essay, a report has a thesis statement or central idea, but unlike an essay, it is organized with headings and subheadings and usually includes graphs/tables to present the results. A report often concludes with evaluation and recommendations.

Essential elements of a report

1. **Title:** A clear and informative title to guide the reader.

2. **Executive summary:** The executive summary summarizes the key points, findings, and conclusion of the report. It gives the reader a preview of the complete document.

3. **Introduction:** The introduction provides background information and context for the subject. It explains the purpose/reason(s) for the study. The introduction ends with a clear thesis statement that is the basis of the complete report.

4. **Body:** The body is subdivided into sections consisting of method/process; results/findings; and analysis/discussion and interpretation of the results.

5. **Conclusion:** The conclusion reiterates the topic and purpose of the report. It sums up the main ideas, evaluates the results, and makes recommendations.

6. **Works Cited** or **References:** This is a list of the resources and references used to write the text. There are different methods, but many use an alphabetical "author–date" list.

7. **Appendices:** Visual information, such as tables, graphs, and charts, is usually included here. The results section often refers readers to the appendices; e.g., "see Table 1," "see Appendix 1".

Report sample

The Issue of Ethical Fashion Consumerism

The executive summary summarizes the key points, findings, and conclusion of the report. It gives the reader a preview of the complete document.

Executive Summary (Summary or Abstract)

The goal of this report was to investigate ethical consumerism and fashion purchases among student populations.

A survey on attitudes toward purchasing fast fashion and ethically produced goods was conducted. The results indicate that the majority of students do not know where stores source the clothing or about factory conditions of workers, and they describe "fair trade" clothes as expensive. The report concludes that more information about company sourcing and factory conditions must be made available to consumers and suggests that a website and app be developed to guide consumers with information about ethical choices and clothing manufacturers.

It is also recommended that Canada Fashion invest resources to develop a directory of suppliers following international ethical guidelines as well as pressure government to provide incentives to enable the production of less expensive "fair trade" clothing.

The introduction provides background information and context for the subject. It explains the purpose/reason(s) for the study. The introduction ends with a clear thesis statement that is the basis of the complete report.

Introduction

On April 24, 2013, the Rana Plaza tragedy in Bangladesh killed more than 1100 garment workers in Bangladesh and wounded more than 2000 more. The incident left consumers all over the world questioning who makes their clothes and in what conditions. Research reports and documentaries have attempted to educate consumers about the high cost of cheap clothing. Consumers, and particularly young people, are becoming much more aware about the costs of the clothing industry and the power they yield with each purchase. This report examines students' attitudes about fast fashion and ethical, fair trade clothing production.

The body is subdivided into sections consisting of methods/process; results/ findings; and analysis/discussion and interpretation of the results.

Methods

This research was conducted by online questionnaire on college websites. There were 110 respondents to an online questionnaire of 20 questions about fashion purchasing habits, ethics, and fair trade manufacturers. The survey used Likert-scale and open-ended questions. The survey was voluntary and anonymous.

Results

The results show that low price is the main motivation for fast fashion purchases (80 percent of respondents). In contrast, while 40 percent of respondents expressed concern about unethical factory practices, only 10 percent answered that they regularly researched the fair trade policy of clothing companies. Over 50 percent of respondents knew about the World Fair Trade Organization (WTFO), but most respondents believed that this was mainly concerned with child labour rather than furthering commitments to gender equality and environmental sustainability. Over two-thirds of students surveyed cited that knowledge of child labour conditions was the single most important factor swaying their decision away from fast fashion. Environmental issues relating to clothing production was the second most important factor. Table 1 (in the appendix) shows the respondents' answers.

Discussion

Table 1 shows the reasons why respondents buy clothing from certain manufacturers. Students express concern about factory conditions and child labour practices; however, the availability and affordability of such clothing tend to outweigh these concerns when they make final purchasing decisions. The problems related to fast fashion turnover are linked to the low price of goods imported from factories where environmental and labour laws are not easily monitored (Reference). Respondents expressed feelings of guilt associated with low-cost fast fashion purchases; students at the same time showed that they wanted to support local and fair trade manufacturers.

Conclusion

It is recommended that manufacturers develop practices of transparency and accountability. Legal requirements are being introduced around the world requiring that companies provide detailed information about production and distribution. This information should be easily available to consumers online and through a shoppers' app.

> The conclusion reiterates the topic and purpose of the report. It sums up the main ideas, evaluates the results, and makes recommendations.

Students are aware of environmental and human costs of fast fashion. It is also recommended that Canada Fashion invest its resources to develop a directory of suppliers following international ethical guidelines as well as lobby government to provide incentives for the production of reasonably priced "fair trade" clothing.

Works Cited

Jones, Alan. "Article Title." *Magazine or Journal Title*, 3 Apr. 2016, pp. 6–10.

> The Works Cited or References should list all sources, in alphabetical order.

Appendix

[Table 1]

> Appendices usually include tables, graphs, and charts.

Revising and Editing Strategies

Revising and editing are important steps in the writing process. These occur once you have finished writing a first draft of your text.

During the revision process, you make changes to the text to strengthen its arguments, improve the writing, and ensure you've met the assignment requirements. In the editing process, you check for mistakes in grammar and word choice.

Your first draft will have mistakes and problems—this is okay. Write a first draft knowing that it is not your final version—this way your ideas can flow coherently. Then revise and edit to create a polished final version of your written text.

Revise your writing using the following steps:

1. Task: Read the assignment again. Review the teacher's requirements. Have you answered the question or completed the assigned task? Have you met the teacher's requirements? Are your ideas and examples relevant?

2. Development: Is the main idea of the text clear? Have you adequately supported it?

3. Structure: Do the paragraphs have topic sentences? Do the ideas flow from one to the next? Have you used cohesive devices to link them? Do you conclude by pulling the ideas together?

When you have completed the three steps above, it is time to edit your work. Edit using the following steps:

1. Read the text aloud because this way you will hear awkward sentences, repetitions, and missing links between ideas.

2. Check all your references and citations to ensure you have included all your sources and cited them correctly and according to the assignment requirements.

3. Focus on one paragraph at a time to check for word choice and grammar mistakes. Check

   - verb tenses
   - subject–verb agreement
   - first-, second-, and third-person pronouns
   - contractions
   - plurals
   - punctuation

4. Print and read the revised and edited text very carefully one last time before you submit it to your teacher.

Professional Writing Strategies

In the workplace, you will need to read and write different types of documents such as emails, business letters, and proposals. All professional writing should be clear and concise.

You will also need to speak in formal and informal business situations face to face and on the phone. Formal speaking situations include business meetings, phone calls, and job interviews. Informal situations include communicating on the phone and with colleagues.

Register

Register is the level of formality with which you speak or write. We use different registers in different contexts. The three most common registers are formal, informal, and neutral.

Formal register

The formal register is used in the following contexts:

- when communicating with people we don't know very well
- in work situations such as meetings and job interviews
- in business writing such as emails and reports
- in academic writing such as essays and research papers
- when giving an oral presentation

Characteristics of the formal register include

- use of longer sentences
- use of compound and complex sentences
- use of reported speech (describing what other people have said or written)
- use of indirect questions ("Would it be possible to leave early today?" or "I was wondering if I could leave early today.") instead of direct questions ("Can I leave early today?")
- use of the passive voice
- use of modals such as *could* and *would* for politeness
- use of full forms (*do not*) instead of contractions (*don't*)
- use of the third person (instead of using *I* or *we*)
- limited use of phrasal verbs (for example, in the formal register, you would be more likely to say *discuss* instead of *talk about* and *request* instead of *ask for*)
- frequent use of longer words (often French cognates)

  EXAMPLES

  Your application has been received, and an interview will be scheduled next week.

  The next department meeting will be held on Thursday at 4:00. Could you please ensure you are on time?

  In this presentation, we will examine the causes of childhood obesity and offer some solutions.

Informal register

The informal register is used in the following contexts:

- when communicating with people who are closer to us
- when talking to friends or family
- when talking to co-workers in a social setting
- in postcards and personal text messages and emails

Characteristics of the informal register include

- use of simple, sometimes grammatically incomplete, sentences
- use of contractions (*don't, shouldn't*)
- use of emotional language
- use of humour
- use of slang, exaggerations, and clichés
- use of phrasal verbs (*get into*) and idioms (*piece of cake*)
- use of abbreviations such as those used in text messages (LOL, BTW)

    EXAMPLES

    That film was sick. You really have to see it.

    We met up at 12 for a quick bite then talked about plans for the weekend.

    He is so lazy; I'm sure they'll fire him.

Neutral register

The neutral register is used in the following contexts:

- when discussing or writing about non-emotional topics
- to deliver facts
- in summaries and reviews
- in technical writing

Characteristics of the neutral register include

- use of simple sentences
- use of factual language
- no use of emotional language
- no use of slang

    EXAMPLES

    Amazon plans to use drones in the near future.

    The package will be delivered on Thursday.

    You must meet the following criteria to get a driver's licence.

Exercise 1

Read the following sentences and decide if the register is formal (F), informal (I), or neutral (N).

1. I totally disagree with his opinion. He's so wrong LOL. _____

2. Could you tell me where the conference is? _____

3. There were tons of people at the show last night. We had an awesome time. _____

4. The meeting will be held in room E304. _____

5. To apply for a passport, you must be a Canadian citizen and at least 16 years old. _____

6. The focus of this presentation will be on the advantages and disadvantages of driverless technology. _____

7. According to a recent study, more children are sedentary and at risk for developing diabetes at a younger age. _____

8. It's ridiculous to think that kids are so lazy and spending all day in front of their computers. _____

Business Writing

Business letter

Business letters can be used to make a request, order a product, make a complaint, or build a business relationship.

Business letter dos and don'ts	
Do	**Don't**
• use formal language and tone • use proper business letter format • address your letter to a specific person • be brief and concise • be clear about your purpose • use the pronoun *I* • check your spelling and grammar carefully	• be too informal • use contractions • make jokes • use slang or swear words • make spelling and grammar mistakes • send a letter that is not addressed to someone specific • handwrite your letter

Business letter sample

Use the following template for all types of business letters.

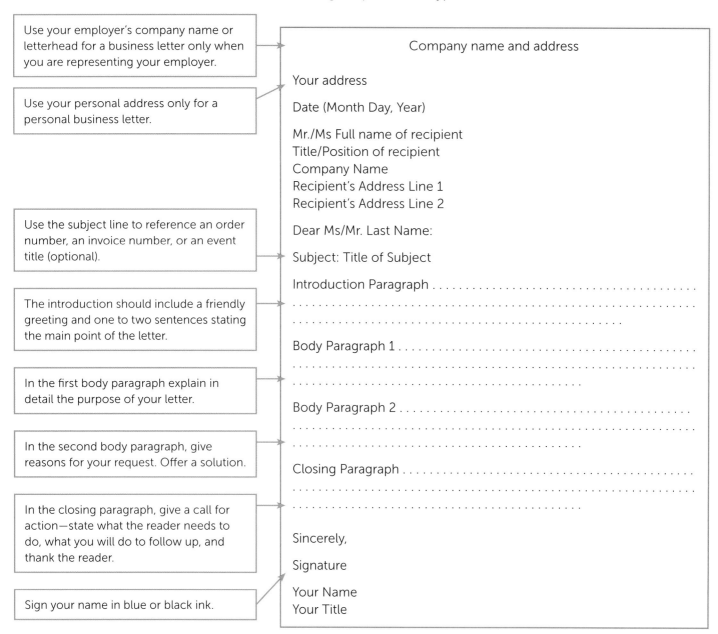

Use your employer's company name or letterhead for a business letter only when you are representing your employer.

Use your personal address only for a personal business letter.

Use the subject line to reference an order number, an invoice number, or an event title (optional).

The introduction should include a friendly greeting and one to two sentences stating the main point of the letter.

In the first body paragraph explain in detail the purpose of your letter.

In the second body paragraph, give reasons for your request. Offer a solution.

In the closing paragraph, give a call for action—state what the reader needs to do, what you will do to follow up, and thank the reader.

Sign your name in blue or black ink.

Company name and address

Your address

Date (Month Day, Year)

Mr./Ms Full name of recipient
Title/Position of recipient
Company Name
Recipient's Address Line 1
Recipient's Address Line 2

Dear Ms/Mr. Last Name:

Subject: Title of Subject

Introduction Paragraph . . . .
. . . .
. . . .

Body Paragraph 1 . . . .
. . . .
. . . .

Body Paragraph 2 . . . .
. . . .
. . . .

Closing Paragraph . . . .
. . . .
. . . .

Sincerely,

Signature

Your Name
Your Title

Email

Email is the most common form of business communication in the workplace today. On average, people receive and send more than 100 emails a day at work. Emails should be short, polite, and clear. Emails should be about six sentences in length and focus on one subject or problem.

Email is less formal than a business letter; however, the level of formality depends on who you are writing to and for what purpose.

Use email when

- you need to reach someone who is difficult to contact by phone
- you need to attach an electronic file
- you need to communicate the same message to many people
- you want to have a written record of the communication

Email sample

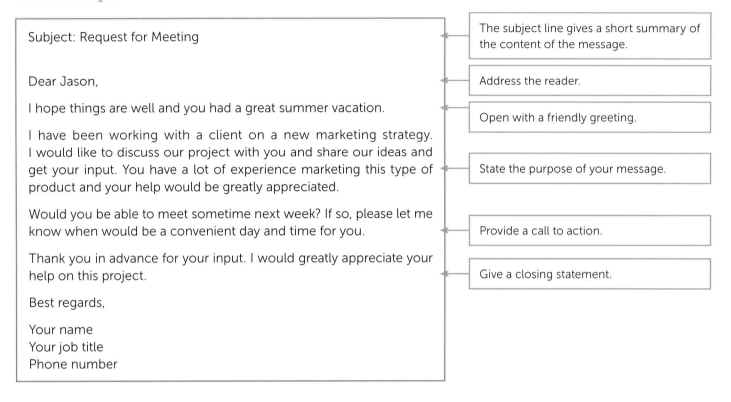

Subject: Request for Meeting → The subject line gives a short summary of the content of the message.

Dear Jason, → Address the reader.

I hope things are well and you had a great summer vacation. → Open with a friendly greeting.

I have been working with a client on a new marketing strategy. I would like to discuss our project with you and share our ideas and get your input. You have a lot of experience marketing this type of product and your help would be greatly appreciated. → State the purpose of your message.

Would you be able to meet sometime next week? If so, please let me know when would be a convenient day and time for you. → Provide a call to action.

Thank you in advance for your input. I would greatly appreciate your help on this project. → Give a closing statement.

Best regards,

Your name
Your job title
Phone number

Exercise 2

Imagine you are working in law firm as a legal assistant. Write an email to your supervisor asking for an extension on a project that you must hand in the following week.

Proposal

Proposals are used to ask for formal support for an idea or a plan of action. For example, you might write a proposal to get permission to do a project, to conduct research, to make a large purchase for your company, or to create a new product.

Outline of a proposal

Introduction: background, issue, explanation of situation or problem, and solution(s)

Body: propose solution, plan, method, timeline, budget

Conclusion: restate need for solution and validity of the proposed plan

Proposal dos and don'ts	
Do	**Don't**
• think about your audience: What do they already know about the topic? What do they care about? • be clear about your purpose • include a timeline (and budget, if applicable) • research your idea	• be too informal • use jargon or overly complex language • be vague about how you will accomplish your plan • make spelling and grammar mistakes

Business proposal sample

To: Canada Small Business Funding

Business Expansion Funding Grant

Introduction: Protein ice cream is new to the North American market. It tastes like ice cream, but is much healthier. It is low fat and low sugar. It contains more protein (15 grams per 125 ml) and fewer carbs and can be used as a nutritional supplement for weightlifters. People are more health conscious today and protein ice cream is a great alternative to high-sugar dessert.

We need funding to market our ice cream to gyms and sports teams.

Body: We will do the following to promote our product:

• We will send free samples to gyms and sports teams
• We will prepare advertising brochures with a well-known advertising company explaining the benefits of our product
• We will develop an attractive website
• We will spend money on research to make the ice cream taste better

Conclusion: People are more health conscious today. This new, delicious, high-protein snack will fulfill the needs of health-conscious people (not just athletes). It will be sold in gyms as well as health-food stores and even in supermarkets.

The Job Search

Cover letter

When you submit your resumé, you will also submit a cover letter. In the cover letter, you explain why you are the ideal candidate for the position. You will highlight your hard skills (technical skills that specifically relate to the job) as well as your soft skills (people skills such as communication skills needed to succeed in this position), and explain how they match the position's requirements. You should highlight your hard skills in your cover letter and resumé and emphasize your soft skills in the interview. Before you write your cover letter, research the company. Understanding its mission, philosophy, and culture can help you tailor your cover letter to better match the position. Your cover letter should not exceed one page.

Cover letter dos and don'ts	
Do	**Don't**
• write only one page • check your grammar • address your letter to a specific individual • use simple language • use action verbs • make your letter different from your resumé	• lie • be vague • use informal language • use contractions • be negative • make spelling and grammar errors

Soft skills that employers are looking for

communication skills	teamwork	organizational abilities	the ability to multitask
adaptability	problem solving	critical thinking	conflict resolution

Exercise 3

With a partner discuss which soft skills you have, and give specific examples in school or workplace situations that demonstrate your soft skills.

Action verbs to use with your resumé and cover letter			
accomplished	communicated	facilitated	presented
achieved	coordinated	focused	reviewed
analyzed	delegated	hired	scheduled
applied	delivered	improved	structured
assisted	discussed	managed	supervised
attained	evaluated	participated	updated

Cover letter sample

Include your name, address, and phone number	Frederic Lachance
	322 Saint Paul Street
Include a professional email address (preferably your college or university email).	Montreal, Quebec H4P 1Y5
	f.lachance@abcd.qc.ca
	541-999-7545

March 12, 2018

> Include the name of the person you are addressing the letter to, along with his or her job title and the company address.

ABC Marketing
Mr. David Laufer
Human Resources Director
90 River Drive
Lachine, Quebec
J2P 3P4

> Address the letter to a named individual in the company.

Dear Mr. Laufer:

> The introduction paragraph should
> - express your interest in the position
> - describe some key soft skills that make you an ideal candidate

In response to your job advertisement for a Marketing Manager, I have enclosed my resumé for your review. I believe my creativity, facility with teamwork, and ability to communicate effectively make me an excellent candidate for this position.

> The body paragraphs should
> - describe your educational background
> - talk about your work experience as it relates to the job
> - discuss any other volunteer work or extracurricular activities you have done

I recently graduated with a college diploma in Business Administration and I maintained an average of 80% in all my courses. Previously I worked as a marketing assistant for a large company. In this position, I gained valuable marketing experience, and I was involved in new product launches and developing new product materials.

I have strengthened my communication and teamwork skills through my extracurricular activities. I tutor students in math and play on the soccer team at my college. Furthermore, I worked on our school's newspaper, which allowed me to develop my creativity.

> The conclusion should
> - summarize why you are a good candidate
> - explain that you would like to meet with the employer
> - thank the reader for considering you as a candidate

My strong academic background as well as my excellent customer service skills, negotiation skills, and conflict resolution abilities make me an excellent match for this position. I would be excited to work for a company like yours that values its employees' development. I appreciate your consideration and look forward to discussing this position further in an interview.

Sincerely,

Frederic Lachance

> Use a formal closing.

Resumé

Companies receive hundreds of resumés for each open position. Hiring managers spend less than 30 seconds looking at each resumé. Your resumé needs to be clear, easy to read, and professional. It should not be more than two pages in length.

Resumé dos and don'ts

Do	Don't
• make contact information visible • use key words listed in the job description (electronic scanners will look for them) • include a summary of your strengths	• lie • make spelling and grammar errors

Resumé sample

Frederic Lachance
322 St. Paul Street
Montreal, Quebec H4P 1Y5
514-999-7545

f.lachance@abcd.qc.ca
http://www.linkedin.com/in/fredericlachance

OBJECTIVE: To work in an entry-level position in marketing

SUMMARY

- Two summers of marketing-related experience
- 82% average in accounting courses
- Excellent teamwork and leadership skills
- Creative and innovative
- In-depth knowledge of Microsoft Office and Excel

EDUCATION

Diploma in Business Administration, Marketing Major

2016–Present Cégep Saint Jean-sur-Richelieu, Saint Jean, QC
- Expected graduation date: May 2018

EXPERIENCE

2016–2018 Marketing Assistant, Mount Royal Décor Company, Chambly, Quebec
- Helped prepare online marketing materials, including blogs, social media, and email pieces
- Prepared and conducted marketing surveys
- Collaborated with marketing manager to create new product materials
- Maintained positive relationships with customers and colleagues

2015–2016 Customer Service Representative, Cogeco Communications, Brossard, Quebec
- Handled incoming calls from customers
- Provided detailed product information to customers
- Participated in an in-house training program
- Managed customer complaints
- Provided technical assistance to customers on products and services

EXTRACURRICULAR ACTIVITIES

2015–Present Math Tutor
- Provide one-on-one tutoring
- Help students with their math courses
- Meet and tutor peers weekly

INTERESTS

Soccer, computers, travel

REFERENCES AVAILABLE ON REQUEST

More Advice for the Job Search

Some employers and job seekers are using less conventional tools than the resumé in the job/talent search. Here are some additional tools and advice that can help you in the job search:

- For creative jobs in fields such as marketing, sales, media, and advertising you could create a video resumé to accompany the traditional cover letter and resumé.
- Use social media to build your professional presence.
- Use your social media contacts in your job search.
- LinkedIn is a popular professional network with groups and discussions. Build and update your LinkedIn profile and connect to groups in your field of study.
- Make sure your social media profiles state that you are actively looking for employment.
- Use your social media profiles to showcase your skills.
- Use Twitter to learn about your industry and to follow leaders in your field.
- Network with friends and contacts about your job search.

Applying for a job

Once your cover letter and resumé are ready, you can begin sending them to prospective employers. Make sure to address your cover letter to a specific person. Look at the company's website to find out the name of the human resources director. Your cover letter should be written specifically for each position you are applying for. You should send your resumé as an email attachment and the cover letter can be written directly in the email.

The job interview

You have applied for a job and been invited for an interview. Now it is crucial to prepare for the job interview to give yourself the best chance possible of being hired for this position.

Interview dos and don'ts	
Do	**Don't**
• arrive five minutes early for the interview • bring extra copies of your resumé and cover letter • research the company • prepare answers to possible questions with examples of your experience • dress appropriately • use a firm handshake • maintain eye contact	• be late • lie • complain about your previous employer or co-workers • be negative • be too informal • wear a strong fragrance • make inappropriate jokes or be sarcastic

During the job interview, the following verbal and non-verbal aspects are important:

- **Voice:** Try not to speak too quickly or too loudly or softly. Take a breath before answering.
- **Non-verbal expressions:** Stay positive and smile where appropriate.
- **Self-confidence:** The more you prepare, the more confident you will be during the interview. Don't belittle yourself or your experiences in the interview.
- **Clarity of ideas:** When preparing your answers, focus on a few simple ideas and stick to them.
- **Vocabulary:** Do your research on the company and the field to make sure you are using the correct vocabulary to answer questions.

Top 10 common job interview questions

1. What can you tell us about yourself?
2. Why did you apply for this position?
3. Why should we hire you?
4. Can you describe a time where you handled a difficult situation involving people?
5. Can you tell us about a mistake you made and how you handled it?
6. What are your strengths?
7. What are your weaknesses?
8. What are your career objectives for the next five years?
9. What are your salary expectations?
10. Do you have any questions for us?

Employer approaches to job interviews

Many companies are choosing new approaches to the job interview. Alternative interview approaches include

- **The conversational approach:** the interviewer will have a conversation with the candidate instead of asking direct questions.
- **The consensus approach:** many people interview the candidate at the same time. It can be stressful for the interviewee. It is important to listen carefully.
- **The all-day approach:** interviewers feel this allows them to really get to know the interviewee.
- **The behavioural approach:** the candidate is asked to give examples to demonstrate they have the necessary skills.

Exercise 4

Answer the following questions about resumés, cover letters, and the job interview.

1. What is the most important purpose of a cover letter and resumé?
    a) to get a job
    b) to get a job interview
    c) to show your achievements

2. Who should the cover letter be addressed to?
    a) "Dear madam/sir"
    b) "To whom it may concern"
    c) "Dear [Mr./Ms last name of the person in charge of hiring]"

3. How long should the cover letter be? _____

4. When you email your resumé to prospective employers, you should
    a) send your resumé as an email attachment and the cover letter written directly in the email
    b) include the cover letter and resumé directly in the email
    c) send both the cover letter and the resumé as attachments

5. A resumé should be _____ page(s) in length.
    a) 1   b) no more than 2   c) 3

6. Why do you think it is important to research the company before you go to the job interview?

    Research allows

    _____

    _____

7. Which of the following is a good question to ask at the end of the interview?
    a) What is the average salary for this position?
    b) What skills does this job require?
    c) What are some future projects that the company is working on?

8. You should emphasize your hard skills in
    a) your resumé and cover letter
    b) the job interview

9. You should emphasize your soft skills in
    a) your resumé and cover letter
    b) the job interview

10. You should write a different cover letter for each position you are applying for.   ❏ True   ❏ False

Research Strategies

Research is important to develop a better understanding of a topic. Research helps us expand our ideas on a topic and find solutions to problems. Throughout your college and university studies you will need to do research on topics related to your field of study. In the workplace, you will also need to do research for a variety of purposes.

Asking questions and researching answers is essential to success in both school and work.

Avoiding Plagiarism

Plagiarism is using the work of another person without citing the source and presenting that work as if it were your own. Plagiarism is serious and many students who plagiarize often do so unintentionally. You can avoid plagiarism by being careful and by using proper citations, footnotes, and references where necessary.

When to credit and document the source	When not to document the source
<ul><li>if you use an author's specific words (quotation marks required)</li><li>if you use someone else's ideas, but paraphrase using your own words</li><li>if you copy more than three words in a row, you must use quotation marks</li></ul>	<ul><li>if the information is common knowledge (for example, birth and death dates of well-known people, dates of historical events, general factual information found in many sources)</li><li>if the information is common knowledge in a specific field of study</li><li>when you use your own ideas</li></ul>

Using quotations and paraphrases

Most of your paper should be written in your own words. Choose your quotations carefully, keep them brief, and copy them exactly from the original. Put them in quotation marks and include the reference in your "Works Cited." Introduce your quotation or paraphrase in the paragraph to show how it connects to your paragraph.

Use quotations	Use paraphrases
<ul><li>to demonstrate that an expert supports your point of view</li><li>to present an opinion that you want to comment on</li><li>to present a passage that is extremely well written and whose meaning you do not feel you can express in a paraphrase</li></ul>At the end of your quotation, include the last name of the author and the page or paragraph number. You must include a Works Cited list in alphabetical order.	<ul><li>when you want to express an idea, but not the exact language</li><li>when you are able to express an idea using fewer words than in the original source</li></ul>At the end of your paraphrase, include the last name of the author and the page or paragraph number. You must include a Works Cited list in alphabetical order.

Example of a paraphrase: Nicholas Carr argues that the Internet is affecting our ability to concentrate for long periods of time (Carr 6).

Example of a quotation: In the article "Is Google Making Us Stupid?" Nicolas Carr wrote, "But a recently published study of online research habits, conducted by scholars from University College London, suggests that we may well be in the midst of a sea change in the way we read and think." (Carr 5)

Research and Sources

- Make sure you are clear about the purpose of your research and be specific about your topic.
- Think carefully about and make a list of appropriate English search terms before beginning your research to produce better quality results quickly.
- Begin your research using Google.
- Try Google Scholar for academic and peer-reviewed options.
- Use specialized databases related to your field of study (e.g., your school library may have nursing, science, or other databases).
- Use EBSCOhost. (If your college does not have this database it can be accessed for free through the Bibliothèque Nationale.)

If you are having trouble getting started or finding sources, visit your school library or library website for help with your research.

Evaluating online sources

Remember to consider the ABCD of website evaluation when choosing articles for your research.

- **A (authority):** Who is the author? What are his or her credentials? Is he or she an expert on the subject?
- **B (bias):** Is the information neutral and balanced?
- **C (content):** Evaluate the content. Is it relevant, accurate, and researched? Consult multiple sources.
- **D (date):** Is the article current? If it is not recent, consider whether that is important.

Reliable websites	Be careful with sites that
• provide information about the author(s) and his or her credentials • provide a list of references at the end of the article • include a statement of purpose • give enough detail on the subject	• contain a lot of advertising • do not identify the author • contain grammatical or spelling errors • are poorly designed • appear to be biased • are blogs, forums, or personal websites

You should answer *yes* to the following questions if you have chosen a credible site:

- Does the information come from a reliable website such as a university or government site?
- Does the information come from a news source that you know publishes trustworthy information?
- Is there information about the author and his or her area of expertise?
- Is the information current and up to date?

You should answer *no* to the following questions if you have chosen a credible site:

- Does the information come for a commercial site trying to sell goods or services?
- Does the site contain a lot of advertising?
- Is it difficult or impossible to find out who wrote the article?
- Is the site written by a student or does it appear to be a personal blog?

Information found on social media

Generally, information found on social media has not been verified, and "fake news" often spreads through social media sites. Treat it with caution and use other, more reliable sources.

Domain extensions

Be aware of domain extensions, what they tell you, and their advantages and disadvantages. You cannot decide if a website is credible based on the domain extensions alone, but being aware of them will help you assess a website's purpose.

Domain endings are not as strictly assigned as they used to be. Carefully evaluate all the sites you use for research.

Name	Intended use	Actual use
.com	Commercial	Any person or entity can register. This is the main domain name and is used by all types of entities (e.g. nonprofits, schools, individuals). Many of these sites exist to sell a product or service. The information may be biased.
.org	Organization	Any person or entity can to register. Originally intended for non-profit organizations. These can be useful. Remember that many organizations have a specific mission, and the information on their sites is not always objective.
.net	Network	Any person or entity can to register. Originally intended for domains pointing to a distributed network of computers, or "umbrella" sites that act as the portal to a set of smaller websites.
.edu	Education	Limited to accredited higher educational institutions and almost exclusively used by American colleges and universities. These sites can be useful and reliable; however, many schools offer free *.edu* websites to their students. You would not want to use a student paper as a source.
.gov	US government agencies	Limited to United States governmental entities. These can be useful especially for up-to-date information such as medical news, statistics, and information about laws and legislation.
.ca	Canadian national domain	Limited to Canadian entities: citizens, permanent residents, organizations, Indigenous groups, government, etc.
.biz	Businesses	Meant to relieve the demand for .com names. Must be for business or commercial use.
.info	Unrestricted	Open for any purpose similar to that of the .com, .net, and .org domains. Explicitly created for unrestricted use.

Using Wikipedia

Wikipedia can be useful as a starting point to obtain general information about a subject, but should not be used as a main reference.

- Check the references for links to other sources.
- When using Wikipedia, always check the information with another source that is considered credible.
- Check your instructor's requirements about using Wikipedia for your research.

Works Cited page

You will be doing research for your written assignments and oral presentations. You must acknowledge your sources in the Works Cited section. There are different styles used for citations. For your English course, you will be asked to use MLA style. A good reference for MLA style is the Purdue OWL website.

- Use the title "Works Cited."
- Use alphabetical order, beginning with the author's last name.
- If the author's last name is not known, use the first important word of the title.
- Use hanging indents (the first line is flush left and the following lines are indented).
- Use capital letters for the first letter of all important words in the title and the source.
- Put the title in quotation marks and use italics for the source.
- For a book, list the author, title (in italics), publisher, and date.
- For an article, list the author, title (in quotation marks), source (in italics), and date.
- For an online source, include the URL and the date the website was accessed. The access date is useful but optional, so check with your teacher.

Remember to cite "container" sources. If, for example, you want to cite a short story that is part of a collection of stories, the individual story is the source and the collection of stories is the container. A container can be digital: a television or podcast series comprising many episodes, a website that contains a variety of individual items, or any other intellectual property that is made up of sources within sources.

Book

O'Neill, Heather. *Lullabies for Little Criminals*. Harper Collins, 2006.

Magazine or newspaper article

Andrews, Richard. "Snack-bag of African Nuts Feeds Ambitions of Montreal Entrepreneurs." *Montreal Gazette*, 18 April 2017. http://montrealgazette.com/news/local-news/snack-bag-of-african-nuts-feeds-ambitions-of-montreal-entrepreneurs.

Electronic sources

Websites

Howell, Zachary. "Ways to Land Your Dream Job Fast." *Canada Info*, 21 October 2017. www.isis-canada.org/ways-to-land-your-dream-job-fast. Accessed 4 December 2017.

Lavalée, David. "The Traits of Athletes that can Predict Workplace Success." *Entrepreneur.* 16 January 2015. www.entrepreneur.com/article/241857. Accessed 25 November, 2017.

"Medical Education." *Enclyclopedia Citizendium,* 2012. en.citizendium.org/wiki/Medical_education. Accessed 25 November 20

Article in a web magazine

Carr, Nicholas. "Is Google Making Us Stupid? What the Internet Is Doing to Our Brains." *The Atlantic*, July/August 2008. https://www.theatlantic.com/magazine/archive/2008/07/is-google-making-us-stupid/306868/. Accessed 30 November, 2017.

Online video

Macleon, Shawn. "Basic Essay Structure." You Tube, uploaded by Smrt English, 15 November 2012, www.youtube.com/watch?v=7P4fzbzwwAg.

Exercise 1

Answer the following questions about doing research and avoiding plagiarism.

1. You should never use Wikipedia in your research. ☐ True ☐ False

2. You can decide if a source is credible by looking at the domain ending of the site. ☐ True ☐ False

3. Most colleges use MLA style for referencing in English. ☐ True ☐ False

4. Name two fields of study or subjects where it is very important to find information that is up to date.

   _____

5. Name two fields of study or subjects where it is less important to find information that is up to date.

   _____

6. If you use information that is common to your field of study, is it necessary to document the source? ☐ Yes ☐ No

7. If you use someone else's ideas but explain them in your own words, is it necessary to document the source? ☐ Yes ☐ No

8. In preparing a Works Cited list, what should you do if you do not have the name of the author?

   _____

Speaking Strategies

Giving Effective Oral Presentations

Most people fear public speaking. Still, you will be asked to give oral presentations in college, at university, and at work. The more you prepare and practise, the better you will be at oral presentations.

Prepare your presentation

Review your teacher's requirements for the presentation before preparing any content.

Choose your subject and then brainstorm ideas. Then narrow down your topic and begin to research your subject.

Develop your presentation

Divide your presentation into an introduction, a body section (with three main points), and a conclusion.

Introduction

Your introduction should capture the audience's attention. For instance, begin with an interesting quotation, a shocking statistic, or a thought-provoking question. Then state your topic and give a brief preview of your presentation.

Body

The content of your presentation should be clear and simple. You want to keep the audience's attention and you want people to remember your presentation. People remember information best when it is organized in groups of three, so divide the body of your presentation into three main ideas. Use clear transitions between each idea, so your presentation flows smoothly and the audience knows when you are moving on to the next point.

Sample transitions			
First . . .	Next . . .	Let's move to the next point . . .	Similarly . . .
On the other hand . . .	In addition . . .	Finally . . .	

Conclusion

The conclusion should bring your presentation to a satisfying end. Use transition words to indicate that you are concluding.

Sample conclusions				
To conclude . . .	In conclusion . . .	To sum up . . .	In sum . . .	Lastly . . .

Then refer to the quotation, statistic, or question you mentioned in the introduction. Briefly restate your main points. End with a prediction, suggestion, solution, or call to action.

Deliver your presentation

Presentations should be carefully prepared, but not memorized. Know the content but keep the delivery fresh. Do not use exactly the same words each time you present. Prepare cue cards with key words to help you remember key points and organization. Do not write out your entire presentation and do not read your presentation. Practise your presentation and remember to time yourself. Slow down as you speak to emphasize key ideas.

Acceptable cue cards	Unacceptable cue cards
Self-driving cars—pros – safer – help reduce accidents (research—93%) – disabled people can use them – reduce traffic	Self-driving cars—the positive aspects of this technology – These cars are safer than traditional cars. – These cars will be involved in fewer accidents. Research shows that 93 percent of road accidents are caused by human error. – People who have disabilities can use them. – Traffic can be reduced because speed limits will be increased. In conclusion, self-driving cars have many advantages.
Self-driving cars—cons – expensive – can be hacked – job losses in transport sector – dangerous in extreme weather	Self-driving cars—The negative aspects of this technology – They are much more expensive than traditional cars. – Hackers could hack the computer system and cause accidents. – People in the transport industry such as drivers could lose their jobs. – These cars might not function well in extreme weather conditions such as snow storms. In conclusion, self-driving cars are expensive and can be dangerous in certain situations.

During your presentation, maintain eye contact with your audience. Don't speak too quickly. Smile and maintain good posture. Don't tell the audience you are not prepared or really nervous. Remember the three Es of delivery: Energy, Eye contact, and Expression.

Prepare a slide presentation

Review your teacher's requirements for the oral presentation before preparing any content. Your teacher will give specific guidelines for length and number of slides.

Slide presentation dos and don'ts	
Good slide	**Bad slide**
 **Advantages of Self-Driving Cars** Safer Help reduce accidents People with disabilities can use them Reduce traffic	*Disadvantages of Self-Driving Cars* • *They are very expensive* • *Hackers could find ways to hack them* • *Some peoples could loose their jobs* • *(Taxi drivers, bus drivers, etc....)* • *They could be difficult to operate in* • *Extreme whether conditions* • *In conclusion, there are many disadvantage* *Pay attention* 
Do Use a large, clear, simple font (size 18 to 48 pt) Use a neutral background colour that's easy on the eyes Use a consistent background for all slides Use pictures/visuals/charts Use spell-check and proofread your work Use key words only Use high-contrast colours (e.g., light background with dark text or dark background with light text)	**Don't** Use small, difficult-to-read font Use complex/patterned backgrounds or colours Use low-contrast backgrounds (hard to read) Use different backgrounds for every slide Leave mistakes/typos in your text Write long, complete sentences Write your complete presentation on your slides Overuse bullets Use distracting graphics or too much animation

Reading Strategies

Reading is one of the primary ways to learn new information, build vocabulary, and engage with the world. Building your reading skills will save you time and make you more successful in English at school and work.

Understanding the Main Idea

The main idea describes what the text is about. It is the point the author wants you to remember most. Identifying the main idea can help you understand the ideas and vocabulary in the text.

To find the main idea of a text, read the introduction and conclusion, and a few words from each paragraph. Ask yourself these questions:

- What is the subject of the text?
- What point does the author want to make about the subject?

The main idea will be supported by supporting details, such as examples, reasons, explanations, comparisons, data, and quotations.

When you summarize the main idea of a text, write it in a complete sentence. Include the following elements in the main idea sentence: title, author, type of text (e.g., article, editorial, short story), subject, and controlling idea.

Understanding the Author's Purpose

The purpose of a text is the author's goal for writing it. Most texts you will read in college, university, or the workplace are written to fulfill one of these main purposes:

- to inform (provide information)
- to persuade (convince the reader of something)

Some other purposes of texts are

- to describe (provide details about someone or something)
- to recommend (make a suggestion)
- to explain (describe how or why something works or happens)
- to entertain (amuse someone)

When searching for the author's purpose, ask yourself why the author wrote the text. What does the author want to accomplish? What effect does the author want to have on the reader? What is the tone of the writing?

Identifying bias

When you read a text, ask yourself if the writing shows bias. *Biased* means "one-sided" and implies that the author has not looked at and judged all the available information or evidence. Think about: What evidence is provided? Does the text favour one perspective more than another?

Objective and subjective writing

One clue as to the author's purpose is whether their writing is objective or subjective.

Objective writing is often used when the author's purpose is to inform, explain, or describe. It suggests the author is not trying to make an argument and does not have personal feelings about the subject.

Subjective writing is often used when the author's purpose is to persuade, entertain, or recommend. It suggests the author does have an opinion or point of view on the subject.

Objective writing	Subjective writing

• remains neutral and impersonal (no first or second person)
• refers to facts and observable data
• does not attempt to persuade
• gives both sides of the issue
 	
    EXAMPLES
 	
    The exam lasted 60 minutes.
 	
    Twenty-two people were killed by the bomb blasts.
	• expresses the author's opinion
	• uses first- and second-person pronouns
	• does not give both sides of the issue
	• uses emotionally charged vocabulary
	• asks rhetorical questions
	
	    EXAMPLES
	
	    I thought the exam was really difficult.
	
	    Terrorists murdered 22 innocent people.

Tone

Tone is the way that the writer expresses his or her attitude in the writing. Examples of tone in a text are formal, informal, serious, humorous, sarcastic, critical, etc. Tone is shown through word choice and sentence structure.

Exercise 1

1. Identify the purpose of the following texts.

2. Is the author biased in the texts? If so, which text(s)?

3. Which text is more objective? Why?

4. What is the tone of each paragraph? What words or sentences indicate the tone?

TEXT A: The Quebec provincial government has put forward a proposal for a new bridge. It is expected to ease the congestion at other bridges. To construct this bridge, a mandatory purchase of properties and land will be necessary and certain roads will need to be re-routed. There will be a fee of approximately $5 to use the bridge during peak times and this money will be used for maintenance of both the bridge and local roads. The construction and technological support will bring many jobs to the area.

TEXT B: How much is the ludicrous proposal for an expensive bridge going to cost YOU? Hundreds of homeowners will lose their properties! Family homes will be destroyed by the developers' demolition ball! Countless fields of fertile farmland are to become fields of concrete! Do we really want the noise and pollution of another busy bridge when the government should be supporting public transportation? STOP this madness and appeal to your council to show some sense!

Previewing

Previewing means getting an overview of what the text is about without reading the entire text from start to finish. It is useful to get a general idea of the article's structure, purpose, relevance, and the amount of time and energy necessary to complete the reading task. When you preview, you are able to make an educated guess concerning what the text is about before reading it.

Key steps to use when previewing:

- Read the title and subtitles (if there are any) and ask yourself what you already know about the topic.
- Read the first paragraph and last paragraph. The first paragraph usually develops the main idea of the text and the last paragraph usually contains a summary of the text. You can also read the first line of each paragraph if you need more information.
- Read any headings or words that "jump out" or catch your eye.
- Look at any images, graphs, or charts.
- Read any questions and vocabulary accompanying the text.

Skimming

Skimming involves reading large chunks of text extremely quickly. Skimming allows you to understand the main ideas without paying attention to all the details. Most readers use skimming quite frequently (e.g., reading a long email or a newspaper article) to get an idea of the topic, purpose, and organization of the text. Keep in mind that this should be a fast process. A single chapter should take only a few minutes.

Key steps to use when skimming a text:

- Note any bold print and graphics.
- Start at the beginning of the text.
- Only read a few words of every paragraph, perhaps the first and last sentences.
- Finish skimming before reading in detail.

Scanning

Scanning involves sweeping your eyes (like radar) over parts of a text to find specific pieces of information. It is a focused reading strategy to locate facts, dates, or references. When you find the word, date, or idea you are looking for, you should then read the entire sentence or section surrounding it. You may want to use a highlighter or pencil to identify the information in the text.

Key steps to use when scanning a text:

- After previewing and skimming, identify the section(s) of the text that you probably need to focus on.
- Start scanning the text by allowing your eyes (or finger) to move quickly over a page.
- As soon as your eye catches an important word or phrase, focus and make a note.
- When you locate the information that you are looking for, slow down to read the relevant section more thoroughly.
- Write down the information you need.

Note that when you scan, you will look rapidly over many lines of print at a time. It is not necessary to read the entire text or understand everything.

SQ3R: Reading to remember

The SQ3R method for study reading uses all the above strategies. It is a technique to help you understand what you read and to be able to recall the main ideas when you need them for exams, tutorials, or meetings.

S: Skim through the text to get an overall idea.

Q: Question what is the most important information you should gain from the text; make a list of questions about the text from the headings and subheadings.

R1:   Read for main idea, purpose, and reasoning and take notes.

R2:   Remember—close the book and see what you can recall; try to recite key points aloud.

R3:   Review the material regularly; try to answer your questions from memory; use outlines or flashcards to regularly return to your notes.

Exercise 2

1. Preview the following text. As you look at the title and headings, what do you think it is about?

   _____

   _____

2. Skim to identify the topic sentence or main idea of each paragraph.

   _____

   _____

---

3. Scan for the following references. What information can be linked to these items?

   a) 2000: _____

   b) *Science*: _____

4. What is the main idea of the text? Use a complete sentence.

   _____

   _____

5. List two supporting details the author gives to support the main idea.

   a) _____

   b) _____

6. What do you think the article's main purpose is?
   a) to inform
   b) to entertain
   c) to persuade

7. Use SQ3R to actively read and recall the main ideas of the text. Create three questions.

8. Is the text objective or subjective? Give two reasons.

   _____

   _____

The Benefits of Fiction

Addicted to stories

Reality television, Instagram, Snapchat, and Facebook have taken all our time away from where we once craved to be—in the middle of an incredible story. In the past, we fervently turned each page while missing breakfast, lunch, and sometimes even dinner just to see what would happen next. Involvement in a story promotes empathy, which is a desirable quality for 21st-century leaders. In 2013, a study in *Science* found that reading literary fiction improved participants' results on tests measuring social perception and empathy.

Short attention span

Research has shown that the average human attention span has decreased from 12 seconds in 2000 to 8 seconds in 2016. We can't sit still long enough to read books. Instead, we pick up a book only to then take out our phones and endlessly scroll. When we stop scrolling, we forget why we picked up the book in the first place.

Adapted from Joshua Fechter. "Benefits of Reading Literary Fiction You May Not Know." *Lifehack*, http://www.lifehack.org/307436/7-benefits-reading-literary-fiction-you-may-not-know-2. Accessed 8 November 2017.

Listening Strategies

In study and work environments, you will need to listen and understand information in English presented in a variety of forms. The best way to improve your listening skills is by listening. The more you listen and watch in English, the more you will understand. Listen to radio or podcasts and watch TV or movies in English. You will notice an improvement in your comprehension after a few weeks.

These strategies will help you understand main ideas as well as details.

Before you listen, ask yourself

- What is the context (a news report, a class lecture, a TV show, an exchange in a coffee shop)?
- What do I already know about this subject?
- What do I think I will learn from the listening?
- What kind of words and style of language will the speaker use?

While you listen

- Take notes.
- Pay attention to words that are stressed or emphasized.
- Listen for words that are repeated.
- Pay attention to key words and facts. Speakers often use key words such as *firstly*, *secondly*, *in conclusion*, etc. before introducing key information so listen carefully to information following these or similar words.
- Keep listening until the end and listen again if necessary.
- Pay attention to the main ideas and key points.

After you listen

- Compare your answers or your notes with a partner or the teacher.
- Review, edit, and reorganize your notes.
- Do further research on the topic.
- Check unfamiliar vocabulary.
- Write or speak about the topic; express your opinion.

Note-Taking

Effective note-taking helps you listen actively and become a more critical listener and thinker. It is important to take notes and to use your notes because, according to research, nine hours after listening or watching we have forgotten 60 percent of what we heard. Organize your notes so that they will be useful in recalling key points.

Note-taking dos and don'ts	
Do	**Don't**
• be organized • show main points and details • use point form • use abbreviations that you develop yourself • leave out details • use a note-taking system that works for you	• write down everything you hear • write down things you don't understand • be distracted by your phone or other devices • worry if you don't understand everything or missed some details

Note-taking system

Choose a note-taking system that works for you. Develop your own or use a popular method such as the Cornell method.

Linear or Cornell method

- Divide your page vertically into one-third and two-thirds.
- Use the left side for main ideas and key words and the right side for supporting details.
- The advantage of this method is that it forces you to decide on the key points.

Exercise

Go online and search for a video on a topic related to your field of study or future career and practise listening while you take good notes. Answer these questions after you listen.

- Did you use key words?
- Did you use point form?
- Did you use abbreviations?
- Did you leave out unnecessary details?
- Can you use your notes to explain the details to another student?

Name
Date
Class
Period

Cornell Notes

• Main idea	• Key words & ideas
• Key Question (after notes are completed)	• Important dates/people/places
	• Repeated/Stressed info
	• Ideas/brainstorming written on board/overhead projector
	• info from textbook/stories
	• Diagrams & Pictures
	• Formulas

Summary of your notes in your own words

Vocabulary Strategies

Building your vocabulary is essential to the process of learning a language. These strategies will help you ensure your vocabulary continues to grow as you progress through the textbook.

Understanding the Meaning of New Words

Good readers don't look up every word in the dictionary. That process is slow and doesn't take into consideration the context in which the word is used. The following techniques will help you understand and guess the meaning of new words more efficiently.

Using context to guess the meaning of new words

Authors often provide clues in the surrounding text to help you understand a new word. If you can understand how a word is being used and what it relates to, it will help you guess its meaning.

Follow these steps to use context to understand new words:

- Identify the **part of speech**. For example, if the word is being used as a verb, it probably describes an action.
- Read the sentence carefully to see if there are **context clues** to the meaning. Understanding the topic of the sentence helps you understand what the word means. Look at the sentences before and after the word for clues. This provides context for the sentence and gives you more details about the topic.
- Look for **definition and example clues**. Authors sometimes provide definitions or examples to help explain difficult words.
- Look for **synonyms** (words with similar meanings) and **antonyms** (words with opposite meanings). Writers often give a synonym to explain key terms, or an antonym to define a word by what it is not. If you know these words, it will help you guess the meaning of the new word.

Cognates

Sometimes you can use your first language to guess the meaning of new words. About 35–60 percent of English is of Latin or French origin. This means that there are many English words that look similar to French words and have the same meaning. Words that share origins and meanings are called "cognates," such as *attention, intelligent, maximum*. Sometimes the spelling changes, but the word is still a clear cognate: *pourcent/percent, établir/establish,* and *hôpital/hospital*. If a word looks similar to a French word, use the context to check if it is likely that the meaning is the same.

Be cautious of "false cognates." These are words that look like French words, but have different meanings. For example, *library* in English is a place to borrow books, while *librairie* in French is a place to buy books. *Attend* in English means to be present (at a place or event), while *attend* in French means "to wait." Other common false cognates are *journey* (a trip); *sensible* (reasonable); *assist* (to help); *rest* (to relax); *lecture* (speech).

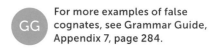

For more examples of false cognates, see Grammar Guide, Appendix 7, page 284.

Exercise 1

Identify the false cognates for the following English words and provide contrasting definitions of the false cognates in English and French.

English word	English meaning	French false cognate	French meaning
actually			
assist			
deception			
demand			
gentle			
lecture			
library			
location			
pass			
sensible			
sympathetic			

Prefixes and suffixes

Learning common prefixes and suffixes can help you guess the meaning of new words.

Prefixes and suffixes are a set combination of letters that can be added to a base word to form a new word. This new word has a new meaning and/or part of speech.

A prefix is one or more letters added to the beginning of a word. The four most common prefixes are *dis-*, *ir-*, *un-*, and *re-*. Adding a prefix usually changes the meaning of the base word quite significantly.

A suffix is one or more letters added to the end of the word. Generally adding a suffix changes the part of speech of the word.

Neither prefixes nor suffixes can stand alone; they must be added to a base word.

Common prefixes

Prefix	Meaning	Example
anti-	against	Many people take anti-depressants.
de-	opposite	The currency has been devalued.
dis-	not	I disapprove of smoking.
em-	cause to	A good manager will empower employees.
en-	cause to	I enclosed a cheque.
im-	not	It is impossible to say no to him.
in-	not	She is not often incorrect.
ir-	not	Some decisions are irrational.
mis-	not correctly	I misunderstood the concept.
non-	not	My patience was non-existent.
over-	more than	We overloaded the truck.
pre-	before	You should precook the beans.
re-	again	I will review the document.
un-	not	Living in the city is unaffordable.

Exercise 2

Complete each word with the correct prefix.

1. _____use of social media can lead to an _____load of information that people cannot process.

2. I think you should _____think leaving your job; it's _____possible to find decent work conditions at the moment.

3. You should _____view your diet; it is _____healthy to eat a lot of sugar.

4. I cannot find my laptop. It has _____appeared.

5. It's _____polite to start eating before everyone receives their meals.

6. I _____viewed the document before the meeting. I dislike being _____prepared.

7. There were too many _____spelled words in his email. I have asked him to _____write the whole document.

Common suffixes

Suffix	Meaning	Example
-able, -ible	adjective—can be done	I am very dependable.
-al, -ial	adjective—having the kind of	My brother is a cynical person.
-en	adjective—made of	I made a woollen sweater.
-er, -or	noun—a person who	He worked as a waiter in LA.
-est	superlative	The CN Tower is the tallest building in Canada.
-ful	adjective—full of	She was thankful for the gift.
-ic	having the characteristic of	My cough became chronic.
-ion, -tion, -ation, -ition	noun—action or condition	Organization is a strength.
-ity, -ty	state of	I was struck by the enormity of the situation.
-ive, -ative, -itive	adjective—tendency or function	The lecture was informative.
-less -ly	adjective—without	The job was thankless.
-ment	noun—action or process	There is more temporary employment today.
-ness	noun—state	I was away due to sickness.
-ous, -eous, -ious	adjective—having the qualities of	She lost consciousness.
-ship	noun—skill, character	We reviewed the membership list.

Exercise 3

Complete each word with the correct suffix.

1. She is a design_____ and her sister is a build_____.

2. Being creative is needed to be success_____ in all fields.

3. I am looking for employ_____ in another province.

4. Employ_____ are looking for candidates who are reli_____.

5. Working in social services can be very stress_____.

6. Leader_____ qualities are essential in management teams.

Build Your English Vocabulary

How many words do you think you need to know in English? What is the best way to add new words to your vocabulary? Are there specialized words that are essential in your field of study or future career? A combination of these techniques can be used to build your vocabulary.

Dictionaries

Paper and online dictionaries are great resources for researching different meanings, pronunciation, collocations, and examples of use of new words. Learning to use dictionary resources well provides more than the word's meaning. The dictionary entry for a word shows

- part of speech: e.g., *n* for "noun" or *adj* for "adjective"; whether the verb is transitive (needs an object; e.g., *admire someone/something*) or intransitive (does not need an object e.g., *work*); and whether the noun is countable or uncountable
- synonyms (words with the same meaning)
- antonyms (words with the opposite meaning)
- collocations (words that go together e.g., *full-time employment; lifelong employment; look for, or seek employment; conditions of employment; employment rights* or *opportunities*)
- pronunciation
- syllables and word stress
- usage and phrasal forms
- number of meanings

Word lists

The New Academic Word List (NAWL) and New General Service List (2013)

The New Academic Word List (NAWL) is a list of words that are frequently used in academic texts; they are not field-specific and are also found in newspapers, on television, and in conversation. If you are familiar with the 2800 most frequently used words that make up the New General Service List in English as well as the 963 words that make up the NAWL, you should be able to understand around 90 percent of any text you read.

To find out whether you know the most frequently used words in English, enter "vocabulary size online quizzes" or "lextutor" in your web browser.

You can browse the word lists by typing *New Academic Word List* or *Academic Word List* website or type *Academic Word List* in your web browser to find other AWL websites. You will find word lists as well as exercises to practise using this vocabulary.

All vocabulary learning requires active involvement and lots of repetition. Visiting these sites, doing related exercises, and writing down unfamiliar words and their definitions will help you build the foundations of your English vocabulary.

Word forms

When you encounter a new word, use a dictionary to confirm its meaning(s), word forms, or parts of speech. Create a chart like this one to record your new vocabulary words. An *X* indicates there is no applicable word.

Target NAWL word	Meaning(s)	Verb	Noun	Adjective	Adverb
utilize	use	utilize	utilization	utilized	X
correlate	connect	correlate	correlation	correlated	X
reliability	dependability	rely	reliance	reliable	reliably
impact	effect	impact	impact	impactful	X
spontaneous	unplanned	X	spontaneity	spontaneous	spontaneously

Mind maps

Mind maps are visual ways to build vocabulary on a topic. When you create a mind map, you make links between new words and words you already know. These links are called associations. The more you think about and use these words, the stronger these links become and the more you will expand your vocabulary.

To make a mind map, think of a word and put it in a box at the centre of your page. Now think of related terms and connect each of them to the main word with a line. For each of those related terms, think of other associated terms and connect them to the related terms with a line. Stop when you can no longer think of words related to the main word.

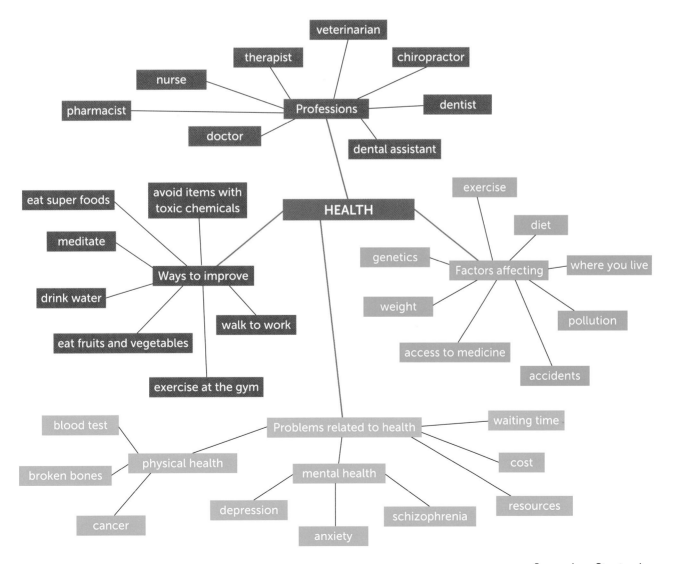

Exercise 4

1. Search online using "word knowledge test" and look for an online resource to test your vocabulary knowledge. Do you know many of the 2000 most frequent words?

2. Create a collocation list of a key word in your field of studies.

3. Create a mind map including at least 10 new words based on a key word in your field of study.

Class challenge

New words are added to English every year. Some are "borrowed" from other languages, and some are new compound words (for example, *skyscraper* was a new word in the 1880s to describe 10- to 20-storey buildings).

Here are some examples of words that are created from two traditional words. Try to match the best definition to these invented compound words. What two words were put together to create each word? Then create another invented word that you think would be a good addition to dictionaries.

chairdrobe (n) _____	a) person or people whose world consists only of knowledge about themselves
afterclap (n) _____	b) the last person who applauds after everyone else has stopped
hiberdating (v) _____	c) when a person ignores friends in favour of a boyfriend or girlfriend
destinesia (n) _____	d) the putting of lots of clothes on furniture other than the wardrobe
youniverse (n) _____	e) when you arrive at the place you want to go to, but cannot remember why you are there

New invented word	Part of speech	Origin and meaning

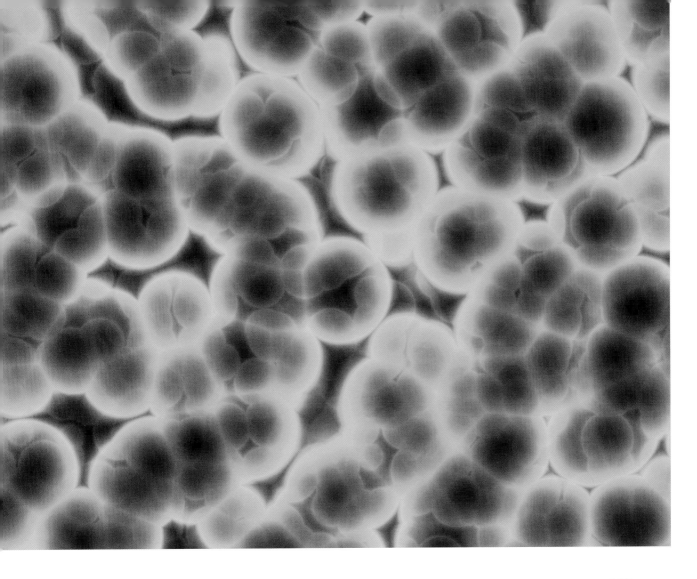

Grammar Guide

CHAPTER 1
Parts of Speech Overview

Go to Explore Online for additional activities using parts of speech.

Chapter 1 reviews the fundamental parts of speech. Identify topics you know well and topics where you need support, and spend more time in the chapters that are most relevant to you.

Understanding parts of speech makes it easier to use accurate sentence structure, subject–verb agreement, and correct grammar. The basic word order of a sentence in English is

subject noun/noun phrase/pronoun + verb + object noun/noun phrase/pronoun

Subject noun/noun phrase/pronoun	Verb (v)	Object noun/noun phrase/pronoun
She	won	it.
The fastest runner	won	the race.

For more information about nouns and pronouns, see Grammar Guide, pages 243 and 251

Nouns (n) are words that name people, animals, places, things, or ideas. Nouns are categorized as
- abstract (an idea or feeling)
- concrete (something physically present)
- common (general items rather than specific ones)
- proper (specific person, place, or organization, spelled with a capital letter)
- countable or uncountable

Pronouns (pn) replace nouns in sentences (*I, me, you, he, she, it, him, her, they, them* . . .) and can be subject or object pronouns.

Type of pronoun	Examples
personal	I, me, he, him, we
indefinite	everyone, each, nobody
reflexive	yourself, herself, themselves
demonstrative	this/that, these/those
possessive	mine, yours, hers
relative	who, that, which, where, when

For more information about determiners, see Grammar Guide, page 246.

Determiners (det) are function words that introduce, limit, modify, or "determine" a noun.

Type of determiner	Examples
articles (definite and indefinite)	the, a/an
quantifiers	some, any, much, every, few
possessive adjectives	my, your, his, her, its, our, your, their
demonstrative	this/that, these/those
numbers/ordinals	one, two . . ./first, second, last, next

Adjectives (adj) describe a noun or pronoun (colour, quality, size, number . . .). Adjectives are usually placed in front of the modified word.

GG For more information about adjectives, see Grammar Guide, pages 251 and 258.

EXAMPLES

Power yoga is a **meditative** exercise, whereas **field** hockey is an **aggressive** game.

She wrote a **long** essay comparing the **different** activities.

Exercise 1

1. Underline the nouns and pronouns.

2. Highlight adjectives.

3. Select and circle the correct determiners for the following sentences. Circle **X** if no determiner is required.

   George is **a/an/X** contract electrician. He works for **the/a/many** different companies. He has **the/a/an/X** college diploma and **the/a/an/X** training in international networks. When he finished **the/a/an/X** training program, he applied for **the/a/an/X** advertised job at **the/a/an/X** local company. He did not get **the/a/an/X** job, but it was **the/a/an/X** great interview. Afterward, he decided to set up **his/her/the/X** own company and offer **the/a/his/X** services to building contractors. He said **the/a/an/X** college diplomas and **the/a/an/X** training provide **the/a/an/X** theoretical approach to electrical problems but he quickly discovered that he needed to develop **the/a/an/X** practical skills. George advises students to look for **the/a/an/X** program offering work internships as part of **the/a/an/X** course.

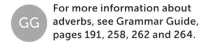

An internship is a work placement or *stage* in French. *Stage* in English refers to either the steps of a process or where actors perform in a theatre.

A **verb** (v) expresses an action (*swim, read, walk, learn*), an occurrence (*happen, become*), or a state of being (*be, exist, stand*). The verb agrees with (matches) the subject of the sentence.

EXAMPLE   Emilie **drives** and the other students **walk** to school.

Adverbs (adv) add information (manner, time, place, degree) to verbs, adjectives, or other adverbs.

GG For more information about adverbs, see Grammar Guide, pages 191, 258, 262 and 264.

EXAMPLES   He moved **quickly**. She is **very** talented.

Exercise 2

Underline the <u>verbs</u>, circle the (adverbs) and highlight the adjectives.

1. Melissa (usually) <u>feels</u> confident in interviews.

2. She said the interview yesterday was really difficult and quite stressful.

3. The first female interviewer asked a very long question.

4. She wasn't very sure she had fully understood.

5. The interviewer stubbornly wanted to know whether she liked spiders.

6. Melissa explained that she had read online about the strange questions that sometimes asked in interviews, but she really wondered what type of caretaking job she was applying for.

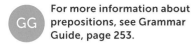 For more information about prepositions, see Grammar Guide, page 253.

Prepositions (prep) provide information about location in space and time.

EXAMPLE   We will go to the library **on** Elm Street **at** 4:00 **on** Monday afternoon.

Preposition	Place	Time and date
at	a specific place: *at school, at work, at the corner*	a specific time: *at 10:00 AM, at dinnertime*
on	a street/road: *on High Street* a device/machine: *on TV, on the Web* a state of something: *on fire, on sale*	days and dates: *on Monday, on weekdays, on August 22*
in	a delineated area: *in Ontario, in Montreal, in my program*	a month, year, century: *in June, in 2020, in the 19th century* a delineated part of the day: *in the evening* a shape/colour/size/belief: *in love, in red, in large*

Exercise 3

Select the correct prepositions in the sentences.

1. Zoe looked up car maintenance courses (at/on/in) the Internet, and one is offered (at/on/in) the local college.

2. The class is held (at/on/in) Tuesdays (at/on/in) 6:00 PM (at/on/in) the parking lot.

3. We can meet (at/on/in) January, (at/on/in) Wednesday, (at/on/in) the morning (at/on/in) the library.

4. Turn (at/on/in) the corner and then continue walking. The restaurant is (at/on/in) West Street and we have a reservation (at/on/in) 8:00 PM.

5. We can join you (at/on/in) the lobby or (at/on/in) the table.

 For more information about conjunctions, see Grammar Guide, pages 254 and 266.

Conjunctions (conj) connect or join words, phrases, or clauses together.

EXAMPLES   *because, as, for, and, nor, but, or, yet, so*

Interjections (int) usually express strong emotions such as love, hate, disgust, surprise, etc. and are commonly followed by an exclamation mark. Interjections are not usually used in professional or academic writing.

EXAMPLES

Oh no, it's raining again!   Wow, did you see that!   Hey!

Exercise 4

Use the information above to identify the parts of speech in the following sentences using abbreviations.

EXAMPLE   n subj   v det   adj   n
             Medicine/is/a/demanding/program.

1. The student union election is tomorrow.

_____

2. Damn! I work this weekend.

_____

3. I am excited about working for the theatre.

   _____

4. Felix always cycles to work.

   _____

A **phrase** is a group of words that adds meaning to a sentence. A phrase is not a sentence because it is not a complete idea with a subject and verb (and predicate).

   EXAMPLES

   The full moon . . .

   Students in college . . .

A **clause** is a group of words with a subject (noun), predicate (verb), and often a complement or object.

   EXAMPLES

   The full moon is shining.

   Students at college work hard.

A **dependent or subordinate clause** does not express a complete idea and cannot stand alone. A dependent clause is often marked by subordinating conjunctions such as *after, although, because, before, even though, if, unless, when,* and *while.*

An **independent or main clause** expresses a complete idea and contains a subject (noun), predicate (verb), and sometimes an object. An independent clause is a **sentence**.

   EXAMPLE   Samuel   works   at the hotel.
                     S   V   O

Exercise 5

Identify whether the following are phrases (P), dependent clauses (DC), or independent clauses (IC) (sentences). Where there is both a dependent and an independent clause, label each clause.

   EXAMPLE   He passed the test (because he studied).
                        IC   DC

1. when it snows

2. she should work harder

3. the older members of the committee

4. she went to the library after class ended

5. if she gets the job, she will be very happy

6. when it stops raining, I'll walk the dog

7. supporting women and children

8. don't buy them unless they are really comfortable

9. because he was driving too fast

10. the children were playing outside until the sun set

CHAPTER 2
Present Tenses

Simple Present

Go to Explore Online for additional activities using the present tense.

We use the simple present tense to talk about **facts**, **generalizations**, and **repeated actions** (e.g., routines and habits).

    EXAMPLES   School **costs** more in 2017 than it did in 1960. (fact)

                   Most people **want** the same things. (generalization)

                   I **wake** up at 7 AM every day. (repeated action)

We also use the simple present to express future scheduled events.

    EXAMPLE

    The train leaves at 4:00 PM.

For more information, see pages 213 and 214.

Forming the simple present

	Affirmative	Negative	Question
for all verbs except *to be*	I work You/We/They work He/She/It works	I do not work They do not work He does not work	Do you work? Does he work? Does he/she/it work? When do I work? Where does he work?
for *to be*	I am You/We/They are He/She/It is	I am not They are not She is not	Am I . . .? Are you/we/they . . .? Is he/she/it . . .? When is the exam? Why are you late?

Spelling: Final -*s* for third-person singular

Spelling rule	Examples
for most verbs, **-s** is added for third-person singular	speak → speaks answer → answers walk → walks write → writes
if the verb ends in **-ch**, **-sh**, **-s**, **-x**, **-z**, **-o**, add **-es**	watch → watches pass → passes fix → fixes go → goes buzz → buzzes
if the verb ends in a **consonant + -y**, change the **y** to **i** and add **-es**.	study → studies try → tries
if the verb ends in a **vowel + -y**, add **-s**	pay → pays employs → employs

Frequency adverbs

Adverbs are placed before the verb, except with the verb *to be*, where the adverb comes after the verb.

> **EXAMPLES**   Jules **usually** drives to work.
>
> Marie is **always** punctual.
>
> My dad doesn't **often** call me.

We can use *often*, *usually*, *sometimes*, and *occasionally* at the beginning of a sentence.

> **EXAMPLES**   Sometimes, I have lunch at my desk.
>
> Occasionally, she meets her clients at a restaurant.

100% of the time								0% of the time

| always | almost always | usually | often | sometimes | occasionally | rarely | almost never | never |

Ever is often used in questions and negatives—*ever*, meaning "at any time," or *not ever*, meaning "never."

EXAMPLE

Do you ever work on Sundays?
I don't ever work on Sundays.

Exercise 1

get up early	play games	go to the library
drive	work in a laboratory	work in a team
wear a suit/uniform	attend meetings	check email
research	create	be stressed
study	repair	speak to the team
write a report	give a presentation	go to the gym

1. Use the simple present tense to write four sentences using the frequency adverbs and some of the words in the box to describe a routine or habit related to your field of study.

> **EXAMPLE**   A graphic designer **often** uses email to communicate with clients.

a) _____

b) _____

c) _____

d) _____

2. Write two negative sentences using the frequency adverbs.

> **EXAMPLE**   A computer programmer does not **usually** have to wear a suit to work.

a) _____

b) _____

Exercise 2

Complete the following with statements, negatives, and questions in the simple present tense.

1. Habits _____ (be) behaviours that are wired so deeply in our brains that

we _____ (perform) them automatically. A habit _____ (allow) us to follow the same route to work every day without thinking; this _____ (free) the brain to think about other things, such as what to eat for lunch.

2. Psychological research _____ (suggest) that insignificant activities such as shopping _____ (provide) insights into personality traits and the way a person _____ (approach) life in general. For example, what _____ (your shopping and eating habits, reveal, *quest.*) about you? At the pharmacy, how _____ (select, you, *quest.*) a new product? _____ (look, you, *quest.*) at the ingredients on each tube of toothpaste until you find one that suits your needs? Or _____ (you, choose, *quest.*) a product quickly and assume that you know exactly how it _____ (work)?

3. That first type of consumer _____ (be) what scientists call an "**explanation fiend**"; the second is an "**explanation foe**." A series of experiments published in 2012 found that explanation fiends _____ (score, usually) high on measures of cognitive reflection; this _____ (mean) they _____ (analyze) information and prefer lots of detail about products. Explanation foes, on the other hand, _____ (score, *neg.*) high on measures of cognitive reflection; they _____ (want, *neg.*) as many details and prefer more general information.

4. Food-related behaviours and eating habits can also say a lot about our personalities. Specifically, a slow eater _____ (like) to be in control and _____ (know) how to appreciate life. A fast eater _____ (tend) to be ambitious and goal oriented. Which _____ (you, think, *quest.*) is most open to new experiences? Finally, _____ (you, know, *quest.*) people who separate different foods on their plate? Reports _____ (indicate) these people are inclined to be detail oriented and disciplined.

Exercise 3

The simple present is also used to describe people and things and to summarize events in the plot of a movie or book.

1. Read the two examples below and circle the verbs.

   a) An epidemiologist is a medical doctor who studies and analyzes patterns, causes, and effects of health states in populations. Epidemiologists specialize in the study of epidemics or pandemics. An epidemiologist trains in all areas of medicine and then does particular research in statistics and public health policy.

explanation fiend (n) a consumer who makes decisions based on a lot of research

explanation foe (n) a consumer who makes decisions based on intuitive feelings

b) The film *Seven* is a 1995 American psychological thriller. It stars Brad Pitt and Morgan Freeman. The story unfolds in an unnamed American city. The film tells the story of a young detective and his older partner as they investigate a murder. Soon it becomes clear that the murderer is a serial killer who leaves signs at the crime scenes. Each murder represents one of the seven deadly sins.

2. Write a description (2–3 sentences) of either a professional person (e.g., electrician, dental hygienist) or a piece of equipment (e.g., microscope, camera) in your field of study.

3. Write a summary (5–6 sentences) of the plot of a film or book that you know well.

Present Progressive

We use the present progressive to express actions that are happening now, are in progress, or are temporary. The present progressive is also used to describe changing states or situations. To form the present progressive, use the **present tense of the verb *to be* + base form of the verb + *-ing***.

EXAMPLES   I **am meeting** her right now.

Hamish **is volunteering** for the international film festival at the moment.

I**'m not working** on Monday if you want to meet for dinner.

The world **is getting** more dangerous.

The number of cars on the roads **is increasing**.

We also use the present progressive to talk about future arrangements. A future arrangement is a plan that you have decided on and organized.

EXAMPLES

I'**m going** to Croatia on my week off.

We **are coming** home on Thursday.

For more information about expressing the future, see Grammar Guide Chapter 4, page 210.

Forming the present progressive

Affirmative	Negative	Question
I am working You/We/They are working He/She/It is working	I am not working You/We/They are not working He/She/It is not working	Am I working? Are you/we/they working? Is he/she/it working? Why are you waiting here? How is he feeling today?

Spelling *-ing* verbs

Verb ending	Simple form	*-ing*	Rule
-e	live hope	loving hoping	*-ing*: drop the *-e* and add *-ing*
One syllable: One vowel + one consonant	win stop	winning stopping	Double the consonant for one-syllable verbs ending in one vowel and one consonant.
Two syllables	permit occur	permitting occurring	Double the consonant for two-syllable verbs when the second syllable is stressed.
-ie	die	dying	change *ie* to *y* and add *-ing*.

Exercise 4

Look at the images below. Write as many sentences as possible about them using the present progressive. Be attentive to subject–verb agreement. Use as many different verbs as possible and prepare at least two questions (and answers) about each picture.

Exercise 5

Describe how things change using the present progressive and verbs such as *get*, *become*, *increase*, *decrease*, *change*, and *develop*. Write two sentences describing how each of the following is changing.

EXAMPLE   phones

Landlines are **becoming** extinct. Mobile phones are **getting** more powerful and the visuals are **becoming** clearer with each update.

1. computers

2. medical care

3. transport

4. population

Stative verbs

The present progressive describes actions. Some verbs are non-action or stative and are rarely used in the progressive even if we are talking about "right now." Stative verbs are verbs that express feelings, the senses, relationships, physical descriptions, beliefs, or possessions (e.g., *possess*, *think*, *hate*, *love*, *fear*, *believe*).

Some verbs express both an action and non-action (stative) meaning.

EXAMPLES

She **is having** a baby. (the birth is in progress) *versus* She **has** a baby.

Alan **is thinking** about food. *versus* Alan **thinks** food should be cheaper.

Exercise 6

Fill in the blanks using either the simple present or present progressive of the verbs in parentheses.

A: Look outside! It _____ (snow)!

B: Yes . . . it _____ (snow) every winter. I _____ (understand, *neg.*) why you are excited!

A: I _____ (love) the snow. _____ (the weather, affect, *quest.*) your mood? I _____ (feel) really happy each time it _____ (snow).

B: Right now I _____ (think) about moving to Barbados. I _____ (think) winter is too long in Canada.

A: _____ (you, think, *quest.*) you will miss anything about Canada?

B: Well, I _____ (love) hockey even if I _____ (like, *neg.*) winter!!

Exercise 7

Fill in the blanks using either the simple present or present progressive of the verbs in parentheses.

An illustrator _____ (use) a variety of tools and techniques to create visual images and illustrations. Most illustrators _____ (be) self-employed or freelance. This means that they _____ (need) to be self-motivated.

Deciding to work in the arts _____ (require) self-confidence and self-knowledge. You need to know absolutely that you _____ (want) to be an illustrator because if you _____ (have) a vague plan it will be hard to sustain over time. Becoming established in the field _____ (take) self-belief and determination; it also _____ (involve) time.

Emma _____ (work) as an illustrator. She _____ (love) drawing and every morning when she _____ (wake) up, she _____ (feel) extremely grateful that she _____ (make) her living as a freelance illustrator. She started a blog when she was 18 and she _____ (still, write) and drawing on the same blog. Emma _____ (say) that the positive feedback is encouraging.

Emma _____ (say) that she _____ (try) hard to maintain an online presence. "I _____ (update) my blog every week and social media is a wonderful thing. I _____ (know) many illustrators who _____ (get) most of their work through Twitter," she says. "At the moment I _____ (work) regularly and I _____ (run) workshops for new freelance artists."

Question Formation

The word order for asking most questions is

Question word(s) + Auxiliary (helping verb) + Subject + Verb + rest of sentence (QASV)

Q	A	S	V	Rest of sentence
Where	does	Sarah	work?	
	do	the children	go	to school?
Why	does	the teacher	study	until midnight?
Where	is	the car?		
When	are	the exams?		
What	are	the children	playing?	
When	is	Jenny	working?	
Who	do	you	know	in your class?
*Who			works	at the bar?
*What			is	the best solution?
How	are	your parents?		

* In this case, the question word is the subject of the sentence, so QASV is not used.

NOTE

1. Do not use *do/does* with the verb *be*.

2. Use *does* with third-person singular (*he/she/it*)—the main verb is the base form (no -s).

Exercise 8

Write appropriate questions for the following answers. The first is completed for you.

1. Where ___**do you work**___? How often ___**do you work in the city**___?

    I work in the city every day.

2. How _____?

    Mel cycles to work.

3. What _____? How often _____?

    Once a month Remy takes the Eurostar train between London and Paris.

4. What _____?

    I am taking driving lessons this afternoon.

5. What _____?

   The library opens at 7 AM and closes at 10 PM.

6. Where _____?

   They are meeting in the entrance hall.

7. Where _____? When _____?

   Sara studies in the library most weekends

8. Where _____?

   Ms. Baxter lives in the same building as we do.

9. When _____?

   We are driving to Nova Scotia next weekend.

10. Who _____?

    I think Jenny is the best person for the managerial position.

Exercise 9

Practise using auxiliaries to give short answers to the *Yes/No* questions.

EXAMPLES

Do you go to the gym? Yes I do./No I don't.

Are you enjoying class? Yes I am./No I'm not.

In short answers, when the answer is *yes* the auxiliary verb is not contracted.

Correct	Yes, she is.
Incorrect	~~Yes, she's.~~

1. Are you listening to the teacher? **Yes, I am./No, I'm not.**

2. Do you usually arrive in class on time? _____

3. Do you like your program? _____

4. Do you cycle to school? _____

5. Does your friend text you during classes? _____

6. Are you learning other languages? _____

Review Exercise

1. Select the most appropriate verb from the choices in parentheses. The first answer is provided.

   What (**do you know**/are you knowing/you know) about photosynthesis?

   sunlight
   carbon dioxide + water ⟶ glucose + oxygen

When we (walking/are walking/walk) along the street, we often (do think/do not think/are not thinking) about the scientific processes that (is taking/takes/are taking) place all around us. Photosynthesis (is/are/are being) the process by which plants (makes/is making/make) their own food using carbon dioxide, water, and sunlight. *Photo* (is meaning/mean/means) "light" and *synthesis* (signify/signifys/signifies) "putting together." The plant (is gathering/are gathering/gathers) carbon dioxide from the air through small pores or holes in the leaves. The roots of the plant (is absorbing/absorbs/absorb) water, and chlorophyll in the leaves (absorbs/absorb/are absorbing) sunlight.

Some of the glucose that plants (are producing/is producing/produce) during photosynthesis is stored in fruits and roots. These foods (are providing/provide/provides) energy for humans and animals. Photosynthesis (are/is/are being) also responsible for balancing oxygen and carbon dioxide levels in the atmosphere. Plants (is absorbing/absorb/absorbs) carbon dioxide from the air and they (is releasing/releases/release) oxygen during the process of photosynthesis.

2. Fill in the blanks with the simple present or present progressive of the verbs in parentheses.

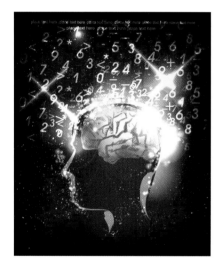

What _____ (happen) in your brain right now? _____ (think, you, *quest.*) your brain is changing? New research _____ (show) that the brain's structure _____ (be, *neg.*) permanent and it _____ (stop, *neg.*) changing. Brain plasticity or neuroplasticity _____ (refer) to the brain's ability to change and adapt as a result of experience. When people _____ (say) that the brain _____ (possess) plasticity, they _____ (suggest, *neg.*) that the brain is similar to plastic. *Neuro* _____ (mean) neurons; neurons _____ (be) the nerve cells or the building blocks of the brain and nervous system, and *plasticity* _____ (signify) the brain's malleability.

Modern technology _____ (demonstrate) that the brain _____ (continue) to create new neural pathways. This _____ (mean) the brain _____ (alter) existing pathways to adapt to new experiences; all the time we _____ (learn) new information and creating new memories. Genetics _____ (influence) the process and the environment _____ (play) an important role. In his book *The Brain That Changes Itself*, Norman Doidge _____ (explain) how environmental changes can lead to dramatic changes in the brain.

3. Use the present tense to write five to six sentences explaining a concept or a product or process in your field of study.

Communicative Activities

1. Guess the film: Think of the story of a film you have seen or book you have read recently. Using the present tense, describe the summary of the story and see if your partner can guess which film or book you are describing.

    EXAMPLE

    James Bond—*Live and Let Die*

    A secret agent is in New Orleans to investigate the murder of three of his colleagues. In the film, the secret agent avoids getting killed by several assassins and discovers a heroin operation run by a villain called Mr. Big. There is a very well-known scene in which the agent meets a beautiful tarot-card reader.

2. "Find someone who . . . ." Write questions for these prompts and then ask your classmates the questions. Find a different person who answers *Yes* for each question.

    EXAMPLE

    plays hockey

    Q: Do you play hockey?

    A: Yes I do (write down student's name to use in your response) _____

    Response: Pierre plays hockey.

Prompt	Question	Response (with name)
a) works at a supermarket		Leila works at a supermarket.
b) speaks Spanish		
c) studies humanities		
d) lives in an apartment		
e) has a dog		
f) walks to school		
g) drinks coffee		
h) practises yoga		
i) has a birthday in October		
j) works in a bar		
k) is wearing contact lenses		
l) plays guitar		

CHAPTER 3
Past Tenses

Simple Past

 Go to Explore Online for additional activities using past tenses.

We use the simple past tense to talk about an activity that occurred at a specific time in the past: an event that began and ended at a definite time in the past (e.g., last week, yesterday, in 1950).

The simple past is formed with the **base form of the regular verb + -ed** and using the simple past forms for irregular verbs.

> **EXAMPLES** New students **arrived** in September.
>
> Julia **went** to New Zealand last year.
>
> It **was** cold yesterday.
>
> James **ran** earlier.

For a list of common irregular verbs, see Appendix 4, page 280.

Forming the simple past

	Affirmative	Negative	Question
regular verbs	I walked You/We/They walked He/She/It walked	I did not walk You/We/They did not walk He/She/It did not walk	Did you walk? Did we/they walk? Did he/she/it walk? Why did you walk there? Where did they walk to?
to be	I was You/We/They were He/She/It was	I was not You/We/They were not He/She/It was not	Was I . . .? Were you/we/they . . .? Was he/she/it . . .? Why were you at the store? When was he in Europe?
irregular verb *to have*	I had You/We/They had He/She/It had	I did not have You/We/They did not have He/She/It did not have	Did you have . . .? Did we/they have . . .? Did he/she/it have . . .? Why did she leave?
irregular verb *to go*	I went You/We/They went He/She/It went	I did not go You/We/They did not go He/She/It did not go	Did you go? Did they go? Did it go? When did they go?

Spellings of simple past -ed forms

Spelling rule	Examples
for verbs ending in **-e**, add **-d** to the verb	love → loved
for verbs ending in two consonants, add **-ed** to the verb	melt → melted
for verbs ending in a **consonant + -y**, change the **y** to **i** and add **-ed**	study → studied
for one-syllable verbs ending in a vowel and a consonant, double the consonant* and add **-ed**.	stop → stopped
for one-syllable verbs ending in two vowels and a consonant, no double consonant, add **-ed**	rain → rained need → needed
for two-syllable verbs ending in a stressed syllable, double the consonant, add **-ed**.	prefer → preferred
for two-syllable verbs ending in an unstressed syllable, add **-ed**	listen → listened visit → visited
for verbs ending in a **vowel + -y**, add **-ed**	play → played
for verbs ending in **-ie**, add **-d** to the verb	die → died

* **EXCEPTIONS**: do not double *w* or *x*. For example, *snow–snowed*; *tax–taxed*.

Exercise 1

Correct the **-ed** verb form errors in the text. The first is completed as an example. There are 15 more errors.

appeared

Yesterday I played tennis with Sally. She **appearred** to be unhappy and

explainned that she needed help for her chemistry class. She complainned

that no one in class had offerred to help. I listenned and tryed to understand.

I pointted out that if she studyed and planed to meet the teacher, she

might get some help. She admitted that I had offerred a reasonable plan,

but she prefered to find her own solution. She hopped she hadn't stoped

me from enjoying the game of tennis. I omited to mention that I was not

worryed because I was winning because she was so distracted.

Information questions (*Wh*- questions)

The word order for asking most information questions is

Question word(s) + **A**uxiliary (helping verb) + **S**ubject + **V**erb + rest of sentence (**QASV**)

	Q	A	S	V	Rest of sentence
simple past (except *to be*)	Where	did did	Peter the students	go? study	English?
to be	Where When	was were	Peter the exams?		last night?

Exercise 2

Change the following statements into negative statements and questions in simple past.

EXAMPLE   In 2016 Henry **worked** on a farm. (original)

He **did not work** on a farm. (negative)

When did he work on a farm? (question)

1. The class started at 3 PM.

    _____

    _____

2. He went to a wedding last week.

    _____

    _____

3. Jane and Joseph took pictures of the space shuttle launch.

    _____

    _____

4. Drones were invented by the US military.

    _____

    _____

5. Researchers found that Internet use affects attention span.

    _____

    _____

6. Sarah felt sad after watching the movie.

    _____

    _____

Exercise 3

Fill in the blanks with the correct form of the simple past.

Tony Sarg _____ (be) born in Guatemala to German parents in 1880. He _____ (have) success as an illustrator, cartoonist, and puppeteer. Sarg's family _____ (return) to Germany in 1887 and he _____ (grow) up familiar with old world marionette techniques; his maternal grandmother was an artist and _____ (have) an extensive collection of puppets, miniature houses, and mechanical toys, which he _____ (inherit). This _____ (lead) to a lifelong fascination with puppetry. In Germany, Sarg _____ (study) in the German military academy and _____ (begin) to show publishers his drawings. Sarg _____ (marry) an American and in 1915 they moved to New York City. Within two years he was in demand both as an illustrator and puppeteer, illustrating for the *Saturday Evening Post*. In 1921, Sarg _____ (draw) images for the film *The First Circus*.

In 1928, he _____ (design) and _____ (build) tethered inflatable figures (helium-filled balloons), up to 40 m long, that could be paraded down Broadway for Macy's. The largest was a dragon and it _____ (take) 50 handlers to operate it.

A few years later, he _____ (create) the first set of the store's animated window displays for Thanksgiving and Christmas. Perhaps the summit of Sarg's creative career _____ (come) at the 1933 Chicago World's Fair, where he _____ (win) several awards; he _____ (understand) the value of his unique "brand" and _____ (sell) puppets for both the Chicago and New York World's Fairs. Nonetheless, his techniques _____ (stay, *neg.*) up to date and competing puppet studios _____ (hire, *neg.*) him. He _____ (become, *neg.*) rich and in 1939 he _____ (lose) more business and declared bankruptcy. He _____ (withdraw) from the city; however, he _____ (make) puppets, books, and puzzles until he _____ (die) in 1942.

Exercise 4

It is 1939 and, while working as a journalist for the *New York Times*, you have been asked to conduct an interview with Tony Sarg.

Create a series of questions in which you ask about his childhood, family, early career, and inventions, and the process of creating cartoons or puppets—use your imagination! You can also ask his "opinion" about the context of his work (World War I, the Great Depression, and World War II).

1. _____

2. _____

3. _____

4. _____

5. _____

6. _____

7. _____

8. _____

9. _____

10. _____

Exercise 5

1. Use the information in the text as well as your own information to complete this past tense timeline about Tony Sarg.

1880	1887	1914	1915	1918	1921	1929	1933	1939	1941	1942
									Japan attacked Pearl Harbor and America entered WW2.	

Past Progressive

We use the past progressive for actions that were in progress in the past. It often describes the background past: actions that were happening at the same time (simultaneous actions) or were interrupted. Like the present progressive, the past progressive is rarely used with non-progressive (stative) verbs.

EXAMPLES

As I **was talking** on the phone, the line went dead.

While Sam **was driving** home, the wind **was blowing** and it became harder to see the road.

We **were walking** when it started to snow.

Forming the past progressive

Affirmative	Negative	Question
I was working	I was not working	Was I working?
You/We/They were working	You were not working	Were you working?
He/She/It was working	He was not working	Was he working?
		Short answer
		Yes, you were.
		No, I wasn't.
		Yes, he was.

Information questions using the past progressive

The word order for asking most information questions is:

Question word(s) + **A**uxiliary (helping verb) + **S**ubject + **V**erb + rest of sentence (**QASV**)

Q	A	S	V	Rest of sentence
What	were	the children	playing?	
When	was	Jenny	working	at the café?

204   Explore 2

Exercise 6

1. Answer the following questions using the past progressive.

   a) What were you doing last night?

   _____

   b) What were you doing at 7:00 this morning?

   _____

   c) What were you doing when you heard Donald Trump had been elected president of the US?

   _____

   d) What were you doing before you came to class today?

   _____

2. Make questions with the past progressive for the following underlined responses.

   a) The illustrator was designing the campaign.

   _____

   b) The illustrator was designing the campaign.

   _____

   c) Crowds were lining the streets of New York to see the parades.

   _____

   d) People were gathering in the streets of New York to see the parades.

   _____

3. Change the answers you wrote in question 1 to negative statements.

   EXAMPLE   I was eating before class. → I was not eating before class.

Exercise 7

Fill in the blanks with correct forms of the simple past and past progressive.

Amelia Earhart _____ (be) 10 when she _____ (see) her first airplane at a state fair, but it wasn't until she _____ (attend) a stunt-flying exhibition, almost a decade later, that she _____ (become) seriously interested in aviation. A pilot _____ (spot) Earhart and her friend, who _____ (watch) from a field, and he _____ (fly) toward them. Earhart _____ (tell) reporters that she _____ (feel) a mixture of fear and pleasure, but she _____ (stand) her ground. She _____ (say) that as the plane _____ (fly) nearby, something inside her awakened.

"I _____ (understand, *neg.*) it at the time," she admitted, "but I believe that little red airplane _____ (bring) something to me as it swished by."

On December 28, 1920, pilot Frank Hawks _____ (give) her a ride that would forever change her life. "By the time we _____ (fly) two or three hundred feet off the ground, I knew I had to fly. While Hawks _____ (show) me the controls, I _____ (already, plan) my airborne future."

Although Earhart's convictions were strong, she had to overcome challenging prejudicial and financial obstacles. Earhart _____ (take) her first flying lesson on January 3, 1921, and, in six months, _____ (make) enough money to buy her first plane. She _____ (buy) a second-hand Kinner Airster, a two-seater biplane painted bright yellow—Earhart _____ (name) it *The Canary*— and _____ (use) it to set her first women's record when she _____ (rise) to an altitude of 4267 m.

One afternoon in April 1928, while Earhart _____ (work), she _____ (receive) a phone call.

She said she initially _____ (think) it was a prank and said she _____ (*neg.* want) to take the call. It wasn't until the caller _____ (give) excellent references that she _____ (know) the man was serious. "How would you like to be the first woman to fly the Atlantic?" he asked, to which Earhart promptly _____ (reply), "Yes!"

Exercise 8

Time expressions and time clauses such as *while, when, at the age of 22, the following year, two years later,* and *when she was 10* are useful for recounting events in the past as they link the ideas from one sentence to the next and help the reader follow a cohesive and coherent story.

Use the following notes from a talk that you attended about the life of Amelia Earhart. Use a variety of verbs, simple past and past progressive, time clauses, and complex or compound sentences to write a 10- to 12-sentence report.

- June 17, 1928: departure with Bill Stulz and Slim Gordon from Trepassey Harbour, Newfoundland. 21 hours later arrival in Burry Port, Wales, UK
- August 1928: first woman to fly solo across North America and back
- 1929: promoting development of passenger airline service
- 1930: official at National Aeronautic Association; President of the Ninety-Nines, an organization of female pilots
- February 7, 1931: marriage to publicist George Putnam; feminist "partnership"
- May 20, 1932: solo flight Newfoundland to Paris; weather and mechanical problems forced landing 14 hours and 56 minutes after departure in Londonderry, Ireland
- January 11, 1935: the first person to fly solo across the Pacific from Honolulu to Oakland, California
- 1935 Purdue University: women's career counsellor and technical advisor in Department of Aeronautics
- June 1, 1937: Earhart and navigator, Fred Noonan, leave Miami for 40 075–km circumnavigation of the globe eastward in a Lockheed Electra 10E
- June 29: arrival in Lae, New Guinea
- July 2: zero Greenwich time, departure for Howland Island, 4113 km away from Lae, in the mid-Pacific
- 7:42 AM "We must be on you, but we cannot see you. Fuel is running low."
- 8:45 AM Last message: "We are running north and south."

Expressing past habits with *used to*

We describe a past habit or a situation that is no longer true or no longer occurring with ***use(d) to* + simple form of verb**.

EXAMPLES

I **used to live** in Madrid. (Now I live in Montreal)

Did you use to live in Madrid?

I **didn't use to drink** coffee. (Now I do)

I **never used to drink** coffee. (Now I do)

Exercise 9

1. Fill in the blanks with correct forms of the simple present, present progressive, simple past, and past progressive.

What _____ (know, you, *quest.*) about the changing workplace? _____ (have, your grandparents, *quest.*) stable lifelong jobs? _____ (be, the situation, *quest.*) the same for your parents? _____ (think, you, *quest.*) will find work easily when you leave college or university?

In the past, Canadian high school graduates _____ (use) to be able to leave school and be employed in secure permanent positions. In the 1980s young people _____ (use) to be able to select a university subject that they _____ (enjoy) and then they _____ (apply) for "graduate" entry-level positions. Employment opportunities worldwide _____ (change) and temporary work _____ (growing) at a faster pace than permanent positions. The number of temporary workers in Canada _____ (reach) a record 2 million in 2012, according to Statistics Canada. This _____ (consist) of 13.6 percent of the work force, compared with 11.3 percent in 1997, when this type of data collection _____ (begin).

Temporary contract work _____ (give) many employers a more flexible work force; this _____ (mean) they can adapt rapidly to the ebbs and flows of demand for workers. Some people _____ (want, *neg.*) to be tied down to one employer and prefer contract work; however, for many workers contract work _____ (lead, *neg.*) to freedom. On the contrary, precarious work conditions are causing uncertainty, underemployment, and stress.

A study by McMaster University in February 2013 _____ (find) four out of ten people in the Greater Toronto region _____ (be) in some degree of precarious work. Researchers _____ (define) this as "employment that lacks security or benefits." They _____ (find) that there _____ (be) almost 50 percent more contract jobs in 2013 than in 1993. They also _____ (report) that contract workers often _____ (have, *neg.*) enough work and they rarely _____ (get) benefits.

Nevertheless, some human resource specialists _____ (claim) that temporary work _____ (bring) benefits for employers and employees. It _____ (let) both try each other out before committing to permanent positions. It _____ (be) a good entry point into the labour market. Temporary contracts frequently _____ (lead) to offers of permanent work.

2. Create questions about work conditions. The first answer is provided as an example.

a) Where/work/you?
   Where do you work?
   _____

b) Look/you/for a job/at the moment?
   _____

c) Be/your first job/what?
   _____

d) How/get/you/the job?
   _____

e) You/have/a permanent job?
   _____

f) Offer/your job/benefits?
   _____

g) Be/how long/your contract?
   _____

h) Work/you/where/after college?
   _____

i) Take/how long/you/to get a permanent job?
   _____

j) Like/you/about temporary work/what?
   _____

k) What/the disadvantages of temporary work/be?
   _____

Review Exercise

1. Identify an important inventor or contributor from your field of study (e.g., Thomas Edison, Louis Pasteur, Marie Curie, Sigmund Freud, Pablo Picasso).

2. When was the person born? What did he or she achieve?

3. Create a timeline for this person's life and important world events of the time. Indicate both the year and the achievement or event.

4. Write a brief paragraph of five to six past tense sentences. Your topic sentence should state the key contribution, importance, and identity of the person. Then support your claim with facts and evidence of the person's work.

5. Be ready to share the text with other students and to ask questions about other key figures.

_____

_____

_____

_____

_____

_____

Communicative Activities

1. Complete the timeline with information about your own life and events that have happened during your lifetime. Share your timeline with a partner and ask questions for more information.

   2000   2001   2005   2010   2012   2015   2016   2017

2. Work with a partner. Take turns talking about the following events. Listen to your partner and ask at least two questions about what he or she tells you.
   a) What did you do last summer? Where were you working? Where were you studying? Where were you living? Use a variety of verbs in the past tenses to describe what you did.
   b) You had an interview for a job, a work placement, or a course. Use a variety of verbs in the past tense to describe what you said or did.
   c) Imagine you are 40 years old. What did you learn at college? What did you use to do in class? What was your life like? Use a variety of past tense verbs to describe what you did in college.
   d) Describe a favourite memory. Where were you? What happened? Who was there? Use a variety of past tense verbs to describe the memory.

CHAPTER 4
Future Tense

Go to Explore Online for additional activities using the future tense.

We use the future tense to talk about events that will occur at a time later than now. There are two ways to form the future: **will + verb** and **be going to + verb**.

Time expressions used when talking about the future

today	**this** + time period
tonight	this week
tomorrow	this year
tomorrow evening	this month
later tonight	this afternoon
in + time period	**next** + time period
in 10 minutes	next Friday
in five years	next week
in 10 months	next month

Future Using *will*

We use **will + verb** to talk about future predictions and to give facts about the future.

EXAMPLES

Many people **will use** 3D printers in the near future.

Soon drones **will deliver** goods for Amazon.

We use **will + verb** for decisions that are made at the moment of speaking.

EXAMPLE

A: The phone is ringing

B: I **will get** it.

We use **will + verb** for promises.

EXAMPLE   I **will help** you clean the garage tomorrow.

Affirmative		Negative		Question
I will (I'll) You will (You'll) He/She/It will (He'll, She'll, It'll) We will (We'll) They will (They'll)	. . . finish the internship this year.	I will not (won't) You will not (won't) He/She/It will not (won't) We will not (won't) They will not (won't)	. . . finish the internship this year.	Will you finish your internship this year? Will they finish the internship this year? When will you finish your internship?

Information questions (*Wh-* questions) using *will*

Question word(s) + **A**uxiliary (helping verb) + **S**ubject + **V**erb + rest of sentence (**QASV**)

Q	A	S	V	Rest of sentence
Where	will	you	study?	
Where	will	Ben	go	to school next year?

Exercise 1

Fill in the blanks with the correct form of *will*.

1. In the future companies _____ (use) drones to deliver goods.

2. In the future 3D printers _____ (cost, *neg.*) as much as they do now.

3. She _____ (get) a promotion this year.

4. Where _____ (work) when you finish your internship?

5. The workplace _____ (be) very different in the next 10 years.

Exercise 2

Write questions to match the answers using *will*.

1. _____

   The workplace will be very different in the future.

2. _____

   Driverless technology will be safe in 10 years.

3. _____

   Drones will soon be able to deliver pizza to our homes.

4. _____

   Workers will change jobs so often because they want more fulfillment.

Future Using *be going to*

We use **be going to + verb** for future predictions, future facts, and future plans.

> **EXAMPLE**   I'm **going to study** accounting next year.

We use **be going to + verb** for decisions made before we speak.

> **EXAMPLE**   I am thirsty. I **am going to get** a drink.

Affirmative		Negative		Question
I am (I'm) You are (You're) She/He is (She's/He's) We are (We're) They are (They're)	. . . going to spend the summer in Mexico.	I am not (I'm not) You are not (You're not) She/He is not (She's/He's not) We are not (We're not) They are not (They're not)	. . . going to spend the summer in Mexico.	Is she going to spend the summer in Mexico? Are they going to spend the summer in Mexico? Where are you going to spend the summer?

Information questions (*Wh-* questions) using *be going to*

Question word(s) + Auxiliary (helping verb + Subject + Verb + rest of sentence (**QASV**)

Q	A	S	V	Rest of sentence
What	is	everyone	doing?	
When	are	Jenny and Jace	coming to visit	Montreal?

Exercise 3

Fill in the blanks with the correct form of *be going to*.

1. I _____ (live) in London for a year.

2. We _____ (travel) to Quebec City for the weekend.

3. She _____ (come, *neg.*) for dinner. She's busy.

4. _____ (we/study) at the library this afternoon?

Communicative Activity 1

With a partner or a small group, look at the following topics. Make predictions about these topics using *will* or *be going to*.

1. technology

2. space travel

3. transportation

4. education

5. poverty in the world

6. population growth

7. pollution

Future Using *will* or *be going to*

Will and *be going to* are used interchangeably to make predictions and to give facts. Sometimes only one expression—*will* or *be going to*—is appropriate.

We use only ***will* + verb** when

- making decisions at the moment of speaking
- making promises

We use only ***be going to* + verb** for

- decisions made before we speak
- future plans

Exercise 4

Fill in the blanks using phrases with *will* or *be going to*.

1. We are excited about our trip to Europe this summer. _____ (visit) London and Paris.

2. I feel really tired. I think I _____ (go) to bed.

3. She has made her decision. She _____ (get) a job in Toronto next year.

4. A: Oh no. I forgot my wallet.

   B: I _____ (lend) you some money.

5. There is a conference next week in Quebec City. She _____ (drive) there on Monday.

Future time clauses

With the following time clauses, we use the simple present tense to talk about the future.

when	before	after	as soon as	if	as long as	unless

EXAMPLES

When people **use** the Internet a lot for many years, their ability to concentrate gets worse.

After she **finishes** her internship, she will get a job in her field of study.

As soon as I **get** home, I will take the dog for a walk.

Exercise 5

Fill in the blanks with the present tense or future tense.

1. When the teacher _____ (arrive) the class _____ (start).

2. I _____ (visit) you as soon as I _____ (finish) work.

3. After I _____ (get) work experience, I _____ (find) a better job.

4. She _____ (travel) for a year before she _____ (begin) university.

5. I _____ (travel) a lot before I _____ (have) children.

6. As soon as she _____ (complete) her degree, she _____ (get) a job in Vancouver.

Future Using the Simple Present and Present Progressive

We also use the present tenses to talk about the future.

The simple present tense is used to talk about a future schedule that always occurs at the same time.

> **EXAMPLES** The train **leaves** at 6:00 PM.
>
> The class **starts** at 8:00 PM.

The present progressive is used to talk about events that we have arranged to do in the future.

> **EXAMPLES** I **am meeting** my boss for lunch today.
>
> We **are leaving** on Saturday.

Exercise 6

Choose between simple present and present progressive.

1. The party _____ (begin) at 7:00 PM.

2. People _____ (arrive) sometime between 7:00 and 8:00 PM.

3. Lisa _____ (come) over for dinner tonight.

4. My flight _____ (leave) at 9:00 AM next Saturday.

Communicative Activity 2

With a partner, use the key words to make questions and then answer them together.

1. Robots/replace/humans

   _____

2. Robots/our jobs/take

   _____

3. People/live/longer

   _____

4. Technology/change/future

   _____

5. Life/easier/more difficult

   _____

6. Money/future/be like

   _____

CHAPTER 5

Present Perfect Tense

We use the present perfect tense for

- activities or situations that occurred or did not occur at an **unspecified time in the past**. When asking questions, *ever* and *never* are often used.

    EXAMPLES

    I**'ve** already **gone** on a fishing trip.

    Have you ever **gone** fishing?

- **duration** using *since* or *for*—when something began in the past and continues in the present.

    EXAMPLE   I**'ve taken** piano lessons since I was five/for most of my life.

- activities that were **repeated** several or many times; the exact times are not specified.

    EXAMPLE   I**'ve seen** U2 in concert about ten times.

- activities or situations in a time frame that is **not yet completed**.

    EXAMPLE   Karin **hasn't made** dinner yet. (she will soon)

- activities that occurred in the **recent past**, often used with *just*.

    EXAMPLE   He**'s just cut** his finger.

The present perfect is formed with the auxiliary ***have/has*** **+ past participle** of a verb. For regular verbs, use an **-ed** ending.

 Go to Explore Online for additional activities using the present perfect tense.

For a list of common irregular verbs, see Appendix 4, page 280.

Affirmative	Negative	Question
I have worked	I have not worked	Have I worked?
You have worked	You have not worked	Have you worked?
He/She/It has worked	He/She/It has not worked	Has he/she/it worked?
We/They have worked	We/They have not worked	Have we/they worked?
Irregular verbs		
I have spoken	I have not spoken	Have I spoken?
You have spoken	You have not spoken	Have you spoken?
He/She/It has gone	He/She/It has not gone	Has he/she/it gone?
We/They have been	We/They have not been	Have we/they been?
		Where has she been all summer?

Exercise 1

Use the present perfect (**have/has** + past participle) of the verb in parentheses.

> **EXAMPLE** (hear, you, ever, *quest.*) **Have you ever heard** of Steven Pinker?

1. Psychologists _____ (study) human behaviour for many years.

2. Have _____ (meet, you, ever, *quest.*) with a psychologist?

3. Pascale _____ (teach) psychology at the university since 2010.

4. Steven Pinker _____ (write) about human behaviour and language learning.

5. Pinker _____ (work) in the US for several years.

6. The field of medicine _____ (advance) enormously since the 19th century.

7. In the last fifty years, researchers _____ (make) many medical discoveries.

8. Car manufacturing _____ (change) considerably in recent years.

9. Globalization _____ (lead) to increased levels of pollution.

10. Elizabeth Gilbert _____ (speak) around the world about creativity.

11. Gilbert _____ (do) at least two Ted Talks.

12. _____ (go, you, ever, *quest.*) to a Ted conference?

Time Expressions

The present perfect expresses duration using *since* and *for*.

Since indicates the specific point in time when the activity began.

> **EXAMPLE** I**'ve played** a musical instrument **since** 2010/**since** last year/**since** yesterday.

For indicates the length of time or the duration.

> **EXAMPLE** I**'ve played** a musical instrument **for** five years/**for** a long time/**for** a while.

Exercise 2

Use the present perfect and *since* or *for* to complete the following sentences.

1. We _____ (be) in class **for/since** an hour.

2. I _____ (live) in my apartment **for/since** ten years.

3. We _____ (work) together **for/since** 2014.

4. Scientists _____ (study) the roots of creativity **for/since** many years.

5. Neurologists _____ (research) brain plasticity **for/since** they discovered the brain could change.

Present Perfect Progressive

We use the present perfect progressive tense to express how long an activity has been in progress—its duration. Some verbs do not change meaning if they are in progressive or simple form (e.g., *live, work, teach*). Non-progressive/non-action verbs are not used in the present perfect progressive (e.g., *believe, understand, hear*).

The present perfect progressive is formed with the auxiliary **have/has + been + verb + -ing**.

Affirmative	Negative	Question
I have been studying.	I have not been studying.	Have I been studying?
You have been studying.	You have not been studying.	Have you been studying?
He/She/It has been working.	He/She/It has not been working.	Has he/she/it been working?
You/We/They have been travelling.	You/We/They have not been travelling.	Have you/we/they been travelling?

Exercise 3

Use the present perfect and present perfect progressive to complete the following sentences.

1. I _____ (teach) biology since 2010.

2. Tom _____ (study) science at McGill for a year.

3. Gilbert _____ (write) two novels so far.

4. The team _____ (research) cancer treatments for three years;

    they _____ (publish, *neg.*) their results yet.

5. I _____ (speak) to Human Resources about work conditions.

6. I _____ (pay, *neg.*) my registration fees yet.

7. Mohammed and Mona _____ (read) all evening, but they still

    _____ (finish, *neg.*) their assignment.

8. Hugh _____ (fly) planes for Air Creebec since 2015.

9. Sally _____ (come, *neg.*) home for the past three months.

10. Ali _____ (work) at Labtech for two years.

Present Perfect and Simple Past

The simple past expresses an activity that occurred at a specific time in the past.

The present perfect expresses an activity that occurred at an unspecified time in the past, a repeated past action, or an action that began in the past and continues in the present.

EXAMPLES

SP: I **was in** Sydney in 2015.

PP: I **have been** to Sydney.

SP: I **ate** at the restaurant last night.

PP: I**'ve eaten** at the restaurant several times.

Exercise 4

Use either simple past or present perfect of the verbs in parentheses.

Since 2000, autonomous vehicles _____ (gain) a lot of interest. Many inventors, academics, and entrepreneurs _____ (be) involved in different projects. Google's self-driving car project _____ (start) in 2009 under the leadership of Sebastian Thrun, a Stanford University professor. Thrun _____ (begin) his research on driverless vehicles at Stanford. In 2005 he _____ (design) the Stanley robot car, which _____ (win) the 2005 DARPA Grand Challenge; it _____ (drive) 212 km on its own. In 2009, Google _____ (launch) its project in California. Since then, testing _____ (expand) to include rainy and desert conditions. The company _____ (develop) GPS, sensors, cameras, radar, and lasers to allow the cars "to see" the world around them. The test cars _____ (drive) over 3 million km in four cities around the US, and the cars _____ (learn) how to sense cyclists and pedestrians. The technology of autonomous vehicles _____ (advance) since 2009; however, in February 2016, a Google car _____ (cause) an accident; it was travelling at only about 3 km an hour when it _____ (hit) a bus. Google _____ (fail) so far to commercialize its cars, and the company _____ (lose) some of its best innovators to other companies. Google _____ (want) to launch a fully autonomous vehicle for over ten years now.

Exercise 5

Use either simple past, present perfect, or present perfect progressive of the verbs in parentheses.

EXAMPLE   (hear, you, ever, *quest.*) **Have you ever heard** of Boyan Slat?

Boyan Slat _____ (create) a foundation to clean up the world's oceans when he _____ (be) only 17 years old. Slat says he _____ (invent) things since he was a child. When he _____ (be) 16, he was diving in Greece and was shocked to see more plastic than fish in the water. He _____ (decide) to look for a solution; he used the idea as the topic of a high school science project. In February 2013, Slat _____ (drop out) of an aerospace engineering program to start The Ocean Cleanup.

He _____ (found) The Ocean Cleanup to use technology to solve the enormous problem of plastic and other debris in the ocean. The Ocean Cleanup's technology _____ (develop) long floating rubber barriers with nets below the surface that act as a sort of artificial coastline, catching debris using ocean currents. When the current _____ (pull) debris to one location, boats can then transport the plastic from the ocean and it can be sold as recycled material to manufacturers.

The Ocean Cleanup _____ (grow) since 2013; in 2014, Slat _____ (raise) $2.2 million through a crowd-funding campaign. Over the past few years, he _____ (raise) another $10 million from entrepreneurs in Silicon Valley and in Europe. Slat _____ (receive, also) money from the Dutch government.

Ecologists and scientists _____ (test) Slat's technology since last summer. Scientists _____ (investigate) a 100-metre-long segment of the barrier for four months in the North Sea. Researchers _____ (collect) data to see how successful the barriers are at actually trapping the plastic.

The goal is to create a 100-km barrier that will first be used in what's known as the Great Pacific Garbage Patch. This area _____ (accumulate) marine debris—including plastic—over many decades.

In 2015 Boyan Slat _____ (win) the UN Champion of the Earth prize and *Time* magazine _____ (choose) The Ocean Cleanup as one of the best 25 inventions.

Exercise 6

Use either simple present, present progressive, simple past, past progressive, present perfect, or present perfect progressive of the verbs in parentheses.

Steven Pinker is an experimental psychologist who writes extensively about language, the mind, and human nature. Pinker _____ (live) in Boston and _____ (work, currently) at Harvard University.

Pinker _____ (be) a renowned writer who _____ (make) vast contributions to understanding human behaviour. Pinker _____ (be) born in 1954 in the English-speaking Jewish community of Montreal. He _____ (have) a bachelor's degree in experimental psychology from McGill. While he _____ (study) at McGill he _____ (become) interested in language. Pinker _____ (continue) his doctoral and postdoctoral work at Harvard and MIT. He _____ (research, presently) language, cognition, and the mind at Harvard.

Pinker _____ (write) extensively about language learning since the 1980s. He _____ (publish) several studies about the genetics and neurobiology of language. In 1994 he _____ (write) *The Language Instinct* and _____ (follow) this in 1997 with *How the Mind Works*. Both books _____ (be) international bestsellers and have been translated around the world. Pinker _____ (change) the way we talk about talking and think about thinking. Pinker _____ (win) prizes from the National Academy of Sciences and the American Psychological Association. He _____ (also, receive) eight honorary doctorates from universities around the world. In 2004 *Time* magazine _____ (include) Pinker in its list of "The 100 Most Influential People in the World Today."

Pinker regularly _____ (write) for newspapers such as *The New York Times* and *The Guardian* about language, morals, and human behaviour.

Until Pinker, most 20th century psychologists _____ (describe) the mind as a blank slate or a computer without programs. Pinker _____ (agree, *neg.*) with this comparison.

In *The Language Instinct*, Pinker _____ (use) ideas from Darwin and _____ (argue) that the human mind is a genetically based word processor based on natural selection.

Pinker _____ (discuss) the role of biology, but he _____ (stress) that biology is not destiny.

"Nature," he quotes Katharine Hepburn's character in *The African Queen* as saying, "is what we were put in this world to rise above."

Exercise 7

Answer one of the following questions with four to five sentences using a variety of verb tenses.

1. "Have you ever heard of . . .?" Describe the achievements and career of a significant person working in your field of study. What has the person invented or created?

2. What designs or innovations have changed your field of study? Explain the role of these innovations.

Communicative Activities

1. For this interview dialogue, use either simple past, past progressive, present perfect, or present perfect progressive of the verbs in parentheses. Then add questions and answers and practise the dialogue with a partner.

   A: Thank you for coming in for an interview, Ms. Higgins. _____ (have, you, *quest.*) any problems finding the offices?

   B: No. It _____ (be) very easy. Your assistant _____ (give) very clear directions.

   A: _____ (be, you, how long, *quest.*) out of work?

   B: I _____ (look) for a new job for the past month. I _____ (work) at Pricelane until last month. The location I _____ (work) at in the city _____ (close) down. There _____ (be) major building work on the street outside the store and businesses _____ (suffer) since early this year.

A: I _____ (hear) about the problems there; it must have been difficult. _____ (work, you, *quest.*) at Pricelane for a long time?

B: I _____ (start) working there immediately after I _____ (graduate) from university. I _____ (work) there for five years and _____ (consider) a change of job since earlier this year.

A: What _____ (learn, you, *quest.*) at Pricelane?

B: Five years ago I _____ (arrive) at the company directly after my marketing internship. I _____ (have) many new ideas, but I _____ (find) it difficult to implement them. I _____ (learn) how to develop projects and to work in teams. I _____ (work) in sales and in the past year I _____ (manage) a sales team. Our store _____ (win) several corporate awards for its marketing plans.

A: What _____ (be, *quest.*) your responsibilities?

B: I _____ (be) responsible for team meetings . . .

Using a variety of verb tenses, continue this interview dialogue with two more questions and answers.

A: _____

B: _____

A: _____

B: _____

2. Create an online interview with either Boyan Slat, Steven Pinker, or Sebastian Thrun. Ask at least 10 questions (*when, where, what, why, how long*, etc.) using simple present, simple past, and present perfect. Write appropriate answers using information from the unit or information you find online.

3. Write eight to ten sentences to apply for a job related to your field of study. Use the **simple present** to describe skills you have and statements of fact. Use **present perfect** to describe what you have done prior to this time and to describe the duration of your experiences (how long you have worked or studied). Use **simple past** to describe specific experiences you had (e.g., what you did in your summer job).

   EXAMPLE   I **have studied** dental hygiene for the past three years.

4. Share your sentences with a partner. Ask at least two questions about the information your partner shares and then write a recommendation/reference letter of four to five sentences to support your partner's job application.

   EXAMPLE   I recommend Manuel for the position because he works hard. He has studied aircraft maintenance for three years and last year he received the highest grade in his class.

Review Exercise

Correct the verb tense errors in the following sentences.

1. Steven Pinker is born in 1954. _____

2. Pinker have had a lot of publications. _____

3. In the 1970s he has studied at McGill. _____

4. Pinker is publishing papers every year. _____

5. He become interested in the brain while he were studying. _____

6. He has published *The Language Instinct* in 1994. _____

7. Pinker write for several newspapers. _____

8. Pinker will winning prizes for his work. _____

9. Pinker is living in Boston since he studied at Harvard. _____

10. Several students become experimental psychologists under Pinker's guidance. _____

CHAPTER 6
Modal Auxiliaries

Modal auxiliary (or helping) verbs are used to indicate functions, attitude, or mood such as ability, making requests, expressing possibility, asking or giving permission, giving advice, expressing obligation (something you have to do), etc. A modal auxiliary verb is always used with a main verb. Common modals include *can*, *could*, *may*, *might*, *must*, *should*, and *would*.

EXAMPLES

I **could** come by on Thursday.

You **should** accept that job offer.

May I ask you about your experiences?

Common Modal Auxiliaries

Modal	Meaning	Past tense of modal	Example
can	to express ability	could; was able to	She can speak three languages. She was able to speak Japanese as a child.
	to make a request		Can I borrow your phone?
	to give an option		We can work at school or at home.
could	to express past ability	could	She could speak Japanese as a child.
	to make a polite request		Could you lend me your class notes?
	to express possibility		It could rain tomorrow.
may	to express possibility		I may be late for work.
	to ask for permission		May I use your phone?
might	to express possibility		She might go to Spain this summer.
should	to give advice		You should research the company before the job interview.
must	to express obligation	had to	You must arrive on time for the job interview.
must not	to express prohibition	did not have to (didn't have to)	You must not be late for work.
have to*	to express obligation	had to	I have to hand in my lab work today.
do not have to	to express lack of obligation	did not have to (didn't have to)	You don't have to wear formal clothing at the office.
will	for the future tense		I will go to Toronto this weekend.
would	to make a polite request		Would you please send me the report?
	for an unreal conditional		I would buy an electric car if I had enough money.
would rather	to express preference		I would rather drive than take the bus.
would like	to express desire		I would like to work in advertising.
be able to*	to express ability	was/were able to	She was able to express herself clearly in English.

Have to and *be able to* are conjugated like other verbs.

Some modals have more than one meaning. Most modals are not conjugated like other verbs. Their form never changes. For questions and negatives, modal auxiliaries do not need an additional auxiliary.

Negative Subject + modal + *not* + verb + rest of sentence

>**EXAMPLE** We might not make it to the event.

Questions Question word + modal + subject + verb + rest of sentence

>**EXAMPLE** What should she study at university?

Exercise 1

Change the following sentences into negative statements and questions.

>**EXAMPLE**
>
>Laura can find a summer job.
>
>Laura cannot find a summer job.
>
>Can Laura find a summer job?

1. Driverless cars could be safer than traditional cars.

   Negative: _____

   Question: _____

2. She should spend more time working on the project.

   Negative: _____

   Question: _____

3. Justin must move to another city to find a job in his field.

   Negative: _____

   Question: _____

4. Rooftop farming could become popular in many cities.

   Negative: _____

   Question: _____

5. Marianne would rather see a show tonight.

   Negative: _____

   Question: _____

Exercise 2

Fill in the blanks with the correct modal. The meaning is given in parentheses. Sometimes more than one answer is possible.

1. You _____ (obligation) always bring extra copies of your resumé when you go to a job interview.

2. You _____ (advice) prepare questions to ask at the end of the job interview.

3. We _____ (possibility) rent a cottage this summer. We are not sure yet.

4. We _____ (obligation) hire a new manager this summer.

5. I _____ (ability) speak three languages.

6. You _____ (prohibition) interrupt the speaker. You can ask questions at the end of the presentation.

7. She _____ (possibility) study engineering. She is not sure.

Have to and *be able to*

The only modals that are conjugated are *be able to* and *have to*. They can be used in the past, present, and future.

EXAMPLES

I **was not able to** complete the homework, but I **will be able to** hand it in tomorrow.

He **had to** travel for work last week.

Exercise 3

Fill in the blanks with the correct form of *be able to*. Make sure to use the correct verb tense.

1. Do you think you _____ finish the report by Friday? I know you are very busy.

2. The technician _____ fix my computer last week.

3. I _____ speak three languages fluently.

4. She _____ meet you next Friday.

5. I _____ save $5000 last year.

Must and *have to* (affirmative and negative)

Present tense	Meaning	Past tense
must	to express obligation	had to
must not	to express prohibition	did not have to (didn't have to)
have to*	to express obligation	had to
do not have to	to express lack of obligation	did not have to (didn't have to)

*Notice that *must* and *have to* have the same meaning in the affirmative, but not in the negative. Also, *had to* is used for the past tense of both modals.

Exercise 4

Fill in the blanks with *have to*, *must*, *don't have to*, or *must not*. Make sure to conjugate *have to*. Sometimes more than one answer is possible.

1. I _____ finish the report by tomorrow.

2. She _____ find a better job.

3. You _____ speak English to work at this company.

4. You _____ come to my graduation if you are busy.

5. You _____ wear a suit at work.

6. You _____ chew gum during a job interview.

Using modals for polite requests

Politeness in the workplace is very important. We can use modals to make requests more polite and less direct. We use *can, could,* and *would* to make requests. *Could* and *would* are more polite than *can*.

EXAMPLES

Can we meet to discuss some problems?   **Could** you drive me to work?

Would you be available next week?

Exercise 5

Look at each statement below and write a polite request.

1. You want to ask your boss for Friday off.

    _____

2. You want to ask your teacher for an extra day to finish an assignment.

    _____

3. You need help with a report.

    _____

4. You want to cancel a meeting.

    _____

Using modals for deductions

We can make deductions about the present using modals.

> *must be*: very sure that it is possible—99 percent
>
> *can't be*: very sure that it is not possible—99 percent
>
> *may/might/could be*: it is possible—50 percent

EXAMPLES

That **can't be** Michael on the phone. He's away this week.

You **must be** exhausted after running the marathon.

Lisa **might** come over later depending on when she finishes work.

Exercise 6

Fill in the blanks with the correct modal of possibility in the present tense. Choose between *must be, can't be,* and *might be*.

1. She isn't in her office. She _____ out.

2. They _____ away for the weekend. I am not sure.

3. She didn't sleep well last night. She _____ tired.

4. Jason is stuck in traffic. He _____ late for the meeting.

5. He _____ from the US. He doesn't speak English.

6. The exam _____ easy. We don't know.

We can also make deductions about the past using modals.

must have + past participle: very sure it was possible—99 percent

can't have + past participle: very sure it was not possible—99 percent

may/might/could + *have* + past participle: it was possible—50 percent

Exercise 7

Choose the correct past tense modal of deduction.

1. Charles is not here. I looked everywhere. He **must have/can't have** left the office early.

2. It **must have/might have** been a mistake to go out the night before the test.

3. Ana **can't have/might have** finished the exam already. It started 15 minutes ago.

4. Martina **must have/can't have** studied a lot for the exam. She got 95 percent.

Communicative Activity 2

In groups of four think of three problems related to your fields of study and think of three or more ways to solve each problem. Use a variety of modals in your answers.

EXAMPLE

Problem: In the field of medicine, there are not enough family doctors for everyone.

Solution: We should train more family doctors. Doctors must take more patients. Canadian doctors should not leave the country.

Review Exercise

Choose the correct modal for each sentence.

1. You **should/may** arrive five minutes early for the job interview.

2. I **might/must** find a job this summer. I am not sure.

3. You **must/can** be tired. You didn't sleep well last night.

4. When I was younger, I **could/can** play the piano.

5. I **am able to/could** work in teams and alone.

6. She **would rather/may** work in the city than in the suburbs.

7. Last year, she **had to/must not** complete an internship.

8. You **don't have to/must not** wear a helmet to go skating, but it is a good idea.

9. She **can't have/might have** forgotten our meeting. I reminded her yesterday.

10. She **shouldn't/couldn't** worry so much about her future. There are a lot of job opportunities in her field of study.

CHAPTER 7

Gerunds and Infinitives

Go to Explore Online for additional activities using gerunds and infinitives.

Verbs that are followed by other verbs sometimes take a gerund (**verb + -ing**) and sometimes take an infinitive (***to* + verb**). Some verbs can take both a gerund and an infinitive.

Verbs followed by a gerund (verb + *-ing*)		Verbs followed by an infinitive (*to* + verb)	
EXAMPLE		**EXAMPLE**	
I **enjoy meeting** my friends.		She **decided to look** for a job as a designer.	
admit	explain	agree	get
advise	finish	appear	hope
avoid	keep	ask	like
consider	like	choose	need
discuss	mention	come	promise
dislike	postpone	decide	wait
don't mind	suggest	demand	want
enjoy	understand	deserve	wish
		expect	would like

Exercise 1

Complete the sentences with the gerund or the infinitive.

1. I like _____ (work) in teams.

2. She wants _____ (live) in the country after she graduates.

3. Millennials expect _____ (change) jobs many times during their careers.

4. He admits _____ (be) nervous about giving oral presentations.

5. I would like _____ (study) in a foreign country.

6. I would consider _____ (move) to another city for work.

7. She expects _____ (find) challenging work after graduation.

Sometimes whether a verb is followed by a gerund or an infinitive changes the meaning of the sentence; sometimes it does not.

Verbs followed by a gerund or an infinitive—no change in meaning	Verbs followed by a gerund or an infinitive—the meaning changes
• She **likes working** with people. • She **likes to work** with people. like love dislike hate begin start attempt	**remember** • I never **remember to lock** the door. (I often forget to do it.) • I can't **remember locking the door**. (Maybe I locked it, maybe I didn't. I can't remember if I did it or not.) **forget** • Don't **forget to hand in** your assignment. (I would like you to hand in the assignment.) • I **forget meeting** him. (I don't remember meeting the person before.) **stop** • I **stopped to take off** my sweater. (I stopped running so I could take off my sweater.) • I **stopped drinking** energy drinks. (I read an article about their dangers, so I stopped drinking energy drinks.) **regret** • I **regret spending** too much money last summer. (I spent a lot of money in the summer and now I don't have enough money.) • I **regret to inform** you that your flight has been cancelled. (I am sorry to be giving you the bad news that your flight has been cancelled.) **try** • I can't lose weight. Have you **tried going** to the gym? (When you try doing something, you are doing it as an experiment.) • I **tried to find** a summer job in my field of study, but I couldn't. (I made an effort to find a job.)

Exercise 2

Fill in the blanks with the gerund or infinitive.

1. I remember _____ (go) to the beach as a child with my parents.

2. I remembered _____ (buy) milk and eggs on my way home from work.

3. I forgot _____ (call) my boyfriend today at work. I was so busy.

4. I forget _____ (study) this topic. Is there going to be a test on it?

5. I am trying _____ (save) money for my trip next summer. I am careful about my spending.

6. I tried _____ (finish) my project, but I didn't have enough time. I handed it in late.

7. She stopped _____ (smoke) two years ago. She is very happy she quit.

8. We stopped in London _____ (visit) my cousin before going to Paris.

9. I regret _____ (tell) you that you were not chosen for this position.

10. She regrets _____ (change) programs. She preferred the other program.

Communicative Activity

With a partner, complete the following sentences using a gerund or an infinitive.

1. When I am not studying I enjoy . . .

2. In the next year I plan . . .

3. To succeed in my field of study, I want . . .

4. I don't mind . . .

5. I don't expect . . .

6. I would never postpone . . .

7. I hope . . .

8. I would love . . .

9. I usually avoid . . .

10. People working in my field always need . . .

CHAPTER 8

Conditionals

Conditional sentences are used to talk about possibility or probability.

Conditional sentences contain two parts: an *if* **clause** that describes a condition and a **result clause** that describes the result. There are different types of conditionals depending on whether the result is certain, likely, or unlikely to occur.

 Go to Explore Online for additional practice using conditionals.

Conditional	Use	Form	Example
zero conditional	used to describe facts, truths, and situations that are certain	*if* **clause:** simple present **result clause:** simple present	Affirmative: If I am tired, I sleep. Negative: If it doesn't rain, the plants get dry.
first conditional (real)	used to describe a situation that will likely happen	*if* **clause:** simple present **result clause:** future	Affirmative: If I can get this weekend off work, we will go skiing. Negative: If I cannot get this weekend off work, we will not go skiing.
second conditional (unreal)	used to describe a situation that will probably not happen	*if* **clause:** past tense **result clause:** *would* + verb	Affirmative: If I had more time, I would get a second job. Negative: If I didn't have to pay off my credit card, I wouldn't get a second job. With the verb *to be*:* If I were you, I would get a second job. If I were you, I wouldn't get a second job.
third conditional	used to talk about impossible conditions that are in the past and cannot be changed	*if* **clause:** past perfect **result clause:** *would have* + past participle	Affirmative: If I had studied more, I would have passed the exam. (I did not study enough) Negative: If I hadn't gone away last weekend, I wouldn't have failed the exam.

*When we use the verb *to be* in the second conditional, *were* is used for all subjects.

The sentence can start with the *if* clause or can end with the *if* clause. Use a comma only when the sentence starts with the *if* clause.

EXAMPLES

If I had more time, I would get a second job.

I will study nursing next year if I am accepted into the program.

Communicative Activity 1

Work in pairs and complete each sentence for the type of conditional given.

1. If I work hard this semester . . . (first)

2. If I get a job this summer . . . (first)

3. If I get accepted into university next year . . . (first)

4. If I could change one thing about myself . . . (second)

5. If I had the opportunity to change the world . . . (second)

6. If I could do any job . . . (second)

7. If I could travel in time . . . (second)

8. If I had the opportunity to work in another country . . . (second)

Exercise 1

Fill in the blanks with the correct form of the first conditional.

If you want to find your dream job, you _____ (need) to follow your passion. If you _____ (be) passionate about your work, you _____ (be) successful in your career. If salary _____ (be) your main criterion for choosing a job, it is unlikely you _____ (find) a dream job. If you are looking for any work that will pay, you _____ (find) something, but it is unlikely to become a dream job. If, on the other hand, you are a professional who is looking for work where you apply your talents and education in a way that is meaningful to you, then it _____ (become) a dream job for you.

Exercise 2

Fill in the blanks with the correct form of the second conditional.

1. If you _____ (find) a wallet with a lot of money in it, what _____ you do?

2. If you _____ (have) the opportunity to live in another country, where _____ you live?

3. If I _____ (have) enough money, I _____ (buy) a big house.

4. If I _____ (live) in Australia, I _____ (be) far away from my family.

5. He _____ (call) her if he _____ (have) her phone number.

6. She _____ (get) a promotion if she _____ (have) more experience.

7. If Stanley _____ (be) at work, he _____ (have) helped with the project.

Remember: When we use the verb *to be* in the second conditional, *were* is used for all subjects.

Exercise 3

Change these sentences into the third conditional.

1. She failed the exam because she didn't study.

   _____

2. He missed the plane because he arrived at the airport too late.

   _____

3. I didn't know that they were hiring employees at Ubisoft. I want to work for that company.

   _____

4. We didn't know Sarah was at the party. We wanted to say hello.

   _____

Exercise 4

Fill in the blanks with the first, second, or third conditional.

1. If it _____ (rain) tomorrow, I _____ (take) my umbrella.

2. If she _____ (go) to the meeting yesterday, she _____ (meet) the new sales manager.

3. If she _____ (can) cook, she _____ (make) dinner for her friends (but she cannot cook).

4. Mathew didn't get the job. He _____ (get) the job if he _____ (prepare) more.

5. If I _____ (be) rich, I _____ (donate) money to charity.

6. If I _____ (be) accepted into my program, I _____ (move) closer to the university.

Using *wish* and *hope*

Wish is used when the speaker wants the reality to be different from or opposite to what it is.

We use **wish + past tense** to talk about present wishes.

   EXAMPLE   She **wishes** she **had** more time.

We use **hope + present tense** to express a desire for something in the future. It is very possible this will happen.

   EXAMPLE   I **hope** I **get** a good job this summer.

Exercise 5

Fill in the blanks with *wish* or *hope*.

1. I _____ scientists find a cure for cancer soon.

2. She _____ she had more money to spend this Christmas.

3. He _____ he lived in a warmer country. The winters are very long in Canada.

4. We _____ politicians take global warming seriously.

5. I _____ I spoke Spanish. It is very helpful when travelling in Latin America.

6. We _____ people won't use 3D printers to print guns illegally.

7. I _____ I had more time to do volunteer work.

Communicative Activity 2

With a partner, discuss these medical/moral dilemmas.

1. If you could clone a dead famous person, who would you clone?

2. If you could choose the sex of your baby, would you?

3. If everyone were using genetic manipulation to make sure their babies were tall, strong, smart, and healthy, would you use it?

4. If you could make money testing a new drug, would you take the risk?

5. If a heroin addict asked you for clean needles, would you give them to him?

Think of your own medical/moral dilemmas and share them with your partner.

CHAPTER 9

Quoted and Reported Speech, and Passive Voice

Quoted and Reported Speech

In reports and academic writing, we use quoted or direct speech and quotation marks ("_____") to write the speaker's exact words.

Reported or indirect speech conveys the speaker's idea, but uses pronouns and changes verb forms to the past tense.

Go to Explore Online for additional activities using the passive voice and quoted and reported speech.

Quoted speech	Reported speech
Max said, "I want a job."	Max said (that) he wanted a job.
He said, " I have a lot of experience."	He said (that) he had a lot of experience.
He said, "I am studying."	He said (that) he was studying.
He said, "I studied."	He said he had studied.
He said, "I have studied."	He said he had studied.
He said, "I have been studying."	He said he had been studying.
He said, "I will study."	He said he would study.
He said, "I may study."	He said that he might study.

Common verbs for introducing quotations or reported speech are *admit, answer, ask (if* or *whether), explain, state, report, write.*

Exercise 1

The quotes in the box on page 236 are answers to interview questions.

1.   What questions were asked to elicit these responses?

> **EXAMPLE**   The interviewer asked, "Do you like children?"

Tell or say

Tell must be followed by a noun/pronoun object.

> **EXAMPLE**
>
> He told **me** he studied.

Say does not require a noun/pronoun object.

> **EXAMPLE**
>
> He said he studied.

2. Use formal English to report the interview responses.

> **EXAMPLE**   Melanie stated that she liked working outside. She also said . . .

> "I want to work at Camp Kuringai this summer."
>
> "I like working outside and I like children."
>
> "I worked at a summer camp."
>
> "I have worked at the same camp for three years."
>
> "I have never had any accidents at the lake."
>
> "I took advanced CPR training earlier this year."
>
> "I will be available from May until the end of August."

Passive Voice

In academic and professional writing, we sometimes use the passive voice when we want to focus on the result rather than the person doing the action.

The passive voice is formed by conjugating the auxiliary **be + past participle** of the main verb. Only transitive verbs (verbs followed by an object) can be used in the passive voice.

The object of the active sentence becomes the subject of the passive voice sentence.

EXAMPLES

Dental hygienists clean teeth. → Teeth **are cleaned** by dental hygienists.

The professor gave a lecture. → A lecture **was given** (by the professor).

The passive voice is used when

- the focus is on the result rather than the person doing the action

  The company invented a new product → A new product **was invented** (by the company)

- it is obvious or not important who is actually doing the action

  Parliament will pass the bill. → The bill **will be passed**.

- the speaker wants to be polite or to be evasive about who is responsible

  Someone did not do the dishes. → The dishes **were not done**.

Tense	Active voice	Passive voice
simple present	I study English. He studies English.	English is studied (by me). English is studied (by him).
present progressive	I am studying English. He is studying English.	English is being studied.
simple past	I studied English last year.	English was studied last year.
past progressive	I was studying English.	English was being studied.
future/modals	She will study English next. They should study English.	English will be studied next. English should be studied.
present perfect	She has studied English since Grade 1.	English has been studied since Grade 1.
past perfect	She had studied English before she studied German.	English had been studied before German.

Exercise 2

Highlight the active (A) and passive (P) voice forms in the text. Identify which verb tenses are used.

Do you know where your clothes were made?

In April 2013 a garment factory in Dhaka, Bangladesh, collapsed Over 1000 people were killed and hundreds were injured. This tragedy brought the world's awareness to worker safety issues and the human costs of cheap, fast fashion. Some reforms have been put into place but a lot of work still has to be done to ensure the rights and safety of Dhaka's garment factory workers. In Germany a social media campaign was released last year. It shows people arriving at a vending machine that is placed in a busy street. The people are attracted to the machine by the promise of cheap fashion. A shirt is being sold for only a few dollars. After they select their size, they are shown the harsh realities and menial wages that go into manufacturing the low-priced garment. The shoppers are then given the choice to continue with their purchase or to donate to charity. The campaign is designed to shine a light onto the darker realities of the clothing and fashion industry. Campaigners want to increase awareness and it is hoped that people will be inspired to spend money ethically. Most of the people filmed decided against the new shirt and they chose to make a donation to charity.

Exercise 3

Make passive voice sentences using the groups of words provided. Use the verb tense or modal in parentheses.

EXAMPLE

Workers/clothes/factories/make (present)

Clothes are made in factories (by workers).

1. Work health and safety rules/by inspectors/impose (present)

2. Textiles/on looms in homes/in 18th century England/weave (past)

   _____

3. The factory site/inspect/by international inspectors (present perfect)

    _____

4. Fashion designer/interview/on the radio at the moment (present progressive)

    _____

5. Clothes/assemble/when the fire alarm/raise (past progressive and simple past)

    _____

6. Many people/by firefighters/before the factory collapsed/save (past perfect)

    _____

7. Money/the public/donate (future)

    _____

8. Factories/annually/by international agencies/inspect (modal: *must*)

    _____

9. Consumers/about the origins of their purchases/inform (modal: *should*)

    _____

10. Media statements/tomorrow/release (future)

    _____

11. The tragedy/about by journalists around the world/write (present perfect)

    _____

12. Factory owners/in 2016/guilty of neglect/find (past)

    _____

Exercise 4

Change the active sentences to passive voice sentences.

EXAMPLE

Bangladesh makes clothes to export to the rest of the world.

Clothes are made by Bangladesh to export to the rest of the world.

1. The Industrial Revolution changed clothing manufacturing in the United Kingdom.

    _____

    _____

2. In 1733 John Kay invented the Flying Shuttle; the Flying Shuttle improved the process of weaving.

    _____

    _____

3. Thomas Saint invented the first sewing machine in 1790 to sew leather and canvas.

    _____

    _____

4. In the 19th century, factories in England manufactured textiles for European markets.

   _____

   _____

5. Garment factories in Bangladesh employ approximately 4 million workers.

   _____

   _____

6. The clothing industry in the United Kingdom employs 140 000 people.

   _____

   _____

7. The fashion industry has created a desire for fast, disposable clothes.

   _____

   _____

8. European markets sell 60 percent of the garments made in Bangladesh.

   _____

   _____

9. Bangladesh garment factories make the majority of clothes sold in stores.

   _____

   _____

10. Western companies have outsourced production to India, China, and Bangladesh since the 1940s.

    _____

    _____

11. Researchers stated that factories sometimes employed children to work 64-hour weeks.

    _____

    _____

12. On average factories pay garment workers in Bangladesh, Cambodia, and India 70 cents an hour and employ them for 12-hour workdays.

    _____

    _____

Negatives and questions in passive voice

The verb **be** is the auxiliary, so do not add the auxiliary **do** in passive voice negative statements and questions. Compare the following statements.

> Health Canada does not promote smoking. *versus* Smoking is not promoted by Health Canada.
>
> Tim did not eat the chocolates. *versus* The chocolates were not eaten by Tim.
>
> Does Health Canada promote smoking? *versus* Is smoking promoted by Health Canada?
>
> Where did you buy the car? *versus* Where was the car bought?

Exercise 5

Change these active sentences to passive voice sentences.

> EXAMPLE   The company did not employ any college students last summer.
>
> College students were not employed last summer.

1. The company does not hire high school students.

    _____

2. How many new employees does the company need?

    _____

3. The company is not interviewing candidates until June.

    _____

4. A management committee was assessing interns all last week.

    _____

5. They did not hire any interns last year.

    _____

6. Does the company sponsor work visa applications for overseas students?

    _____

7. How will they contact new employees?

    _____

Exercise 6

Select the correct verb tense and use active or passive voice to complete the text.

I _____ (write) to reply to your enquiry about business planning. Last week you _____ (write) and _____ (ask) about writing the business plan and I _____ (tell) by staff that you still have questions. Another link to the instruction manuals _____ (activate) by our team. I _____ (hope) that these explanations answer your questions, but if you _____ (have) further questions a meeting _____ (can, arrange) next week and we can complete the business plan together.

First of all, the business plan program that _____ (send) to you when you _____ (register) your business number _____ (must, install). Your email _____ (can, use) as your identification and you _____ (ask) to select a new password. Numbers and letters _____ (must, combine) to create your new password. As soon as you access the program you _____ (require) to choose a template. The business plan _____ (write) by completing the template.

The template _____ (design) to answer all business planning questions. It _____ (use) by hundreds of clients. An example of a completed template _____ (attach) to this email. The business plan _____ (save) by the program automatically and it _____ (can, access) from any computer.

If you _____ (have) any other questions, I _____ (recommend) you reply to this message and a customer service representative _____ (require) to answer in the next 24 hours.

Yours sincerely,

Communicative Activities

1. Think of a building you visited recently. Use the passive voice and make a list of activities that are done in this place. Use as many different verbs as possible.

   EXAMPLE   At a library:

   Books are read.

   Computers are used.

   Lectures are given.

   Late fines are paid.

2. Think of a procedure or task related to your field of study. Use the passive voice to write 8–10 sentences describing the concept.

   EXAMPLE   When a new product is launched in the financial services industry, information is provided to the sales team. Details of the product, as well as sales incentives and goals, are discussed. Meetings are held in which the teams discuss sales strategies. Reports are run to target clients that will be interested in the new product. Calls are made to the most important clients first. The sales representative must be prepared to answer the questions they have.

Exercise 7

Correct the passive voice errors.

Shoplifting is often see as victimless, but in fact it costs the UK's retail industry £335m a year. Some of this cost are pass on to consumers as they force to pay higher prices. The ways buildings and streets design can help reduce shoplifting. A range of techniques is be implement by architects, city planners, and law enforcement teams to tackle this issue. For example, the strategy of restricting people's access to certain areas while directing them to others test by Crime Prevention Through Environmental Design (CPTED). Potential shoplifters is persuaded to reflect on the costs and risks of stealing. Retail design is using to encourage spending and to deter shoplifting.

A retail environment can describe as cues, messages, and suggestions that can use to manipulate shoppers' behaviours.

CHAPTER 10

Nouns, Articles, Determiners, and Pronouns

Nouns

A noun is a person, place, thing idea, concept, or quality. Nouns are divided into countable nouns and uncountable nouns.

 Go to Explore Online for additional activities using nouns, articles, determiners, and pronouns.

Countable nouns

Countable nouns are people, places, or things that can be counted. They have a singular and a plural form.

Singular, countable nouns take a singular verb and plural countable nouns take a plural verb in the present tense.

Singular and plural forms of countable nouns

Countable nouns	Singular form	Plural form
for most nouns, add **-s**	book presentation job	books presentations jobs
for nouns that end in **-ch**, **-s**, **-sh**, **-ss**, **-x** and **-z**, add **-es**	watch box address brush	watches boxes addresses brushes
for nouns ending in **consonant + -y**, change **-y** to **-ies**	library theory	libraries theories
for nouns ending in **-o preceded by a vowel**, add **-s**	radio piano	radios pianos
for nouns ending in **-o preceded by a consonant**, add **-es**	potato hero	potatoes heroes
for most nouns ending in **-f** or **-fe**, change **-f** to **-ves** (there are some exceptions)	half life knife wolf	halves lives knives wolves
for nouns ending in **-is**, change **-is** to **-es**	analysis crisis hypothesis	analyses crises hypotheses

Countable nouns		Singular form	Plural form
common irregular nouns		child	children
		deer	deer
		fish	fish
		man	men
		person	people
		tooth	teeth
		mouse	mice
		woman	women

Uncountable nouns

Uncountable nouns are things or concepts that can be measured but cannot be divided or counted. They are always singular and followed by a verb conjugated in the third-person singular form of the verb in the present tense.

abstract concepts	advice, happiness, homework, information, knowledge, love, peace, progress, research
groups of similar objects	clothing, food, furniture, money, transportation
food and liquids	bread, cheese, fruit, juice, meat, milk, oil, rice, water

Exercise 1

Decide if the following nouns are countable (C) or uncountable (U).

_____ innovation	_____ suitcase	_____ advertisement	_____ farm	_____ marketing
_____ leadership	_____ money	_____ education	_____ tea	_____ technology

Articles

Articles are words that introduce a noun and indicate if it is general or specific. The definite article *the* indicates a specific item; the indefinite article *a* or *an* indicates a general item.

Use of articles with countable and uncountable nouns

Article	Type of noun	When to use it	Example

a/an	• singular countable nouns	• use with nouns that are unspecified
		  • use **a** with a word that begins with a consonant sound
		  • use **an** with a word that begins with a vowel sound
			She bought an electric car.
			
			They are working on a new marketing strategy.

the	• singular countable nouns • plural countable nouns • uncountable nouns	• use with nouns that are known to the listener • use with nouns that were mentioned before • use when referring to a specific item • use with some countries	The company I worked for last year is hiring. The vegetables grown at Lufa Farms are fresh. The information we got at the meeting was useful. the United States, the Netherlands, the Philippines
zero (no article)	• plural countable nouns • uncountable nouns	• use when talking about nouns in general • use for meals, places, and transport • use with most countries	Driverless cars will solve many problems. I drink coffee at work. I go to university. She is from Canada.

Exercise 2

Fill in the blanks with **a/an** or **the**, or leave the space blank if no article is required.

1. You can control _____ drone with _____ smartphone.

2. Driverless cars will make _____ roads in big cities safer.

3. Would you take _____ exercise pill to lose weight?

4. _____ boss has purchased _____ furniture for our new office.

5. I work for _____ company that offers _____ unlimited vacation time to employees.

6. _____ creativity is important in _____ workplace.

7. _____ head-hunter is often used by _____ companies to fill positions.

8. _____ doctorate degree is required to become _____ psychologist.

9. My grandfather was born in _____ Scotland.

Determiners

Determiners are function words that introduce, limit, modify, or "determine" a noun.

Demonstrative pronouns *this, that, these, those*

This, *that*, *these*, and *those* are demonstrative pronouns or demonstratives. They are used to show that something is near or far from the speaker in space or time.

Demonstrative pronoun	Use	Example
this	refers to a singular noun near the speaker (in space or time)	This is my friend Jeremy.
these	refers to a plural noun near the speaker (in space or time)	These are the awards I got at camp.
that	refers to a singular noun far from the speaker (in space or time)	That was a fun evening.
those	refers to a plural noun far from the speaker (in space or time)	Those didn't work.

Much, many, and *a lot of*

Much, *many*, and *a lot of* are quantifiers. We use them to talk about quantities, amounts, and degrees.

Determiner	Use	Example
much	• used with uncountable nouns • usually used with negatives and questions	I don't have much time to finish the assignment. How much money do you make?
many	• used with plural countable nouns • used with affirmatives, negatives, and questions	I've been trying to get a job with that company for many years. There aren't many opportunities to get together. How many times did you try to call me?
a lot of	• used with plural countable nouns and uncountable nouns • used with affirmatives, negatives, and questions • We use *a lot* as a short answer.	He had a lot of questions. She didn't play a lot of sports in high school. Do you do a lot of cardio at the gym? Q: How many friends did you make on your trip? A: A lot.

Exercise 3

Fill in the blanks with *much*, *many*, or *a lot of*. Sometimes more than one answer is possible.

1. McGill University receives **many/much** applicants for medicine every year.
   _____

2. Q: How **much/many** time did you spend preparing for the exam? _____

   A: **A lot./Much.** _____

3. The company doesn't have **much/a lot of** money left. _____

4. There is **a lot of/much** pollution in Shanghai. _____

5. She learned **a lot/much** during her internship. _____

A little and *a few*

(A) little and *(a) few* are quantifiers meaning "some." *A little* and *little* are used with uncountable nouns. *A few* and *few* are used with countable nouns.

A little and *a few* have neutral meanings.

> **EXAMPLES**
>
> I have **a little** time before my next meeting. We can go for coffee.
>
> I have **a few** minutes to discuss this problem now.

Little and *few* have negative meanings. We use them to mean "not as much as may be expected or wished for."

> **EXAMPLES**
>
> I have **very little** time before my next meeting. I won't even be able to have lunch.
>
> She has **few** close friends. She spends a lot of time alone.

Exercise 4

Fill in the blanks with *a little*, *little*, *a few*, or *few*.

1. There are _____ women in top positions in companies. There should be more.

2. He has _____ money to live on because he earns a small salary.

3. There are _____ people at the office who are bilingual. The company needs to hire more bilingual staff.

4. I have _____ more pages to write for the assignment. I should be finished by tomorrow.

5. He applied to _____ university programs. He will decide which one to go to.

6. She has _____ self-confidence. She is very nervous meeting new people.

7. He had _____ extra time to review for the exam this morning. He got a good mark.

8. There are _____ openings this summer. Most positions have been filled already.

Some and any

Some and *any* are quantifiers and are used to express the quantity or amount of something, when the exact quantity, amount, or number is not known.

Determiner	Use	Examples
some	• used with plural countable nouns and uncountable nouns • used in the affirmative • used in questions when offering or requesting something	She has some time on Monday to discuss the project. Q: Would you like some food? A: I'd like some coffee.
any	• used with plural countable nouns and uncountable nouns • used in the negative and interrogative form.	He doesn't have any ideas to share. Do you have any thoughts on global warming?

Exercise 5

Choose *some* or *any* to complete the sentences.

1. I need to do **some/any** work this evening.

2. Charles doesn't have **some/any** free time this weekend.

3. There aren't **some/any** empty parking spaces at the mall.

4. I met **some/any** interesting people on my trip last summer.

5. Would you prefer to have **some/any** extra time to finish your report?

Every and each

Every and *each* are used before a singular noun to talk about the entire group. They have similar meanings, but there is sometimes a difference between them. *Each* refers to members of a group as individuals. *Every* refers to the group as a collection of members.

EXAMPLES

I go to school **every** day.

Each student is given a locker at the beginning of the semester.

Exercise 6

Choose the correct sentence.

1. a) Each cover letter should be addressed to a specific person.
   b) Each cover letters should be different.

2. a) Each candidates gave a five-minute presentation.
   b) Each candidate gave a five-minute presentation.

3. a) Every house on the street are different.
   b) Every house on the street is different.

Both, either, and neither

Both, *either*, and *neither* are used to discuss the relationship between two things. *Both* means one and the other. *Either* means one or the other. *Neither* has a negative sense, meaning not one or the other.

Exercise 7

1. Fill in the blanks with *both*, *either*, or *neither*.

    a) _____ of us want to study law next year. It is our dream.

    b) _____ of us wants to study psychology. We want to study engineering.

2. Correct the mistakes in the following sentences.

    a) She speaks either Spanish nor Italian.

    _____

    b) It was a great tennis match. Neither players played well.

    _____

    c) I will go to both college or university after graduating.

    _____

    d) I went to Barcelona and Madrid. I liked either cities very much.

    _____

Partitives

A partitive is a word or phrase that indicates a part or quantity of something. We use partitives with uncountable nouns to make them countable. Partitives are often used with food and liquids.

EXAMPLES

a piece of advice

a cup of coffee

a teaspoon of sugar

Exercise 8

Match the partitive with the noun.

Partitive	Letter	Noun
1. a piece of		a) water
2. a bottle of		b) clothing
3. a pair of		c) silence
4. a loaf of		d) advice
5. a bar of		e) scissors
6. a drop of		f) bread
7. a moment of		g) soap
8. an item of		h) blood

There is and *there are*

We use *there is* and *there are* to say something exists or doesn't exist.

	Use	Example
there is	• use with singular countable nouns and uncountable nouns	There is a piece of pizza left. There isn't much time to get there.
	• can be used with **any** to indicate a zero quantity of something	There isn't any rain in the forecast.
	• To form a question, place **is** in front of **there** (can be used with **any**).	Is there a storm coming? Is there any reason to wait?
there are	• use with plural countable nouns	There are many ideas about how to help refugees. There aren't many women in my class.
	• can be used in the negative with **any** to indicate a zero quantity of something	There aren't any tests left.
	• To form a question, place **are** in front of **there** (can be used with **any**).	Are there any houses for rent?

Communicative Activity 1

Work with a partner. Take turns thinking of an object related to work or to your field of study. Your partner will ask you questions using articles and determiners to try to guess the object.

EXAMPLES

Does it sit on a desk?

Would I have any in my bag?

How many of them would be in a typical office space?

Communicative Activity 2

With a partner, take a photo of an interesting scene outside the classroom. Describe the people and things in the photo using *there is* and *there are*.

EXAMPLES

There is a man crossing the road.

There are two people talking on their phones.

Communicative Activity 3

With a partner, look around your classroom. Describe what you see using *there is* and *there are*. Use articles and determiners (*a/an, the, some, many, a lot of*) in your descriptions as well.

Pronouns

Pronouns are words we use instead of nouns to avoid repeating nouns. Pronouns refer to something or someone that was previously mentioned.

Pronouns and possessive adjectives

Subject pronoun (comes before the verb)	Object pronoun (comes after the verb)	Possessive adjective (used with a noun)	Possessive pronoun (replaces the noun)	Reflexive pronoun (used when the object is the same as the subject)
I	me	my	mine	myself
you	you	your	yours	yourself
he	him	his	his	himself
she	her	her	hers	herself
it	it	its	its	itself
we	us	our	ours	ourselves
you	you	your	yours	yourselves
they	them	their	theirs	themselves

A possessive adjective modifies the noun that comes after it to show possession.

his: belonging or connected to a man or boy

He met **his** friend at school.

her: belonging or connected to a woman or a girl

She turned on **her** cellphone.

Exercise 9

Fill in the blanks with the correct object pronoun, possessive pronoun, or possessive adjective.

1. Lisa got _____ first job in a telemarketing company.

2. I forgot _____ (my laptop) in my schoolbag.

3. She reviewed _____ (the reports) this morning.

4. I met _____ (Sylvie and Jason) for lunch.

5. She read _____ (the newspaper) after breakfast.

6. We had dinner with _____ boss on Friday night.

7. He gave _____ (Justine) some advice on how to succeed.

8. I don't think this USB key is _____.

9. She got a job at _____ father's office.

10. She has her own company. It is _____.

Exercise 10

Fill in the blank with the correct reflexive pronoun (*myself, yourself*, etc.).

1. Watch out or you will hurt _____.

2. She takes _____ very seriously.

3. They treated _____ to a trip.

4. He enjoyed _____ at the party.

5. Your presentation was excellent. You should be proud of _____.

Indefinite pronouns

Indefinite pronouns replace nouns and do not refer to a specific thing or person. They always take a singular verb.

Indefinite pronoun	Use/Meaning	Example
people		
anyone anybody someone somebody	to refer to one person	Anyone can apply for the job. I don't know anybody who studies music. Someone must have a map. Somebody knocked at the door last night.
everyone everybody	to refer to a group	Everyone loves Fridays. Everybody likes to get a raise.
no one nobody	not a single person	I rang the bell but no one was home. Nobody admitted to making the mistake.
things		
anything something	to refer to one thing	He couldn't think of anything to say. I need something to wear to the interview.
everything	to refer to all the things of a group	Everything is on sale.
nothing	not a single thing	There was nothing he could do.

Exercise 11

Choose the correct sentence.

1. a) Nobody know when the exam will take place.
   b) Nobody knows when the exams will take place.

2. a) I don't like nothing on the menu at this restaurant.
   b) I don't like anything on the menu at this restaurant.

3. a) Does anybody work in this office?
   b) Does nobody work in this office?

4. a) The store is closed. Everyone has gone home.
   b) The store is closed. Someone has gone home.

5. a) Nobody is driving that car. It is driverless.
   b) Anybody is driving that car. It is driverless.

CHAPTER 11

Prepositions

A preposition is a word that connects a noun or pronoun to other words in a sentence. A preposition shows direction, location, or time, and can also be used to introduce an object. There are hundreds of prepositions and prepositions have various functions. For example, the prepositions *at* and *to* have more than 15 functions including for movement and place.

Go to Explore Online for additional activities using prepositions.

Prepositions of Time

Prepositions of time show when an action takes place.

Preposition of time	When it is used	Example sentence
at	for exact times	The meeting starts at 10 o'clock.
in	for months, years, centuries, and long periods	I will begin my new job in September.
on	for specific days and dates	The conference is on Saturday January 15.

Exercise 1

Fill in the blanks with the correct preposition of time.

1. The meeting will begin _____ 2 o'clock.

2. The office party will be held _____ December 15.

3. My final exams will take place _____ December.

4. His internship finishes _____ January.

5. We will go to the park _____ Tuesday.

Prepositions of Place

Prepositions of place are used to refer to a place where someone or something is located.

Preposition of place	When it is used	Example sentence
in	inside; or a defined area	She is waiting in the restaurant.
at	the exact place or position	I will meet you at the corner.
on	in a position above and touching	The phone is on the table.
beside	next to; by the side of	She ran the race beside me.
between	in the location that separates two people, places, or things	A stranger sat between us.
behind	at the back of	I parked behind your car.
in front of	in the position just ahead of	He sits in front of me in class.
under	lower than something	I found my pen under my desk.
over	above or higher than something	The sign is over the door.
across	on the other side of	My office is across from yours.

Communicative Activity 1

With a partner, use prepositions of place to write six to eight sentences about the objects in the classroom.

Prepositions of Movement

Prepositions of movement are used to show movement from one place to another.

Preposition of movement	When it is used	Example sentence
across	moving from one side to the other	She biked across the country.
along	in a line corresponding to the direction of	We walked along the shore.
from	to show where something starts	The bus from Halifax was early.
into	to the inside of	I went into the building.
through	in one side and out the other side	The plane travelled through the clouds.
to	in the direction (following the verb *go*)	I go to church down the street.
toward	in the direction of	We drove toward the border.

Exercise 2

Choose the correct preposition of movement.

1. The train went **through/across** the bridge.

2. I go **to/from** the supermarket on my way home from work.

3. We drove east **toward/across** the ocean.

4. She walked **through/along** the beach.

5. In the morning, we drive **from/to** home **to/from** work.

6. Our offices are **across/along** the street from the subway station.

Prepositions with verbs *get, go, arrive, depend, listen, wait*

Here are some common verb–preposition combinations.

When it is used	Example sentence
arrive in a town or country	Anais **arrived in** Spain last month.
arrive at other places	I **arrived at** the airport early this morning.
depend on someone or something	I **depend on** my bicycle for transportation.
get to a place	I **got to** the dentist's office an hour late because of traffic.
go to a place	They **went to** the hospital for their training.
go by a form of transport	Eric **went by** bus to New York.
listen to someone or something	I **listened to** a report about global warming.
wait for someone or something	I **waited for** my package to arrive.

Prepositions for Other Relationships

Preposition	When it is used	Example sentence
after	later than a certain point in time	I went home after work.
before	earlier than a certain point in time	We will buy supplies before going on the trip.
by	before (and including) a certain point in time	I need to write my essay by Monday.
until	to show the end of a period of time	The restaurant is open until 11 PM.
since	a point in time in the past	I have worked at the pet store since 2011.
for	an amount of time	Shelley has played the flute for three years.
ago	a certain time in the past	I started reading this book two weeks ago.
during	from the beginning to the end of a certain time period	It is hard to sleep during the day.
while	to represent two actions that are happening at the same time	I was sleeping while he was watching TV.

Exercise 3

Fill in the blanks with the correct preposition.

1. We have been coming to this place _____ we were children.

2. We went to the gym _____ starting work in the morning.

3. She was working on the report _____ I was talking on the phone.

4. _____ visiting France, I decided to move there _____ a year.

5. I fell asleep _____ the meeting.

6. I am waiting _____ I get paid to buy a couch.

7. If I don't hear from you _____ Saturday, I will give your ticket to someone else.

8. I decided to go into marketing two years _____ .

Noun–preposition combinations

addiction to	He has an **addiction to** prescription drugs.
approach to	I tried a new **approach to** this experiment.
response to	Her **response to** the question was brief.
solution to	They found a **solution to** the problem.
cure for	I hope scientists will find a **cure for** cancer in the future.
need for	There is a **need for** speech therapists in Canada.
passion for	He has a **passion for** helping people.
talent for	She has a **talent for** music.
advantage/ disadvantage of	The **advantage of** online learning is that you can learn from home.
knowledge of	He has extensive **knowledge of** marketing.
belief in	He has a **belief in** hard work.
decrease/increase in	There has been an **increase in** the number of accidents.
interest in	I have an **interest in** learning sign language.
rise in	There is a **rise in** obesity among young people.
report on	I watched a **report on** driverless technology.
information about	She is looking for **information about** criminology programs in Canada.

Communicative Activity 2

Write five sentences using noun–preposition combinations with information about your field of study or future work environment. Then, share your sentences with a partner.

EXAMPLES

I have a passion for helping people; that is why I am studying social work.

We need to find a solution to the increase in poverty in Canadian cities.

Phrasal Verbs

A phrasal verb (also called a multi-word verb) consists of a verb plus another word, usually a preposition. This combination has a different meaning from the verb alone. There are thousands of phrasal verbs in English. You will increase your vocabulary as you learn more phrasal verbs.

Common phrasal verbs related to work

Phrasal verb	Definition	Example sentence
call off	cancel	Tomorrow's meeting is called off.
deal with	take care of/handle a problem	I have a lot of problems to deal with.
fall through	fail; be unsuccessful	The new design project fell through.
fill in	replace	I filled in for the boss at the meeting.
get ahead	become successful in a career	She wants to get ahead in her field.
hand in	submit; to give to someone to a person in authority	I handed in my research proposal.
look into	to try to find out about something/ investigate	A customer hasn't received his shipment yet. Could you look into it?
put off	postpone; push to a later date	I put off my vacation this year.
report back	to give information that you have discovered	We have to report back to the supervisor.
think over	think carefully/consider	You need to think over your decision to quit your job.

Exercise 4

Fill in the blanks with the correct phrasal verb. Use the correct verb tense.

1. I have a big decision to make about my career. I need to _____ what I will do.

2. She will _____ her studies for a year to travel.

3. I will _____ for my friend at work tomorrow. She is on vacation.

4. My travel plans _____ this summer. I don't have enough money. I will stay in the city.

5. He wants to _____ in his job at a marketing company. He wants new challenges and a better salary.

6. As a social worker you have to _____ people's problems.

7. I interviewed a nurse and _____ to the class.

8. His car was stolen last night. The police will _____ the theft.

9. We will _____ the soccer game because of the rain.

10. We _____ our lab report yesterday. It took a long time to finish.

CHAPTER 12

Adjectives and Adverbs

 Go to Explore Online for additional activities using adjectives and adverbs.

Adjectives and adverbs are used to describe or modify other words. Adjectives describe or modify nouns and pronouns while adverbs modify verbs, adjectives, and other adverbs.

Adjectives

Adjectives are words used to describe or modify nouns and pronouns. They never change form. That is, they stay the same in the singular and plural form for both male and female subjects.

Adjectives are usually placed before the noun.

>   **EXAMPLE**   The CEO gave an **interesting** speech.

Adjectives come after the verb **be** and other linking verbs.

>   **EXAMPLE**   She was **calm** about the new sales targets. In fact, she seemed **excited**.

Order

When you use more than one adjective before the noun, place the adjectives in this order.

1.   determiner: *a, an, the, my, your, several*, etc.

2.   opinion: *lovely, boring, interesting, exciting*, etc.

3.   size: *tiny, small, large*, etc.

4.   shape: *square, oval, round*, etc.

5.   age: *old, new, ancient*, etc.

6.   colour: *red, blue, green*, etc.

7.   origin: *British, Canadian, Spanish*, etc.

8.   material: *gold, silver, concrete, silk*, etc.

>   **EXAMPLES**
>
>   My parents live in a lovely, small, ancient, brick house.
>
>   She ordered a delicious, large, round, vegetarian pizza.
>
>   He works in a stimulating, large, open office.

Exercise 1

Choose the correct sentence.

1. a) I work on a wooden, big, white desk.
    b) I work on a big, white, wooden desk.
    c) I work on a white, big, wooden desk.

2. a) She read a book, interesting, new.
    b) She read a new, interesting book.
    c) She read an interesting new book.

3. a) He is a young, caring nurse.
    b) He is a caring young nurse.
    c) He is a nurse, caring young.

The comparative using -er and *more*

The comparative form of an adjective is used to compare two people, places, or things. To form the comparative: **adjective + -er + than** or **more + adjective + than**.

	Rule	Adjective	Comparative
adjectives with one syllable (short adjectives)	add -er to the adjective + *than* **adjective + -er + than**	smart calm	smarter than calmer than
adjectives that end in -y	remove the -y and add -ier + than **adjective + -ier + than**	early noisy	earlier than noisier than

	Rule	Adjective	Comparative
adjectives with two or more syllables (long adjectives)	add *more* before the adjective and add *than* ***more* + adjective + than**	dynamic professional	more dynamic than more professional than
irregular adjectives		good bad far little	better than worse than farther than/further than less than

EXAMPLES

Some people say driverless cars are **smarter than** drivers.

My new place is **noisier than** my old place.

She is **more professional than** my last supervisor.

Today is even **worse than** yesterday.

Exercise 2

Fill in the blanks with the correct comparative form.

1. This year the company was (profitable) _____ than last year.

2. My job is (difficult) _____ than her job.

3. My office is (big) _____ than my assistant's.

4. The university is (far) _____ from my home than the college.

5. My team is (lively) _____ than yours.

The superlative

A superlative form of the adjective is used to compare three or more people, places, or things—to compare one person, place, or thing with all other members of the same group. To form the superlative, begin with **the + adjective + -est** or **the + most + adjective**.

	Rule	Adjective	Superlative
adjectives with one syllable (short adjectives)	add *the* before the adjective, and add *-est* to the adjective **the + adjective + -est**	smart calm	the smartest the calmest
adjectives that end in -y	add *the* before the adjective, and remove the *-y* and add *–iest* **the + adjective + -iest**	early noisy	the earliest the noisiest

	Rule	Adjective	Superlative
adjectives with two or more syllables (long adjectives)	add *the most* before the adjective *the most* **+ adjective**	dynamic professional	the most dynamic the most professional
irregular adjectives		good bad far little	the best the worst the farthest/the furthest the least

EXAMPLES

He is **the smartest** person I know.

The earliest I get up is 6 AM.

Apologizing when you make a mistake is **the most professional** response.

Working together always produces **the best ideas**.

Exercise 3

Fill in the blanks with the correct superlative form.

1. This is the _____ (bad) job I have ever had.

2. Everest is the _____ (high) mountain in the world.

3. The Atacama Desert is the _____ (dry) place on earth.

4. Montreal is the _____ (large) French-speaking city in Canada.

5. The Netherlands is the _____ (happy) country on earth.

Communicative Activity 1

With a partner, make comparative or superlative questions using key words and then take the geography quiz. The first one has been completed for you.

1. mountains/high (comparative)

   Which mountains are higher? _____ (a) the Andes   b) the Rockies

2. pyramids/old (comparative)

   _____ a) the Egyptian   b) the Mayan

3. country population/small (comparative)

   _____   a) Australia b) Japan

4. city polluted (comparative)

   _____   a) New York b) Beijing

5. expensive city in the world (superlative)

   _____   a) Zurich b) Singapore

6. small country in the world (superlative)

   _____   a) Monaco b) Vatican City

7. long river in the world (superlative)

   _____   a) the Nile b) the Amazon

8. populated city in the world (superlative)

   _____   a) Mexico City b) Tokyo

Adjectives ending in -ed and -ing

Some adjectives look like verbs because they end in -ed or -ing. Adjectives that end in -ed describe how a person feels, and adjectives ending in -ing describe how something makes a person feel.

EXAMPLE   The work is boring. *versus* I am bored by the work.

              I am **fascinated** by travel.

              His oral presentation was **interesting**.

Adjectives ending in -ed	Adjectives ending in -ing
interested	interesting
bored	boring
fascinated	fascinating
amazed	amazing
surprised	surprising
confused	confusing

Exercise 4

Complete the sentences with the **-ed** or **-ing** form of the verb in bold.

1. Alice is going to Australia. Planning the trip **excites** her.

   a) She is _____ about the trip.

   b) She thinks it will be an _____ trip.

Choose the correct adjective.

1. My trip to Vancouver was very **bored/boring**.

2. I was very **confused/confusing** by my chemistry assignment.

3. The presentation was **amazed/amazing**.

4. She was **surprised/surprising** to get the award.

Comparing equal attributes

To say two people, places, or things are the same, use **as + adjective + as**.

>   **EXAMPLES**
>
>   She is **as smart as** me.
>
>   He is **as hard-working as** the rest of the team.

We use **not + adjective + as** to say two people, places, or things are not the same.

>   **EXAMPLE**   She is not as busy as her boyfriend.

We can use **as . . . as** to compare actions.

>   **EXAMPLES**
>
>   It doesn't work as well as we'd hoped.
>
>   (We'd hoped it would work better than it does.)
>
>   Michael didn't play as well this week as he did last week.
>
>   (Michael played better last week than he did this week.)

Exercise 5

Use *as . . .as* or *not as . . .as* in the following sentences.

1. Vancouver is _____ (not, cold) Montreal.

2. Toronto is _____ (expensive) Vancouver.

3. Economics is _____ (interesting) psychology.

4. He is _____ (not, experienced) his boss.

5. His English is _____ (good) his French.

Adverbs

Adverbs modify or add information to verbs, adjectives, or other adverbs. Adverbs often end in **-ly** and modify the verb.

>   **EXAMPLE**   Daniel spoke **quietly**. He is **very** shy.

Making comparisons with adverbs

Forming the comparative and superlative using adverbs is the same as with adjectives.

	Adverb	Comparative	Superlative
adverbs ending in -ly	quickly	more quickly	the most quickly
	quietly	more quietly	the most quietly
other adverbs	hard	harder	the hardest
	fast	faster	the fastest
irregular adverbs	well	better	the best
	badly	worse	the worst

Exercise 6

Choose the correct response.

1. Jacob did **better/the best** in math this year than last year.

2. Sarah ran **faster/the fastest** and won the race.

3. My new teacher explained the concept **the most clearly/more clearly** than my last teacher.

4. This exam was **harder/the hardest** I have ever written.

5. During the presentation, I spoke **quicker/more quickly** than usual.

6. She played **worse/the worst** when she knew they wouldn't make the championships.

Communicative Activity 2

With a partner talk about your best and worst jobs. Use the comparative and superlative. Then compare jobs.

Review Exercise

Identify and correct the errors in the comparative and superlative.

1. She is as interested in the job that him.

   _____

2. Calgary is more big than Edmonton.

   _____

3. English is more easy that French.

   _____

4. My school is more farther than my work.

   _____

5. He is the goodest candidate for the position.

   _____

6. The novel was the more interesting book I read this semester.

   _____

7. The math course is most difficult than the chemistry course.

   _____

8. The trip to Paris was fascinated.

   _____

9. He runs more fastly than I do.

   _____

10. She works most efficient than he does.

    _____

CHAPTER 13
Sentence Structure

Go to Explore Online for additional activities using sentence structure.

A complete sentence begins with a capital letter, ends with a period, has a subject and a verb, and expresses a complete idea.

There are three basic types of sentences.

Sentence type	Contains	Example sentences
simple	one independent clause	School starts on Tuesday. I worked all weekend.
compound	two or more independent clauses joined by a connecting word (a coordinating conjunction)	I went to bed early, **and** I woke up late. Class starts at 9 AM, **but** I'm going to be late.
complex	at least one independent clause and one dependent clause	**Although math is Suzanne's favourite subject**, she is going to take economics at university. The test **that I took on Tuesday** was really hard.

Incomplete sentences, or fragments, are common in spoken English, informal emails, and texts. You might say "*so tired working until 2 am to finish.*" However, in formal written English, it is important to use complete sentences.

Exercise 1

Label the following sentences *simple*, *compound*, or *complex*. Underline the subjects and circle the verbs.

> EXAMPLE Stephanie ⟨has⟩ a lot of homework, but she ⟨has⟩ a full week to do it.
> <u>compound</u>

1. When you apply for a job, you must submit a resumé. _____

2. Reading books increases vocabulary. _____

3. Essay planning is essential. _____

4. Essay planning is essential and it always takes a lot of time. _____

5. Although the exam was difficult, most students did very well. _____

Coordinating Conjunctions and Conjunctive Adverbs

Coordinating conjunctions are words that combine two or more independent clauses. There is a comma after the first independent clause and before the coordinating conjunction (CC). The sentence structure looks like this: **independent clause, CC independent clause.**

> EXAMPLE Hamish liked the book, but he did not enjoy the movie.

Conjunctive adverbs are words that show the relationship between ideas. A semicolon (;) is placed before the conjunctive adverb (CA) and a comma follows it. The sentence structure looks like this: **independent clause; CA, independent clause.**

EXAMPLE   The movie was good; however, the book was much better.

Coordinating conjunction (CC)	Use	Example sentence
and	addition of an idea	I like to camp, **and** I go hiking often.
but	shows a contrast	I like to camp, **but** I only like to go in the summer.
or	shows an alternative	I will either go hiking for the weekend, **or** I will take a canoe trip.
so	shows a result	It can get cold at night in the outdoors, **so** I always bring a warm hat.
for	shows a reason	I go camping, **for** I like sleeping under the stars.
yet	shows a contrast	I don't like camping, **yet** we go camping every summer.
nor	adds another (negative) idea	She doesn't like camping, **nor** does she like hiking.

Note *for*, *nor*, and *yet* are less commonly used coordinating conjunctions.

Conjunctive adverb (CA)	Use	Example sentence
in addition **furthermore** **moreover**	addition of an idea	I enjoy camping; **moreover,** I am a skilled at outdoor first aid.
however **on the other hand**	shows a contrast	I have hiked alone; **however,** I prefer hiking with others.
in fact **indeed**	shows emphasis	I don't mind sleeping outdoors; **in fact,** I sleep better.
for instance **for example**	shows an example	You must be prepared when camping; **for example,** flashlights and matches are important tools in an emergency.

Exercise 2

A forensic scientist prepares legal statements for court cases, _____ (and/but/or/so) these scientists do not always work in laboratories. The forensic scientist examines materials _____ (and/but/or/so) he or she reports about traces of substances such as blood, explosives, and drugs. It is a slow process _____ (and/but/or/so) dramatic breakthroughs do not occur very often. The work can be routine and tedious _____ (and/but/or/so) it can be unusual and exciting. The forensic scientist gathers evidence _____ (and/but/or/so) uses techniques like DNA profiling to support reports.

The acronym FANBOYS will help you remember the coordinating conjunctions.

For
And
Nor
But
Or
Yet
So

Exercise 3

Select the correct conjunctive adverb (CA) for these compound sentences.

Many people wonder what studies are required to be a meteorologist; _____, (in fact/for instance/however/furthermore) many people do not know what this career involves. Meteorology is a university course; _____, (in fact/for instance/however/furthermore) it is not one of the most familiar sciences. Meteorologists use mathematical and physical formulas to make predictions; _____, (in fact/for instance/however/furthermore) this work involves a lot of research. Meteorologists study weather patterns; _____, (in fact/for instance/however/furthermore) they cannot always predict natural disasters. A television meteorologist must be knowledgeable; _____ (in fact/for instance/however/furthermore), good communication skills are equally important.

Complex Sentences and Subordinating Conjunctions

A subordinate or dependent clause needs to be attached to an independent clause; this forms a complex sentence. The subordinate clause can be at the end (no comma) or at the beginning (followed by a comma) of the sentence.

Subordinating conjunction	Use	Example
when while as soon as after before	indicate sequence/time	I will call you back **as soon as** I get out of class. **When** you get home, take the dog for a walk.
although even though	indicate contrast/concession	**Although** I like to ski, I haven't been to a mountain in years. I haven't been to a mountain in years **even though** I like to ski.
because as so that	indicate a reason	I chose to go to school in the US **because** I received a scholarship. **As** I am the shortest, I should stand at the front!
how where wherever	indicate place and manner	I chose the park **where** I used to go as a kid.
unless if as long as	indicate a condition	**If** I need anything, I will ask.

Select the correct subordinating conjunction for these complex sentences.

1. (As soon as/Unless/So that) 3D printing becomes the norm, we won't be able to imagine a time without it.

2. (When/Because/Wherever) driverless cars are driven by computers, they are safer.

3. A 3D printer can print tools (if/so that/although) you do not have any around.

4. Creative people are never bored (because/although/before) they can always think of new ideas to amuse themselves.

5. (When/Even though/Unless) creative people discover a problem, they think of many different solutions.

6. (As/Where/After) they know when to trust their intuition, people with emotional intelligence are excellent decision makers.

> ## Communicative Activity
>
> Write one compound sentence and one complex sentence incorporating each of the following independent clauses. Pay attention to punctuation.
>
> 1. I am taking a trip . . .
>
> 2. children today spend too much time online . . .
>
> 3. I did not finish my assignment . . .
>
> 4. the population is increasing . . .

Sentence Problems

A comma splice is the use of a comma between two independent clauses. Instead of using a comma, separate the clauses with a period (full stop) or add a coordinating conjunction after the comma.

> **EXAMPLE**   ~~I went to art classes, they taught me a lot.~~
>
>   I went to art classes. They taught me a lot.
>
>   I went to art classes, **and** they taught me a lot.

A run-on sentence is two independent clauses that aren't separated by any form of punctuation. Correct a run-on error by separating the clauses with a period (full stop), a semicolon (;), or by adding a coordinating conjunction.

> **EXAMPLE**   ~~The job is challenging the company takes on lots of projects.~~
>
>   The job is challenging**.** **T**he company takes on lots of projects.
>
>   The job is challenging**;** the company takes on lots of projects.
>
>   The job is challenging**,** **and** the company takes on lots of projects.

A sentence fragment is a dependent clause—or incomplete thought—that needs to be completed before it can make sense.

> **EXAMPLES**   Because the clock struck 12 . . .
>
>   Before I went to bed . . .

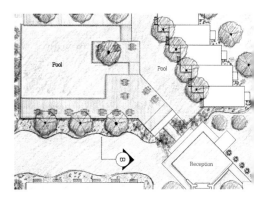

Exercise 5

Identify whether the following sentences are comma splices (CS), run-on sentences (RO), or fragments (FR), and then correct them.

1. Working in an office is not for everyone, studies show that it can take a huge toll on your health. (CS/RO/FR)

    _____

    _____

2. As sitting all day is hard on your body. (CS/RO/FR)

    _____

3. Even though eating at the desk. (CS/RO/FR)

    _____

4. One of the most common issues that arises from sitting at a desk is neck and back pain this can be treated with massage and stretching. (CS/RO/FR)

    _____

    _____

5. Sitting on a yoga ball can help you sit up straight and use your core muscles, using a standing desk can help too. (CS/RO/FR)

    _____

    _____

6. Because experts recommend standing up once an hour. (CS/RO/FR)

    _____

    _____

7. Doing moderate activity during your lunch break and walking to work will help you avoid the dangerous effects of sitting all day stretching regularly will keep you healthy. (CS/RO/FR)

    _____

    _____

    _____

Exercise 6

Correct the following text using coordinating conjunctions, conjunctive adverbs, and subordinating conjunctions. Make sure there are no comma splices, run-on sentences, or fragments. Be attentive to punctuation.

Ideally everyone would know their true calling early in life and would find happiness in their dream job but it often doesn't work that way some research suggests that people expect to change careers three times in their lifetimes lifelong careers may not be the norm any more. Even though many people ask their parents. There are better ways to choose a career than just following in your parents' footsteps or choosing randomly career counsellors advise people to think about what excites and energizes them everyone wants to enjoy what they do and feel happy at work. Being passionate about a job.

CHAPTER 14

Punctuation, Capitalization, Numbers, and Abbreviations

Punctuation

Punctuation shows meaning as much as words and grammar do. What is the difference in meaning between the following?

Go to Explore Online for additional activities using punctuation and capitalization.

>   Eat dad.
>
>   Eat, dad.

Apostrophes

Use an apostrophe in English to show contraction (where a letter has been removed) and to show possession (that a thing or person belongs to or relates to someone or something).

Contraction	
of a subject and its verb	I am → I'm he is → he's you will → you'll they have → they've I had/I would → I'd
of a negative and an auxiliary	is not → isn't are not→ aren't were not → weren't will not → won't cannot → can't had not → hadn't

Possession	
add **'s** for singular nouns, irregular plurals, and collective nouns	The books belong to that girl → that girl's books The books belong to those men → those men's books The president of the country → The country's president
add **s'** for plural nouns	The books belong to those boys → those boys' books
add **'s** with singular nouns even if the noun ends with -s if you would naturally pronounce and extra s when saying the word aloud	The book Lynne Truss wrote → Lynne Truss's book The books belong to Ms. Jonns → Ms. Jonns's books *exceptions: Dickens' novels; Saint Thomas' Hospital
No apostrophe for plural forms of acronyms	CEOs FAQs CÉGEPs
for decades	1990s 2020s
for possessive adjectives	his, her, its (the company's policy → its policy)

Exercise 1

Punctuate the following sentences by inserting apostrophes.

1. Whos the governments representative?

2. The governments policy was refused by the labourers union.

3. Im surprised you didnt see that theyve won the vote.

4. The government proposed its amendment, but its too late to get voters support.

Colons (:)

Use a colon to introduce a list.

> **EXAMPLES** An essay has the following: an introduction, body paragraphs, and a conclusion.

> The successful job applicant needs the following: a science degree, relevant experience, skills with computer spreadsheets, and experience in customer service.

Semicolons (;)

Use a semicolon to join two independent clauses.

> **EXAMPLES** Mohammed applied for the position; he starts on Monday.

> Chinglee worked in telecommunications; however, she's now looking to use these skills in a new field.

Periods/full stops (.)

Use a period (N.Am.)/full stop (UK) at the end of a complete sentence.

> **EXAMPLE** Mr. Hamel has opened a new office.

> Ms. Walker helped the refugees with paperwork while working at the UN.

Commas (,)

Use a comma after introductory words or phrases.

> **EXAMPLES** First, I decided to go to the gym.
>
> As a result, I feel much better.

Use a comma before and after any interruption inserted into a complete sentence.

> **EXAMPLES** Harwinder, who comes from Delhi, is studying computer programming.
>
> Hard work, according to my parents, is inevitable when starting a business.

Use a comma to separate a series of three or more words or phrases.

> **EXAMPLES** Nurses have to work night, weekends, and public holidays.
>
> Marie speaks French, English, Spanish, and Arabic.

Hyphens (-)

Use a hyphen with compound numbers, some prefixes, some compound nouns, and with compound adjectives before a noun.

> **EXAMPLE** eighty-five, ex-boyfriend, mother-in-law, twenty-year-old student

Quotation marks (" . . .")

Use quotation marks before and after direct quotes. Capitalize the first letter of the quote and put end punctuation (question mark or period) inside the quotation marks.

> **EXAMPLE** Sylvie asked, "When will we receive our results?"

Numbers

In professional business writing, use numbers instead of words in statistics and financial statements. In sentences, the numbers one to ten are written as words.

> **EXAMPLE** The employment agency met 45 people. There were three candidates for the actual position.

In academic writing, numbers are generally written as words:

- for numbers under one hundred (e.g. ninety-five)
- rounded numbers (e.g. six million)
- ordinal numbers (e.g. second, twenty-first)

Use numbers when writing addresses, dates, degrees, measurements, pages, prices, and percentages.

> **EXAMPLE** In 2005, the text book cost $30; it now costs 50 percent more; I paid $45 and my sister in the UK paid £20.

Exercise 2

Correct the errors with numbers.

1. At least 3 public health experts have stated that government guidelines aim to reduce sugar intake over 5 years by 20 percent. _____

2. Officials had more than 40 meetings with concerned parties, 9 meetings with manufacturers, and 3 meetings with health professionals. _____

3. In a survey of 250 people, 85 percent of respondents wanted to reduce their sugar intake. _____

4. Breakfast cereals currently have approximately fifteen grams of sugar in one hundred grams of cereal. _____

5. Children are sometimes consuming 3 times the recommended amount of sugar, so tooth decay is a major health problem for children aged 5 to 9 years old. _____

Abbreviations

An abbreviation is the shortened version of a word; some abbreviations are initials of groups of words that become acronyms.

EXAMPLES		
	NAFTA	North American Free Trade Agreement
	NASA	National Aeronautics and Space Administration
	UK	United Kingdom
	Corp.	Corporation
	Mr.	Mister
	i.e.	in other words
	e.g.	for example

Use *Ms.* for women rather than *Mrs.* or *Miss*, which are dependent on the woman's marital status.

Exercise 3

What does each abbreviation mean? Go online to find out if you do not know.

1. RCMP _____

2. EU _____

3. CSIS _____

4. MRI _____

5. CEO _____

6. CFO _____

7. UN _____

8. WTO _____

Capitalization

The following words are capitalized in English:

- the first word of a sentence

    Cars break down. Accidents happen.

- proper nouns and all the words in addresses, place names, etc.

    Xavier Dolan, Lake Ontario, Cabot Square, Main Street, Herzing College

- the pronoun *I*

    My sister and I travelled together.

- days of the week, months, and holidays

    Monday, February, Christmas Eve, Labour Day, Fourth of July

- languages, nationalities, and religions

    Canadians might be Christians, Muslims, Jews, Buddhists, or have other beliefs. They might speak English, French, Algonquian, Hindi, Mandarin, or other languages.

- titles of individuals, courses, books, and articles

    Professor Tremblay, President Obama, Chemistry 101, *The Heart of the Matter*

NOTE Articles and prepositions in the middle of a title are not capitalized.

Exercise 4

Capitalize the words where necessary.

last monday august 15th, i had an interview at whole foods on high road, kensington. the manager, ms. chiang, asked which languages i spoke. i told her that I spoke english, french, and some hindi. she asked how i had learned the languages, so I told her about my semester at the london school of economics as well as my travels to mumbai, india. she told me about human resources and workplace health and safety policies. i'm going to go on a training course and will begin work after labour day.

Exercise 5

Punctuate and capitalize the following text appropriately.

plant based diets are often shown to be healthy but canadians eat a lot of meat and are sometimes reluctant to completely cut meat from their diet so its important to know that eating a plantbased diet which often means being vegetarian doesnt have to mean becoming vegan

plantbased diets are high in vegetables wholegrain bread and cereals legumes and whole fruits yet can still contain small amounts of meats and dairy products

a survey of over 3000 north americans found that 70 percent thought that a plant based diet would achieve the following prevent disease lead to longer lifespans and reduce obesity dr hamid from the canadian health commission said statistics show that those following a plant based diet might live longer but statistics dont show a link between obesity and plant based diets

Overview of Verb Tenses

Simple present

Usage: facts, generalizations, repeated actions (routines and habits)

Key words: *usually, always, every day*

Statement	I usually drive to work. She drives an electric car.
Negative	I do not usually drive to work. She does not drive an electric car.
Question	(How often) do you drive? (What car) does she drive?

Present progressive

Usage: happening now, in progress, temporary

Key words: *now, right now, at the moment, today, this week, this month*

Statement	I am driving to work at the moment. She is driving an electric car.
Negative	I am not driving to work at the moment. She is not driving fast.
Question	(Where) are you driving to now? (What car) is she driving?

Simple past

Usage: action or event that began and ended at a definite time in the past

Key words: *yesterday, last Monday/week/month/June/year/summer,* (duration of time) + *ago,* X *years ago, in 2010*

Statement	I drove to work yesterday. She drove an electric car when she was in LA.
Negative	I did not drive to work yesterday. She did not drive an electric car when she was in LA.
Question	When did you drive to work? Where did she drive an electric car?

Past progressive

Usage: duration in the past, atmosphere, simultaneous past actions

Key words: *while, when*

Statement	I was driving to work when I broke down. She was driving too fast in the school zone.
Negative	I was not driving to work. She was not driving too fast.
Question	(Why) were you driving fast? (Why) was she driving too fast?

Future

Usage: predictions, plan (be going to), promise (will)

Key words: *next year, soon, tomorrow*

Statement	I will drive to work next year. She is going to drive her dad's sports car.
Negative	I will not (won't) drive. She is not going to drive his car to the cottage.
Question	(Why) will you drive to school? (When) is she going to drive home?

Present perfect

Usage: unspecified time in the past, duration from past to now, repeated several times, not yet completed

Key words: *since, for, how long*

Statement	I have driven to work since I passed my driving test. She has driven to work for six months.
Negative	I have not driven since I passed my driving test. She has not driven to work for six months.
Question	(How far) have you driven since you passed your test? (How long) has she driven to work?

Present perfect progressive

Usage: duration from past to now

Key words: *since, for, recently*

Statement	I have been driving since I was 18. She has been driving to work for six months.
Negative	I have not been driving since I was 18. She has not been driving to work for six months.
Question	(How long) have you been driving? (How long) has she been driving to work?

Past perfect

Usage: completed past action before another past action

Key words: *already, before*

Statement	I had already driven on the left before I arrived in Australia.
Negative	I had not driven on the left before I arrived in Australia.
Question	(Where) had you driven on the left side of the road before you arrived?

APPENDIX 2

Prepositions and Phrasal Verbs

Common Verb and Preposition Combinations

The following verb and preposition combinations are collocations: two or more words that are frequently used together in a way that sounds natural to a native English speaker.

Verb–preposition	Example sentence
agree with (someone) about/on (something)	I agree with you on the plan.
apply to (a place) for (something)	Jason applied to the law firm for a job.
arrive at (a room, building)	Lisa arrived at work late yesterday.
arrive in (a town, country)	When did you arrive in South Africa?
belong to	That sweater belongs to me.
consist of	The report consists of research and an experiment.
depend on (someone) for (something)	I depend on my alarm clock to wake me up.
dream about/of	She has always dreamed of going to Disneyland.
excuse (someone) for (something)	Please excuse me for forgetting your name.
get in/out/on/off/up	I got in late last night and got up early.
go back	When do you go back to school?
go to	We will go to the park tomorrow.
hear about/of (something) from (someone)	I heard about the job from my friend.
laugh at	I always laugh at my puppy's behaviour.
listen to	Did you listen to the explanation?
look at	Look at that house!
look for	Detectives look for clues.
pay for	I don't know how I will pay for my trip.
point at/to	The teacher pointed at me to answer the question.
put on	Over the summer, I put on weight.
speak to/with (someone) about (something)	I would like to speak to you about your behaviour.
talk to/with (someone) about (something)	Would you like to talk to me about your feelings?
travel to	We are travelling to New York next week.
turn on/off	The lights turned on automatically.
wait for/on/up	I will wait up for you to get home.

Phrasal Verbs

A phrasal verb consists of a verb and preposition or adverb that when put together have a different meaning from that of the original verb.

Verb	Meaning
account for	give a reason
ask out	invite someone out on a date
break up	end a relationship
bring up	raise a topic; raise a child
brush up on	refresh/improve your knowledge of something
bump into	meet by chance
call back	return a phone call
call off	cancel
calm down	become more relaxed
check in	register at an airport or hotel
check into/out	investigate
come across	find by chance; to make an impression
deal with	take care of/handle a situation or problem
die down	decrease in strength; diminish in power
drag on	last longer than expected
drop off	deliver someone or something; to fall asleep
drop out	leave school without finishing
fall through	fail to happen
figure out	understand; find the answer
fill out	complete a form or application
hand in	submit homework or a report
hand out	distribute
join in	participate
keep on	continue
keep up with	maintain the same level as someone
leave out	omit; not mention
look after	take care of
look forward to	anticipate with pleasure
look up to	admire
mix up	mistake
nod off	fall asleep
own up	confess
pay back	reimburse
put off	postpone
put out	extinguish
rule out	eliminate
run into	meet someone by chance
show off	brag or boast
stick up for	defend
take after	resemble in appearance or character
tell off	reprimand
turn down	refuse
watch out	be careful
work out	do physical exercise/find a solution

APPENDIX 3

Non-Progressive Verbs

The following verbs express a state or an emotion rather than an action. They are called non-progressive verbs because they are not usually used in the present or past progressive tenses.

Correct	I like candy.
Incorrect	~~I am liking candy.~~

The verbs with an asterisk (*) can be used in progressive tenses, but the meaning changes, as shown in the examples below.

Senses	Emotions	Mental states	Possession	Other
feel*	amaze	believe	belong	appear
hear	appreciate	desire	have*	be
see*	astonish	expect*	own	cost
smell	care	feel*	possess	exist
taste	envy	forget		include
	fear	imagine		look*
	hate	know		owe
	like	realize		seem
	love	recognize		sound
	mind	remember		
	need	suppose		
	want	think*		
		understand		

The following verbs can be used in the progressive tense, but the meaning changes.

	Example as a non-progressive verb	Example using the progressive tense
expect	He expects to graduate next year. (He thinks he will.)	We are expecting snow this weekend. (It is going to snow.)
feel	I feel good about the job interview. (I feel it was successful.)	I am feeling nervous right now. (I am nervous at this moment.)
have	She has a dog. (She owns a dog.)	We are having breakfast now. (We are eating.) They are having fun on their trip. (They are experiencing a good time.)
look	You look surprised. (appear)	What are you looking at? (watching)
see	She saw some nice paintings at the museum. (noticed)	She is seeing a new guy from school. (dating)
think	I think creativity can be learned. (This is my opinion.)	What are you thinking about? (What is on your mind?)

Irregular Verbs

Here are some of the most common irregular verbs in English.

Base form	Simple past	Past participle
awake	awoke	awoken
be (is/are)	was/were	been
beat	beat	beaten
become	became	become
begin	began	begun
bend	bent	bent
break	broke	broken
bring	brought	brought
build	built	built
burn	burnt/burned	burnt/burned
buy	bought	bought
catch	caught	caught
choose	chose	chosen
come	came	come
cost	cost	cost
cut	cut	cut
dig	dug	dug
do	did	done
draw	drew	drawn
dream	dreamt/dreamed	dreamt/dreamed
drink	drank	drunk
drive	drove	driven
eat	ate	eaten
fall	fell	fallen
feel	felt	felt
fight	fought	fought
find	found	found
fly	flew	flown
forget	forgot	forgotten
freeze	froze	frozen
get	got	got/gotten
give	gave	given
go	went	gone
grow	grew	grown
have	had	had
hear	heard	heard
hide	hid	hidden
hit	hit	hit
hold	held	held
keep	kept	kept
know	knew	known
lay	laid	laid
lead	led	led
leave	left	left

Base form	Simple past	Past participle
lend	lent	lent
let	let	let
lie	lay	lain
light	lit/lighted	lit/lighted
lose	lost	lost
make	made	made
mean	meant	meant
meet	met	met
mistake	mistook	mistaken
pay	paid	paid
put	put	put
read	read	read
ride	rode	ridden
ring	rang	rung
rise	rose	risen
run	ran	run
say	said	said
see	saw	seen
sell	sold	sold
send	sent	sent
set	set	set
shake	shook	shaken
shine	shone	shone
show	showed	shown
sing	sang	sung
sit	sat	sat
speak	spoke	spoken
speed	sped	sped
spend	spent	spent
stand	stood	stood
steal	stole	stolen
strike	struck	struck/stricken
swim	swam	swum
take	took	taken
teach	taught	taught
tear	tore	torn
tell	told	told
think	thought	thought
throw	threw	thrown
understand	understood	understood
wear	wore	worn
win	won	won
withdraw	withdrew	withdrawn
write	wrote	written

Guide for Correcting Writing Errors

Your teacher will use the following codes to identify the type of error you have made. You can then try to correct the error.

Code		Type of error
AWK		The sentence is awkward and needs to be reworded.
C		Capitalization: The word should or should not be capitalized.
		march 15, 2019 **Correct:** *March 15, 2019*
F		French: French is used instead of English.
		She has formation in accounting. **Correct:** *She has training in accounting.*
Frag		Fragment: Indicates that the sentences is incomplete
		Although she was late yesterday. **Correct:** *She was late yesterday.*
P		Punctuation: The punctuation mark is missing or incorrect.
		Creativity, which is the skill of the future is needed in all fields of study.
		Correct: *Creativity, which is the skill of the future, is needed in all fields of study.*
PR		Pronoun: The incorrect pronoun or possessive adjective is used.
		She likes sugar in his coffee. **Correct:** *She likes sugar in her coffee.*
Prep		Preposition: The incorrect preposition is used.
		He went at university. **Correct:** *He went to university.*
SP		Spelling: There is a spelling error.
		He is relable. **Correct:** *He is reliable.*
S/PL		Singular/plural: There is a problem with the singular or plural form.
		I worked as a volunteer because I wanted to help person. **Correct:** *people*
SS	DS	Sentence structure: Double subject. The sentence has two subjects.
		The class it's starting early. **Correct:** *The class is starting early.*
	INC	Sentence structure: Incomplete sentence. The sentence is missing a subject or verb.
		My job in marketing. **Correct:** *My job is in marketing.*
	RO	Sentence structure: Run-on. The sentence is in fact two or more sentences.
		He works at night she works during the day. **Correct:** *He works at night. She works during the day.* or *He works at night; she works during the day.*

Code	Type of error
SVA	Subject–verb agreement: There is a subject–verb agreement error. *He work at a bank.* **Correct:** *He <u>works</u> at a bank.*
VF	Verb form: The wrong verb form is used. *Yesterday we <u>seen</u> a film.* **Correct:** *Yesterday we <u>saw</u> a film.*
VT	Verb tense: The wrong verb tense is used. *Last week, she <u>has worked</u> on the garden.* **Correct:** *Last week, she <u>worked</u> on the garden.*
WF	Word form: The wrong form of the word is used. *He is <u>worry</u> about the test.* **Correct:** *He is <u>worried</u> about the test.*
WO	Word order: The words are in the wrong order. *I study <u>science computer.</u>* **Correct:** *I study <u>computer science.</u>*
WW	Wrong word: The wrong word is used. *She <u>made</u> a good grade in the class.* **Correct:** *She <u>got</u> a good grade in the class.*
X or ✗	Extra word/Delete a word: There is a word that is not necessary. *I put <u>the</u> gas in my van.* **Correct:** *I put gas in my van.*
∧	Missing word/Add a word: There is a word missing. *Driverless cars will exist in future.* **Correct:** *Driverless cars will exist in <u>the</u> future.*
?	Question: The sentence is not clear.
‿	Close up/combine word or sentences *Some times, I forget to set my alarm clock.* **Correct:** *Sometimes*

APPENDIX 6

Commonly Misspelled Words

Accuracy in spelling is important to ensure that academic and business writing is taken seriously. Here is a list of commonly misspelled words. What other words do you have difficulty spelling correctly?

absence	emphasis	occasion
accommodate	exaggerate	occurred
acknowledgement	example	parallel
address	foreign	possession
aggression	government	privilege
apartment	grateful	pronunciation
argument	guarantee	recommend
business	height	responsible
colleague	immediately	separate
company	judgment	siege
conscientious	leisure	strength
definitely	length	technician
department	license (v)/licence (n)	truly
dependent	lose	weight
disappear	maintenance	weird
disappoint	noticeable	which
embarrassment		

In most cases, standard Canadian usage follows British spelling (*theatre, colour*) but elsewhere it follows American spelling (*organize, apologize*). Another example is found in the following:

American/British spelling

judgment/judgement

acknowledgment/acknowledgement

False Cognates

More than 25 percent of words in the English language come from French, which is an advantage for French speakers learning English. However, be careful with false cognates (*faux amis*). False cognates (also called false friends or gallicisms) look the same or similar in French and English but have different meanings.

Common false cognates

French word	English false cognate	Definition of English false cognate	Correct English word	Example sentence
actuellement	actually	in fact	currently/right now	I am currently living in Vancouver.
advertissement	advertisement	a notice promoting a product, service or event	warning	She received a warning for her behaviour.
ancien	ancient	old	former	My former employer wrote a reference letter for me.
commander	command	order	order	We ordered a new printer for the office.
compréhensif	comprehensive	complete	understanding	My boss is very understanding.
conducteur	conductor	orchestra performer	driver	She is a good driver even though she just got her licence.
deception	deception	the act of misleading or cheating	disappointment	It was a disappointment to hear that you are moving.
décevoir	deceive	mislead or cheat	disappoint	I was disappointed that I didn't get the job.
eventuellement	eventually	finally	possibly	The company will possibly be hiring employees in January.
formation	formation	structure	training/background	She has a background in accounting.
gentil	gentle	soft	nice	She is a nice person.
hazard	hazard	danger	chance	We met by chance in Cuba.
lecture	lecture	conference or speech	reading	Our psychology teacher assigned a lot of reading this semester.
librairie	library	a place to borrow books	bookstore	The novels are sold in the bookstore.
location	location	a place or position	rental	She is looking for an inexpensive rental car.
médecin	medicine	the science of diagnosing, treating and preventing disease; drugs	doctor	My doctor prescribed medicine for my pain.
professeur	professor	a university teacher	teacher	My sociology teacher gave an exam yesterday.
propre	proper	real or true; appropriate	clean	I like to keep my office space clean.
publicité	publicity	media attention	advertisement	There are so many advertisements on Facebook.
résume	resume	restart	summarize	He wrote a summary of the article.
réunion	reunion	meeting after a period of separation	meeting	He gave a slide presentation at the meeting.
sensible	sensible	practical, realistic	sensitive	Her skin is very sensitive.
supporter	support	help; assist	put up with	Teachers find it difficult to put up with texting in class.
sympathique	sympathetic	understanding	friendly	My co-workers are very friendly.
vacances	vacant	empty	vacation	We had a great vacation in Europe.

About the Authors

Vanessa Beal has a BA in Art History and a BEd TESL. She also has an MA in Applied Linguistics from Concordia University. She has taught university-level ESL and yoga in Sydney and currently teaches at Cégep Edouard Montpetit.

Sherry Kent received her TESL degree, with distinction, from Concordia University. She also holds an MA in Applied Linguistics from Concordia University. She has taught Inuit learners in Northern Quebec and has also taught in Chile. She currently teaches ESL at Cégep Saint-Jean-sur-Richelieu.

Credits

Unit 1

Photo Credits

1 iStock.com/Mikolette
2 © Rawpixelimages | Dreamstime
4 Axel Bueckert/123RF
6 iStock.com/agsandrew
9 Kaspars Grinvalds/123RF
12 © Andreaobzerova | Dreamstime
13 © Benoit Daoust | Dreamstime
14 rook76/123RF
15 © Science Pics | Dreamstime
18 Tyler Olson/123RF
21 © Kobby Dagan | Dreamstime

Literary Credits

6 Adapted from University of Warwick, Coventry, UK "Self Awareness – Who Am I?"
15 Used with permission of FastCompany.com © Copyright 2018. All rights reserved.

Audio and Video Credits

4 Used with permission of Hogan Assessment Systems. © 2015 All rights reserved.
12 CBC Licensing

Unit 2

Photo Credits

23 iStock.com/KatarzynaBialasiewicz
24 © Georgerudy | Dreamstime
26 Cathy Yeulet/123RF
27 iStock.com/monkeybusinessimages
29 © 2015 by Robert Half. Reproduced by permission
30 © iStock/ Georgijevic
32 ESB Professional/Shutterstock.com
33 © Prathan Chorruangsak | Dreamstime
36 © Kittipong Jirasukhanont | Dreamstime
37 © Rawpixelimages | Dreamstime
38 © Nullplus | Dreamstime
40 © Fredbro | Dreamstime
42 Tyler Olson/123RF

Literary Credits

26 Reprinted by permission of the author.
37 Republished with permission of Mansueto Ventures LLC, from Aaron Skonnard, CEO, Pluralsight. "Does Unlimited Vacation Really Work?," Inc.com, Oct. 7, 2014; permission conveyed through Copyright Clearance Center, Inc.

Audio and Video Credits

32 Used with kind permission from Terry O'Reilly.
36 CBC Licensing

Unit 3

Photo Credits

45 iStock.com/vgajic
46 Akhararat Wathanasing/123RF
47 Christine Langer-Pueschel/123RF
50 © Rawpixelimages | Dreamstime
51 © Panom Bounak | Dreamstime
54 © Gururugu | Dreamstime
56 © Clique Pictures Production
58 © Joy Prescott | Dreamstime
59 Republished with permission of The Atlantic Monthly Group, Inc., from Marc Bain and Jenni Avins, "The thing that makes Bangladesh's garment industry such a huge success also makes it deadly," Quartz, April 24, 2015; permission conveyed through Copyright Clearance Center, Inc.
60 © iStock/ Weekend Images Inc.
61 © Radiokafka | Dreamstime; © Ndoeljindoel | Dreamstime

Literary Credits

45 Care of The William Ready Division of Archives and Research Collections, McMaster University Library
47 Reprinted with permission from Washington Top News.
54 Material republished with the express permission of: O Canada.com, a division of Postmedia Network Inc.

Audio and Video Credits

51 CBC Licensing
56 From Traceable. © 2014 Clique Pictures Production.

Unit 4

Photo Credits

63 iStock.com/Cecilie_Arcurs
64 © Olha Rohulya | Dreamstime
66 © Monkey Business Images | Dreamstime
69 Sergey Nivens/123RF
72 Cathy Yeulet/123RF
73 UCLA
76 © iStock/ DenGuy
77 Jakub Gojda/123RF
79 © Sergey Khakimullin | Dreamstime.com
80 irstone/123RF
82 © Syda Productions | Dreamstime

Literary Credits

66 ANDREW WALKER © The Independent 2018
72 From The Huffington Post, October 30th, 2013 © 2013 The Huffington Post. All Rights Reserved. Used by permission and protected by the Copyright Laws of the United States. The printing, copying, redistribution, or retransmission of the Material without express written permission is prohibited.

Audio and Video Credits

69 PBS NewsHour, "Nicholas Carr's The Shallows: What the internet is doing to our brains." Used with permission of NewsHours Productions LLC.
77 From The Age of the Drone. © 2015 Rebot Films Inc.

Unit 5

Photo Credits

85 iStock.com/Cecilie_Arcurs
86 racorn/123RF
88 iStock.com/tzahiV
89 Irina Moskalev/123RF
91 Michael Warwick/Shutterstock.com; ZUMA Press, Inc./Alamy Stock Photo
93 iStock.com/SpVVK
94 © iStock/ xavierarnau
98 © Pindiyath100 | Dreamstime
102 © Zhykharievavlada | Dreamstime.com
103 © Giovanni Gagliardi | Dreamstime
104 © Michael Albright | Dreamstime

Literary Credits

88 Republished with kind permission permission from Terry O'Reilly.
98 This article was originally published on The Conversation.

Audio and Video Credits

93 CBS News
103 CBC Licensing

Unit 6

Photo Credits

107 iStock.com/izusek
108 © Starastin | Dreamstime
110 © Busakorn Pongparnit | Dreamstime
112 microone/123RF
116 Cisco Customer Experience Report for the Automobile Industry, May 2013
118 Henrik Dolle/123RF
119 © Evgeny Gerasimov | Dreamstime
120 iStock.com/izusek
121 © Julief514 | Dreamstime.com
122 Akhararat Wathanasing/123RF
125 Oleksandr Lypa/123RF
126 © Wavebreakmedia Ltd | Dreamstime
127 © Alenmax | Dreamstime
129 © Takorn | Dreamstime

Literary Credits

112 Republished with permission of The Atlantic Monthly Group, from Adrienne Lafrance, "Self-driving Cars Could Save 300,000 Lives per Decade in America," The Atlantic, September 29, 2015; permission conveyed through Copyright Clearance Center, Inc.
121 © The Globe and Mail Inc. All Rights Reserved.

Audio and Video Credits

Projects

Photo Credit

Learning Strategies

Photo Credits

Literary Credit

Grammar Guide

Photo Credits

Literary Credit

Index